Lecture Notes in Computer Science 7805

Commenced Publication in 1973
Founding and Former Series Editors:
Gerhard Goos, Juris Hartmanis, and Jan van Leeuwen

FoLLI Publications on Logic, Language and Information
Subline of Lectures Notes in Computer Science

Mohan Ganesalingam

The Language of Mathematics

A Linguistic and Philosophical Investigation

 Springer

Author

Mohan Ganesalingam
Trinity College
Cambridge CB2 1TQ, UK
E-mail: mg262@cam.ac.uk

ISSN 0302-9743   e-ISSN 1611-3349
ISBN 978-3-642-37011-3   e-ISBN 978-3-642-37012-0
DOI 10.1007/978-3-642-37012-0
Springer Heidelberg Dordrecht London New York

Library of Congress Control Number: 2013932643

CR Subject Classification (1998): F.4.1-3, I.1.4, I.2.7

LNCS Sublibrary: SL 1 – Theoretical Computer Science and General Issues

Typesetting: Camera-ready by author, data conversion by Scientific Publishing Services, Chennai, India

Printed on acid-free paper

Springer is part of Springer Science+Business Media (www.springer.com)

For Appa and Amma,
with all my love.

Foreword

Since 2002, FoLLI, the Association for Logic, Language, and Information, has awarded an annual prize for an outstanding dissertation in the fields of logic, language, and information. The prize is named after the well-known Dutch logician Evert Willem Beth, whose interdisciplinary interests are in many ways exemplary of the aims of FoLLI. It is sponsored by the E.W. Beth Foundation. Dissertations submitted for the prize are judged on technical depth and strength, on originality, and on the impact made in at least two of the three fields of logic, language, and computation. Recipients of the award are offered the opportunity to prepare a book version of their thesis for publication in the *FoLLI Publications on Logic, Language and Information.*

This volume is based on the PhD thesis of Mohan Ganesalingam, who was a joint winner of the E.W. Beth dissertation award in 2011. We wish to quote here from the jury report on Ganesalingam's thesis.

> This thesis attempts a formalization of the language of mathematical texts (definitions, theorems, formulas), regarded as special natural language texts; the formalization aims to be suitable for being processed by computer systems. It continues pioneering work of Aarne Ranta, extending the scope to 'the whole mathematics', while Ranta focused on mathematical words and did not elaborate symbolic mathematics. M. Ganesalingam applies logico-linguistic tools, mainly Discourse Representation Structures and Typed Terms, to formalize mathematical statements and formulas, typed parsing, ambiguity of mathematical terms and others. The ultimate goal of this research is a computer system, processing mathematical texts. This dissertation provides theoretical foundations for the project.
>
> In her nomination letter Ann Copestake states: "I think there are many reasons why linguists should care about this thesis. In some sense, I believe it helps to validate the whole enterprise of formal compositional semantics. We can see how the compositional semantics developed in DRT for the language of mathematics relates to the underlying logic, and feel confident that the process is complete. [...] The thesis is truly interdisciplinary: it relates to mathematics, philosophy of mathematics, linguistics, computational linguistics and formal computer science." Aarne Ranta writes in his support

letter: "The characteristic feature of the thesis is that, while the author is well versed in previous attempts and theories and scrutinizes them in detail, he takes nothing for granted but develops his own theory from scratch. He builds a view of the language of mathematics as a unique complex of natural language and symbolism, evolving in time both for the community and for each individual mathematician. [...] The notion of ambiguity is central for most of the discussion: while mathematical texts in the end are unambiguous when understood correctly, they look hopelessly ambiguous when viewed from any ordinary point of view of syntax or semantics. The ambition of the thesis is to build a new theory of how ambiguities are resolved; a further ambition is to explain how language evolves in time, touching the fundamental questions of the philosophy of mathematics." The committee agrees with the above opinions. Several members of the committee pointed out the wide scope, interdisciplinarity, originality and possible significance for all three areas of Logic, Language and Computation.

Wojciech Buszkowski,
Chair of the 2011 Beth Prize Committee

Preface

This book is based on a PhD thesis supervised by Ann Copestake and Mike Gordon from the University of Cambridge Computer Laboratory. Its primary purpose is to take mathematical language, of the kind found in textbooks and papers, and analyze it in the way that generative syntacticians and semanticists analyze natural languages.

Mathematical language is exceptionally well-suited to such an analysis for a number of reasons. First and foremost, its semantic content can be completely captured in an appropriate logic. This distinguishes mathematical language from general natural language, in which vagueness and other phenomena prevent logical representations from completely capturing the meanings of sentences. Indeed, to the best of my knowledge, mathematics is by far the largest domain to which deep semantic analysis can actually be applied. As such, it provides a unique testbed for the wealth of semantic theory developed over the last four decades.

Second, mathematicians actually have an explicit, normative standard which specifies the semantics that should be assigned to mathematical statements. This means that the semantic representation that a given semantic theory assigns to the text will either be correct or incorrect; there is no room for argument about whether a particular analysis is appropriate. (There are in fact some problems with the standard semantics assigned to mathematical sentences; Chapter 7 is devoted to repairing these while remaining as close as possible to the source material.)

Third, mathematical texts contain explicit *definitions* of all mathematical terms and notations. These definitions include complete syntactic and semantic information about the term or piece of notation being introduced. An appropriate theory can extract all of this information from definitions, obviating the need for an explicitly specified lexicon. As well as the obvious advantages for any practical applications of the work, this is attractive from a theoretical perspective: excluding an explicitly specified lexicon means that the theory is much more constrained, in that it involves fewer "parameters".

Fourth, from a linguistic perspective, mathematics turns out to be a "Goldilocks" domain. It is large enough to be interesting: It includes phenomena such as presuppositions, anaphors, prepositional phrases, donkey-like sentences, and a range of plural constructions. At the same time, mathematics is small enough not to be overwhelming; for example, it essentially excludes tense, intensionality, modality and most pragmatic phenomena. This limitation in scope enables us to build a total semantic model for mathematics; and this model will cover enough semantic phenomena to be of real interest to linguists.

Finally, there are a number of practical applications of this work. Most notably, there is a community of computer scientists working in theorem proving; methods for extracting the logical content of actual mathematical language seem to be of considerable interest to this community. The presence of this community is potentially valuable to linguists: it means that any programs based on a theory of mathematical language will be extensively tested, providing direct empirical validation or refutation of linguistic theories. This said, I should stress that this book is primarily motivated in its own right: I study mathematical language for exactly the same reasons that linguists study natural languages.

I hope that the work presented here will be of interest to a number of audiences. The book as a whole is rooted in the generative linguistic tradition, and is addressed at linguists; those linguists who do not want to study the subject in depth may find the informal overview given in Chap. 2 useful. Mathematicians are most likely to find the discussion of the foundations in Chap. 7 useful, although they may also be interested in the overview just mentioned and in the discussion of ambiguity in Chap. 4. Chapter 7 may be of particular interest to philosophers, as the material in that chapter is closely connected to the work of Benacarraf and to the structuralist school in the philosophy of mathematics. They may also be interested in Sect. 2.6, which discusses a respect in which the syntactic structure of mathematical language changes as one learns more mathematics. Computer scientists are again likely to find Chap. 7 of some interest, and may also be interested in Chap. 5, which discusses the type system underlying mathematical language, and in Chap. 6, which describes a "type inference algorithm" for mathematical language.

History

The work presented here grew out of a much larger long-term project to construct a computer language for expressing pure mathematics in a way that was as close as possible to real mathematics. I should emphasize that all of the analysis given in this book relates to *actual mathematical language*, not to some putative computer language. Nevertheless, some discussion of the wider context may be of interest to some readers.

In 1999, knowing a small amount of mathematics and an even smaller amount of linguistics, I hit upon the rather ambitious idea of trying to build a parser for mathematical language. The end result was, from a linguistic perspective, crude. The input language which it accepted was at times closer to that of the more accessible theorem provers than to real mathematics, and it produced no semantic output. The main innovation of that parser was an ability to accept definitions written in something resembling their standard form, and to adjust the grammar in response to such definitions.

I showed this parser to Thomas Barnet-Lamb, now my collaborator, shortly before he was due to join me at Trinity College, Cambridge; he was sufficiently enthusiastic about the project to try writing documents for the parser himself. Over the remaining three years of my undergraduate degree in mathematics and the entirety of Thomas's, we spent a great deal of time extracting phenomena from all the mathematical language we were exposed to, both in lectures and in textbooks. Using these observations, we had extensive discussions about how we might make the language accepted by the parser more expressive and closer to real mathematics.

By 2007, we had amassed a wealth of potential improvements to the language, but had encountered many difficult and technical linguistic issues, which were impeding our progress. At this time, I also constructed a second version of the parser; the input language of this parser was still crude, and again the parser produced no semantics, but the language accepted was noticeably improved from the previous version. From that version, we came to appreciate the extraordinary degree of ambiguity found in mathematical language, and so realized that disambiguation would need to be a major focus of any subsequent work.

At this time, I applied to be a PhD student in the University of Cambridge Computer Laboratory, under the expert supervision of Ann Copestake and Mike Gordon. The PhD focused exclusively on linguistic issues, albeit with a greater emphasis on disambiguation than is conventional in mainstream linguistics. The thesis I wrote between 2007 and 2009 forms the basis of this book.

Once I had completed the work presented in this volume, we were finally in a position to create a wide-coverage parser which accepted real mathematical language and compositionally assigned semantics to sentences. From 2011 to 2012, we worked on such a parser. Needless to say, there are some restrictions on what the parser can accept. Many of these correspond to the restrictions discussed in Sect. 1.3; for example, the parser does not accept informal language, in a sense made precise in Sect. 1.3. There are other restrictions, of which the one with by far the greatest effect is a constraint on the accepted "vocabulary": as well as any defined words and phrases, authors are restricted to using "extramathematical" words and phrases from a fixed list. (To give some sense of what this might mean, the current list of acceptable phrases begins "a," "all," "an," "and," "any," "are," "as," "as required," "assume," 'assuming," "at.") Restricting the vocabulary in this way means that we can aim for complete coverage of appropriately restricted sentences; the method is essentially the same as the method of fragments pioneered in Montague (1970a,b, 1973). The list of acceptable phrases is large, but excludes many rare usages. In practice, we have found that this means that approximately half of sentences drawn from textbooks can be expressed without any changes, and most of the remainder require minor word substitutions.

At the time of writing, we have a well-functioning syntactic component, in that the parser accepts every sentence in a reference text, as well as most other sentences that we have tried it on, and post-parsing phases remove a large proportion of the ambiguity present in input sentences. The typeless portion of the semantics is complete except for certain cases involving the interactions of two or more difficult linguistic phenomena, including particularly genericity in various manifestations. We have manually examined the semantics produced for each sentence in the reference text, and ascertained that they are correct and that the introduction of type will remove any remaining ambiguity in all but a few sentences.

It has also proved possible to test the compiler even without type fully integrated into the system. This was done by focusing on a single area of mathematics, in order to cut down on word sense ambiguity and notational collision. The compiler was recently tested in this way on a corpus of unseen discourse fragments produced by a professional mathematician, and the results were extremely promising: the compiler produced the correct semantic output for over 95% of the input. Less than 5% of the input was ambiguous, and it is clear that type will remove all remaining ambiguity.

Note on Collaboration

As noted above, this book is part of a long-term collaborative project. Every part of the book draws indirectly on the understanding of the language of mathematics I gained over ten years of working with my collaborator, Thomas Barnet-Lamb. In addition to this, certain parts of it are directly based on collaborative work:

1. In Sect. 2.6, I discuss a phenomenon called *reanalysis*, whereby the syntactic analysis of notation can change while meaning is preserved. This was discovered and studied collaboratively.
2. Much of the discussion of ambiguity in Chap. 4 is based on joint discoveries and discussions. This includes in particular, Sects. 4.1.4, 4.1.5, and 4.3.2.
3. Chapter 5 contains by far the largest proportion of joint work; in particular, the type system presented in Sect. 5.3 and Sect. 5.4 is the last revision in a long series of type systems we have constructed, each handling slightly more of the difficult phenomena we encountered. Indeed, the only non-collaborative part of Chap. 5 is the initial, more philosophical presentation of the various concepts needed to make sense of the notion of

type, although even here the concepts involved in the failure of extensionality (Sect. 5.2.2) were jointly discovered.
4. Sections 8.2 and 8.3 give brief summaries of pieces of collaborative work.

In addition to these, the status of Chap. 7, discussing the foundations of
mathematics, is unusual. About a year before my thesis was written, I came
up with a primitive notion of "systems and models" (Sect. 7.4), and used these
to outline what I believed to be the correct way of handling the construction
of the various number systems used in mathematics. We then jointly made
considerable effort testing this against the data and ensuring that it could
cope with much more advanced examples, such as the algebraic closure of a
field. There were no specific major advances that I can attribute here, but I
regard this as contingent: in *many* comparable cases, Thomas found a serious
flaw in my analysis, or suggested a major improvement. Also, although I
cannot recall discussing them at this stage, I am certain that we were both
aware of the philosophical problems associated with the standard models of
the foundations.

When I came to write up the material on the foundations, I realized at the
last minute that there were major flaws in the original proposal; indeed, it
was actually unsound. Accordingly, I was forced to abandon it and construct
a rather different and more powerful proposal. Time constraints required that
work to be done in intensive solitude. During that period, I formulated the
notions of time and ontogeny which play a central role in Chap. 7, and spent
some time examining the connections to the philosophy of mathematics. This
substantially changed the way I thought about foundational issues, with the
result that the material presented in the chapter does not resemble our earlier
work. The end result of this process is that I am in the unusual situation
where I can only say, Chap. 7 is related to joint work, without being able
to pinpoint any specific areas or advances which were collaborative. Perhaps
the best way of summing up the situation is to say that the model of Chap. 7
is the successor to a prior, collaboratively constructed model.

Finally, I should note that although I have written all of the text in this
volume myself, I have chosen to use the pronoun "we" throughout the main
text for stylistic reasons.

Acknowledgments

Working on an interdisciplinary project, I find I am always out of my depth;
this book could not have been written without the help of many mathematicians, linguists, computer scientists, and philosophers who have given me
the benefit of expert knowledge. I would like to thank all of them, including
Ted Briscoe, Dan Flickinger, Thomas Forster, Georges Gonthier, Tim Gow-
ers, John Harrison, Martin Hyland, Kasia Jaszczolt, Andy Pitts, Tim Storer,
Henry Wilton, Inna Zakharevich, Ed Zalta, Sarah Zerbes, and many of the individuals I shall name below. As my interest in the language of mathematics

dates back to my undergraduate days, it is likely that this list is incomplete; for anyone I have omitted, both apologies and gratitude are in order.

Others must be thanked individually. Imre Leader and Aarne Ranta provided specific feedback on my work, and it is much improved as a result. Trinity College has funded both my PhD and my postdoctoral position; and above and beyond this, it has been my home for almost ten years. If I thank an institution, it is because there are too many individuals to name; but I am grateful to you all. I must also thank the Computer Laboratory, which has provided remarkable facilities and helped me through a number of technical crises, and especially Lise Gough, who takes such good care of us all.

My intellectual debt is much older than this book. A succession of teachers took great care of a difficult student, and led me to stand where I am now. Many have not only been remarkable teachers but also remarkable friends. I am grateful to all, but must particularly thank a few. Diane Mitchell (then Diane Dupriez) was my first mathematics teacher, and spent an unreasonable amount of her own time and energy taking care of an unruly child. I owe her not only for all she taught me but also for her limitless patience and compassion. Oliver Padel and Maíre ní Mhaonaigh took me in out of kindness long ago. They may not believe me, but they continue to have a great influence on my work. Without them I would feel that my intellectual upbringing was only half complete; and this would be a dry and (to me) unsatisfying half of a book. I will continue to benefit from their generosity for a lifetime. And the last debt is by far the greatest. Michael Davies not only taught me to think about mathematics; he taught me to think. Everything I have done since rests on that foundation; and in every step I take, I can see his influence. If this volume lives up to his standards, I will be content.

Thinking is not all there is to a PhD; persevering and surviving is another matter, which I could not have managed without the support of many friends. There are far too many to mention, but there are some I must particularly thank. To Vladimir Dokchitser, without being too demonstrative, I shall simply say: without you, I would be considerably thinner. My ever-patient, ever-tolerant, ever-cheerful officemate (and Doktorschwester) Aurelie Herbelot and her girlfriend Eva von Redecker have taken care of me through so many of the hardest times in the last two years; I cannot imagine how I would have managed without them. I wish you were my real sister, Aurelie! Without Ann Tucker, who took care of me for so many years, I would never have made it this far; you are always in my heart. And last but not least, I must thank all the children who I have worked with over the last two years, together with their families, who have always been there for me. If the children had not forced me to stop thinking about proofs and pronouns on a regular basis (sometimes by the application of a remarkable amount of force), I am not entirely sure I would be in one piece. Among them I must particularly thank 9-year-old Eloise Stanley for offering to write up my thesis in her best handwriting, so that it would make a good impression; that may be the nicest gift I have ever been offered.

Two years ago, Ann Copestake and Mike Gordon had a stray mathematician turn up on their doorsteps, with a wild and implausible plan. They took a remarkable risk in taking him in, and provided him with an inexhaustible source of advice, support, expertise, reassurance, and sheer patience. One of the reasons that I am most glad to have finished this book is that I have in some small measure repaid their faith in me, which has been far greater than I could ever reasonably have asked for.

Thomas Barnet-Lamb has been my collaborator for many years. In this book I have taken some small steps on my own; but they are steps on a long road that we are walking together. If I were to thank him for his help with my work, I would be doing him an injustice; everything of worth is not mine, but ours, together. Instead I will thank him for his compassion, his incisiveness, his determination, his patience, his empathy, his raw genius and, above all else, his unwavering friendship. And in the end, there are few things I have ever wanted more than this: that for as long as I can lift a pen or write a word, we walk side by side, struggling to understand the world, to see what lies beyond the horizon. Let us reach the end of the road together.

And finally, my parents. I have no words with which to answer to their immeasurable love. I can only say, inadequately: thank you for everything.

October 2012   Mohan Ganesalingam

Contents

1

Introduction

1.1 Challenges

The aim of this book is to give a formal, objective and above all precise analysis of the language used by mathematicians in textbooks and papers. Our analysis will closely parallel the analyses of human languages by syntacticians and semanticians in the generative tradition. In particular, it will let us take mathematical sentences, determine their syntactic structure, and extract their underlying meaning in an appropriate logic.

We face a number of central challenges in this task. Some relate to the scope of the analysis and to our methodology, and some to the nature of mathematics itself. In this section, we will outline these main challenges.

First and foremost, we aim to give an analysis that can potentially encompass all of pure mathematics. This is considerably harder than developing an analysis of the language used in a single, isolated area of mathematics, such as group theory or linear algebra. In order to describe so much mathematics with a compact theory, we develop ways for our theory to *adapt* by extracting mathematical terms, notations and concepts, and all properties thereof, from their explicit *definitions* in mathematical texts. So, for example, our theory will need to be able to extract all syntactic and semantic properties of the word 'group' from the definition of a group, as found in any textbook on group theory.

Second, we will require that *every* mathematical term, notation or concept be extracted from mathematical text rather than being an intrinsic part of our analysis. Even foundational material must be extracted from text; the theory must be compatible with the standard foundational accounts using the ZF(C) axioms, but must not be tied to them. This strategy of *full adaptivity* is considerably harder than allowing some mathematics to be encoded directly into our theory. However, it consistently pays dividends when we reach sufficiently advanced mathematics. For example, it is substantially harder to adaptively extract set theory from mathematical texts than to describe it directly. But if we confront and overcome this problem, we find that the same methods we used to extract set theory from texts can be used to extract category theory from texts. Conversely, if we had directly encoded set theory into our analysis, we would have encountered real difficulties when facing category theory.

Third, mathematics is written in a mixture of words and symbols. These are very different in character. The words resemble words in natural language texts, but have many differences. The symbols superficially resemble symbols in artificial languages but, as we shall show, they behave in a way that is much more complex than in any artificial language. And the interaction between words and symbols is unlike anything found in any other kind of language, natural or artificial; although the two are entirely dissimilar, they are remarkably interdependent. Thus we will need to develop a new kind of theory of language, unlike theories of both natural languages and artificial languages, to give a unified account of mathematics. This requirement will pervade our analyses of individual phenomena.

Fourth, because the theory must describe such a wide range of mathematics, ambiguity becomes a major problem. As we will see, word sense ambiguity, attachment ambiguity, coordination ambiguity and other kinds of ambiguity from natural language recur in mathematics. But moreover, and more problematically, we will show that the syntactic structure of a fixed expression in symbolic mathematics can depend on what kinds of mathematical objects occur in it, i.e. on the *types* of the objects in it. Thus the syntax of symbolic mathematics is type-dependent in a way that has no parallel in any other kind of language, and that requires novel disambiguation techniques. Additionally, we will demonstrate that ambiguity in words and ambiguity in symbols are very different in character but are inextricably intertwined; neither can be resolved without resolving the other. We will also show that existing methods from linguistics and computer science are unable to remove ambiguity in mathematics. Eventually we will remove the ambiguity by developing a novel method which tracks the flow of type information inside mathematical sentences, treating words and symbols in a unified way.

Fifth, we will show that there is a considerable gap between what mathematicians claim is true and what they believe, and this mismatch causes a number of serious linguistic problems. For example, mathematicians claim that all numbers are really sets, but their use of language consistently reflects a belief that this is not the case. Our attempts to understand what is happening here will lead us deep into the foundations of mathematics, and will show us that our linguistic problems are connected to philosophical problems. Resolving them will prove to be a major undertaking.

Last, our focus on adaptivity and our close examination of mathematical material will lead us to the discovery that a notion of time plays a key part in the language of mathematics in a way that has not previously been realised. For example, we will exhibit instances of a heretofore undescribed phenomenon whereby the meaning of a fixed piece of mathematical language can *change* as time passes and one learns more mathematics. Equally, we will derive constraints on our theory based on the fact that mathematics is learned in order, and that certain parts of mathematics may or must be learnt before other parts. All of our descriptions of phenomena in the language of mathematics will need to be compatible with our novel notion of time. Ultimately, this notion will come to play a key part in our analysis of the foundations; it will allow us to find deficiencies in all of the standard accounts of the foundations of mathematics, and eventually to construct an alternative account which resolves these problems.

To sum up, the main challenges that we will face are as follows:

Breadth. The theory must be able to describe all of pure mathematics.

Full Adaptivity. All mathematical content must be extracted from mathematical text.

Words and Symbols. We will need to analyse all phenomena in mathematics by giving a unified description of their relationships to both the words and symbols in mathematics, despite the fact that these are highly dissimilar.

Ambiguity. We will find that ambiguity is utterly pervasive in mathematics, and that it crosses the line between words and symbols in an unprecedented way. Resolving this will require novel techniques.

Belief and Behaviour. We will need to resolve disparities between the claims mathematicians make about certain mathematical objects and the linguistic behaviour of those objects.

Time. We will discover a novel notion of time underlying mathematics, and all accounts of the language of mathematics and the foundations of mathematics will need to be compatible with this.

We will return to discuss these in the conclusion (Chapter 9).

1.2   Concepts

1.2.1   Linguistics and Mathematics

Our analysis of the language of mathematics is related to generative linguistics in two ways. First, our aim is to give a completely formal and precise description of the language of mathematics. Similarly, the central aim of generative linguistics is to give a completely formal and precise description of natural languages, such as English. Thus, in a broad sense, all of the work in this book may be regarded as 'the application of linguistics to mathematics'. In this respect, linguistics gives us general ideas about how we can formally analyse language: it provides us with a mindset which we can use throughout the entire book.

Second, if we restrict ourselves to the part of mathematics that consists only of words, there are clear parallels with natural languages. We need to be careful not to say that these parts of mathematics are written in natural language; as we shall see in §2.3, many of the conventions are different, so that the same sentence might mean different things in mathematical language and in general natural language. Nevertheless, much of the machinery of linguistics may be adapted to describe textual mathematics, before being combined with novel machinery for describing symbolic mathematics. This is, surprisingly, almost untrodden ground; as the only linguist to analyse mathematics, Aarne Ranta, remarks:

> Linguistically, the study of mathematical language rather than everyday language is rewarding because it offers examples that have complicated grammatical structure but are free from ambiguities. We always know exactly what a sentence means, and there is a determinate structure to be revealed. The informal language of mathematics thus provides a kind of grammatical laboratory. Amazingly little use has been made of this laboratory in linguistics; even the material presented below is just an application of results obtained within the standard linguistic fragment containing donkey sentences etc. It is to be expected that a closer study of mathematical language itself will give experience that is useful in general linguistics as well.
>
> (Ranta, 1994)

We should emphasise that Ranta primarily studies the words in mathematics, rather than the symbols (see §1.5.1 for details). We will be concerned with both, and will therefore have to stray further from the linguistic canon than Ranta does.

Linguistics is divided into many branches. Those that will be most useful to us are generative syntax (Chomsky, 1957) and formal semantics in the Montagovian tradition (Montague, 1970a,b, 1973). We will make particular use of the semantic theory called Discourse Representation Theory (Kamp and Reyle, 1993).

There are some significant ways in which mathematics differs substantially from natural languages, which will affect our general approach. Most of these will be described in Chapter 2, which gives a description of the language of mathematics, but one is worth emphasising here. Mathematics has associated with it a clear, external, notion of meaning. Since the publication of Principia Mathematica (Whitehead and Russell, 1910), it has been accepted that the language of mathematics can be given a complete semantic representation in the form of an appropriate logic. Unlike current semantic representations for natural language, these logical representations for the language of mathematics completely capture what mathematical objects 'are' and how they behave.

Further, when mathematicians are writing modern mathematics in a formal register (see §1.3 for details of registers), they intend to formulate meaningful statements in some underlying logic. If it was pointed out that a particular sentence had no translation into such a logic, a mathematician would genuinely feel that they had been insufficiently precise. (The actual translation into logic is never performed, because it is exceptionally laborious; but the possibility of the translation is held to be crucial.) Thus mathematics has a normative notion of what its content should look like; there is no analogue in natural languages.

1.2.2 Time

As noted in §1.1, a novel notion of time will play a major part in this book. In this section, we will briefly sketch the role which this notion plays and then list the parts of the book in which it is elaborated on.

The importance of time in our theory arises from adaptivity, i.e. the way in which our theory derives mathematical terms, concepts and notation from their definitions in texts. We can only refer to a term, concept or notation *after* the appropriate definition has been encountered; correspondingly, we need to pay considerable attention to the *temporal order* in which definitions and other material are encountered.

The notion of time will lie in the background when we discuss adaptivity and definitions (§2.2), but it will first come to prominence in our discussion in §2.6 of a (previously unnoted) phenomenon which we call reanalysis, whereby the meaning of a fixed mathematical expression can change over time, i.e. as an individual mathematician encounters more mathematics. The notion of time will then remain in the background throughout most of Chapters 3, 4, 5 and 6, implicit whenever we discuss operations like definition, where there is an essential distinction between our picture of mathematics 'before' and 'after' the operation. It will, however, occasionally surface more explicitly. Most notably, we will use it to criticise certain disambiguation mechanisms in §4.1.4, to argue that certain pieces of mathematics must not be able to affect each other in §5.3.3, and to argue that certain categories must be able to grow over time in §5.3.5.

It is only when we come to Chapter 7, discussing the foundations of mathematics, that the concept of time will come into its own. In that chapter, we will contrast the notion of time with another notion of time from the philosophical literature (more specifically, from Lakatos (1976)), introduce terminology to reflect this and then use the notion of time as our central tool throughout the remainder of the chapter. It is not too much of a stretch to say that the significance of the chapter lies in its demonstration of the utility of our novel notion of time.

1.2.3 Full Adaptivity

Adopting a linear temporal perspective allows us to state a remarkable property of mathematical language. It is very nearly the case that the language of mathematics is completely *self-contained*: that every lexical, syntactic or semantic property of a mathematical object can be adaptively extracted from the discourse prior to the first reference to that object. It is this property that allowed us to even formulate our goal of describing mathematics using a fully adaptive theory.

In linguistics as a whole, it is normal to slightly idealise the material that is treated. For example, treatment of syntax do not generally concern themselves with hesitation, incomplete sentences, and a number of similar phenomena which are common in actual language. Our notion of full adaptivity involves a small degree of idealisation in the following sense: we do not cope with the case where, say, a mathematician introduces the notion of a point *in* a metric space and subsequently refers instead to a point *of* a metric space. We should emphasise that the degree of idealisation here is very small; disparities like the one just described are relatively rare in mathematical texts.

There are also a few cases where full adaptivity would require a piece of information which is never stated in mathematical texts. For example, if our theory is to be able to completely remove ambiguity, it needs to able to predict that (in a vector space context) '$v_1 \otimes w + v_2 \otimes w$' means '$(v_1 \otimes w) + (v_2 \otimes w)$' rather than '$v_1 \otimes (w + v_2) \otimes w$'. This prediction is based on an underlying convention (discussed in §4.1.5) which is not spelt out in mathematical texts. The absence of this information impedes a fully adaptive approach to disambiguation.

Informational gaps of this kind are extremely rare; they might crop up two or three times in a text. In addition, it is *without exception* the case that a short, local emendation to the text could introduce the information needed for a fully adaptive strategy to work.[1] For these reasons, we do not regard the existence of informational gaps as major impediments to our theory of full adaptivity. Throughout the remainder of this book, we will draw attention to informational gaps in the few places they occur.

1.3 Scope

We will now delimit the scope of our investigations, and of this book, by qualifying exactly what we mean by 'the language of mathematics'.

First and foremost, as stated in §1.1, the theory given here is required to describe all of pure mathematics. To substantiate this point, some background may be required. A very primitive precursor to the theory given here was constructed during my first year studying the Cambridge Mathematics Tripos; the soundness and effectiveness of this theory were then verified via implementation inside a computer program. The theory was then tested against all the mathematics encountered during my subsequent study; this raised a number of difficult linguistic problems which remained unsolved until I undertook the work described in this book. Problems were also contributed by my collaborator Thomas Barnet-Lamb during his own time within the Cambridge Mathematics Tripos and his Ph.D. in algebraic number theory in the Harvard Mathematics Department. In selecting mathematical examples

---

[1] We should emphasise that we are not suggesting that mathematicians change the way they write. The point is that if the relevant information could not be encoded locally in the text, information would be flowing into our fully adaptive theory in a 'mysterious' manner.

for use in this book, we have generally drawn a balance between using material from as many areas of mathematics as possible, in order to demonstrate the generality of the theory, and illustrating remarks using the simplest example that does them justice. Material has also been taken from the standard texts on each subject wherever possible.

Second, mathematics is written in many registers. In particular, the mathematical language written in textbooks varies subtly from the mathematical language presented in university lectures. For example, the latter allows the use of brackets to disambiguate the 'natural language' part of mathematics, but the former does not. We will look only at the register used in the more rigorous, careful textbooks.

Third, even a single register has within it two modes of language, a formal mode and an informal mode. The formal mode consists of assertions whose content is purely mathematical. The informal mode consists of commentary on the ongoing mathematics. Individual sentences in the language of mathematics tend to be either entirely formal or entirely informal, though there are exceptions. It is worth noting that mathematicians have very strong intuitions about the distinction between these two modes.

The distinction between the two modes can be made objective and precise, as follows. Under the standard view of the foundations of mathematics, an object is a mathematical object if and only if it is a set in Zermelo-Fraenkel set theory.[2] A sentence is in the formal mode if and only if it consists only of assertions about mathematical objects and about mathematical facts, so that its semantic content is purely truth-conditional and can be completely captured in an appropriate logic. The difference can be illustrated with respect to the following sentence:

> It would be interesting to go further and characterise the group G_0, *provided with the filtration of the G_i*, but that appears to be much more difficult.
>
> (Serre, 1979, p. 68)

This refers to concepts that cannot be captured in truth-conditional terms, such as 'interestingness' and 'appearance'. Thus this is an informal remark. By contrast, the following assertion refers only to mathematical objects, and mathematically capturable properties of those objects:

> Every bounded monotonic sequence converges.
>
> (Sutherland, 1975, p. 9)

Its content can be completely captured in predicate logic as

$$\forall x. realsequence(x) \wedge bounded\_as\_realseq(x) \wedge monotonic\_as\_realseq(x)$$
$$\Rightarrow converges\_as\_seq(x).$$

---

[2] We will come to criticise this position in Chapter 7, but the diagnostic will be salvageable: we will merely need to say an object is mathematical if and only if it could be constructed as a set in ZF set theory.

Thus this sentence is in the formal mode. The formal mode also includes the expression of relationships between mathematical facts, as in:

By $\underbrace{\text{Theorem 11}}_{\text{mathematical fact}}$, $\underbrace{\text{every bounded monotonic sequence converges.}}_{\text{mathematical fact}}$

From a linguistic perspective, the formal mode is more novel and interesting because it is restricted enough to describe completely, both in terms of syntax and semantics. By contrast, the informal mode seems as hard to describe as general natural language. We will therefore look only at mathematics in the formal mode.

Finally, every mathematical text is written in a mixture of some natural language and symbols. We will only concern ourselves with the case where the natural language in question is English. The theory of mathematics in, say, French is unlikely to be that different to the theory of mathematics in English. But by restricting ourselves to English we gain the ability to abstract away from certain concerns of general language which are orthogonal to our primary concerns. In particular, English-language mathematics can be very effectively captured by an unaugmented phrase structure grammar, and exhibits little in the way of agreement.

1.4 Structure

Chapter 2 presents a descriptive overview of mathematics from a linguistic perspective. §2.6 is of particular importance as it highlights a previously undiscussed way in which the meaning of fixed mathematical expressions may change as more mathematics is encountered; this section may be of interest to philosophers of mathematics.

Chapter 3 sets up the basic linguistic framework which is used in the remainder of the book. Syntax is handled using a context-free grammar, and semantics using a variant of Discourse Representation Theory (Kamp and Reyle, 1993) adapted to better fit mathematical phenomena. The theory constructed in this chapter is comparable to that constructed by Ranta (cf. §1.5.1 below), but covers a much wider range of phenomena and overcomes certain deficiencies noted by Ranta in his own work.

We should note that Chapter 3 concludes the analysis of material for which there is a precedent in the literature; subsequent chapters discuss more advanced topics. Consequently, we make a point of noting particular difficulties that any analysis must face at the beginnings of Chapter 4, Chapter 5 and Chapter 6, and also in §4.4. Chapter 7, discussing the foundations of mathematics, contains a comparable discussion of major difficulties in §7.3.

Chapter 4 discusses ambiguity in detail. It begins by demonstrating that ambiguity is pervasive in both words and symbols in mathematics and then

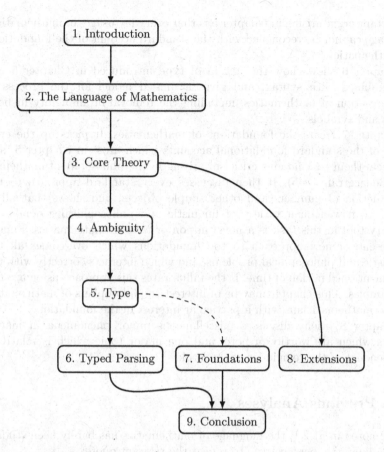

Fig. 1.1 Dependencies between chapters

gives a sequence of examples that show that standard mechanisms for disambiguating formal languages are not adequate for resolving ambiguity in symbolic mathematics, and that the textual ambiguity and symbolic ambiguity in mathematics are too intertwined to be handled separately. Chapter 4 concludes by arguing that a notion of *type* is needed to resolve ambiguity in mathematical language, and mathematics is unique in that the syntax of an expression can depend on the types of the elements it contains.

Chapter 5 begins by showing that showing that the standard notion of 'type' conflates two separate notions, and separates these. It then gives a sequence of examples of the use of mathematical language which narrow down exactly which type distinctions need to be in place to model mathematics. In particular, it demonstrates that mathematics contains *non-extensional types*, which have no parallel in any other kind of language; it then uses the two separated notions of type to characterise and interpret this concept. Finally, it presents the actual formal type system needed to model mathematics. One important point arising in Chapter 5 is that everyday usages of mathematical language cannot be reconciled with the standard account of the foundations of mathematics.

Chapter 6 shows how the notion of type introduced in Chapter 5 can be combined with syntax, and gives a unified model for the process of interpretation of mathematics, including the removal of ambiguity in both words and symbols.

Chapter 7 treats the foundations of mathematics. It picks up the criticisms of the standard foundational accounts which arose in Chapter 5, and connects them to a famous criticism arising in the philosophy of mathematics (Benacerraf, 1965). It then discusses every standard approach to the construction of numbers and other simple objects, and shows that all of these are flawed on a variety of linguistic and philosophical grounds. Its primary tool in this task is a novel notion of *time* in mathematics. Finally, it presents a new approach to the foundations which overcomes all the linguistic and philosophical problems, and which interacts correctly with the aforementioned notion of time. It then illustrates this approach using a range of examples. This chapter may be of interest to philosophers of mathematics and to mathematicians with a particular interest in the foundations.

Chapter 8 briefly discusses miscellaneous minor phenomena in mathematics which are worthy of note, and one major topic which is relatively independent of the remainder of the book.

1.5   Previous Analyses

As we noted in §1.2.1, the language of mathematics has barely been studied from a linguistic perspective. To repeat the relevant quote:

> Amazingly little use has been made of [the language of mathematics] in linguistics; even the material presented below is just an application of the results obtained within the standard linguistic fragment containing donkey sentences etc..
>
> (Ranta, 1994, p. 3)

1.5.1   Ranta

The only substantive work on the language of mathematics appears in papers by Ranta (Ranta, 1994, 1995, 1996, 1997a,b) which operate within the framework of Constructive Type Theory (Martin-Löf, 1984). These papers place a great deal of emphasis on the problem of *sugaring*, that is, the conversion of logical representations into sentences in the language of mathematics. We are not concerned with this problem in this book; our approach follows a more classical linguistic tradition, and is concerned purely with analysis rather than synthesis. Equally, we do not base our analysis on Constructive

Type Theory but on a modified form of Discourse Representation Theory (Kamp and Reyle, 1993) which, as we will show in Chapter 3, is well-suited to describing a range of mathematical phenomena. Nevertheless, there is a substantial amount of material in Ranta's work to which (the earlier parts of) our theory may be compared, and on which our theory improves. In particular, we will solve various problems that Ranta notes in his analyses of plurals (Ranta, 1994, p. 11–12; cf. §3.3.6) and of variables and quantifiers (Ranta, 1994, p. 11–13; cf. §3.5).

Our own work is more ambitious than Ranta's in three respects, which have been introduced in §1.1. First, Ranta exploits Montague's method of fragments (Montague, 1970a,b, 1973) to study small domains in mathematics, such as plane geometry. By contrast, we aim to produce a theory that describes all of mathematics, subject to the restrictions given in §1.3. Thus we are forced to accord much greater weight to ambiguities and notational collisions that arise when the theory simultaneously describes many areas of mathematics.

Second, we extensively analyse symbolic mathematical notation, which is only discussed briefly in Ranta's work. (See §2.4.1 for details of Ranta's analysis). That is, our linguistic theory analyses expressions such as

$$\left| \delta \int_2^\infty \frac{E(t)}{t^{1+\delta}} \, dt \right| < A\delta \int_2^T \frac{dt}{t} + \frac{A\delta}{\log T} \int_T^\infty \frac{dt}{t^{1+\delta}}$$

(Hardy and Wright, 1960, p. 352)

We will find that behaviour of expressions of this kind is complex in a way that has no analogue in natural languages, computer languages, or any other theoretically analysed systems that we are aware of. In addition, there is considerable interaction between such symbolic material and the parts of the language of mathematics that resembles natural language. As noted in §1.1, some of the most challenging problems solved in this book are motivated by the need to find a unified treatment of these two dissimilar parts of mathematical language.

Third, Ranta manually specifies a lexicon for the fragment under consideration. Thus, for example, the theory describing plane geometry is associated with a hand-crafted lexicon containing entries for 'a line', 'a point' and 'the intersection of X and Y'. As noted in §1.1 and §1.2, we do not follow this approach but instead extract all mathematical terms, concepts and notation from definitions.

In addition to these, there are various minor respects in which we extend Ranta's work. For example, Ranta makes little reference to rhetorical structure. Given that mathematics exhibits discourse-level phenomena which do not exist in general language, we need to handle these carefully and explicitly. (Cf. §2.5 and §3.5.) We will highlight such improvements as we encounter them.

Most of the material that directly corresponds to or improves on Ranta's work will be presented in Chapter 3, which presents the basic theoretical framework of the book. (Several minor and self-contained phenomena are relegated to Chapter 8, which outlines miscellaneous extensions to the main theory.) In particular, Chapter 3 will explain how our framework can handle the problems noted by Ranta in his own work. The remainder of the book will introduce more severe problems that arise due to our more ambitious aims, and present solutions to these.

1.5.2 de Bruijn

Parts of this book may be related to de Bruijn's work on a *Mathematical Vernacular* (De Bruijn, 1987), a formal language intermediate between ordinary mathematical practice and formalised computer languages for mathematics (themselves discussed in §1.5.4 below). The Mathematical Vernacular is adaptive (in the sense introduced in §1.1): its lexicon and grammar are not fixed, but expand when definitions in mathematical texts are encountered. Further, de Bruijn's delimitation of the scope of the mathematical vernacular (De Bruijn, 1987) may be compared to our notion of the formal mode (§1.3), with the caveat that the Mathematical Vernacular excludes assertions about relationships between mathematical facts.

Nevertheless, there are significant differences between the our work and de Bruijn's. The Mathematical Vernacular seems to be intended as a practical tool, designed to overcome some of the weaknesses in de Bruijn's computer theorem-proving language Automath. By contrast, we are analysing actual mathematical language from a linguistic perspective. Some consequences of this difference in emphasis are that de Bruijn often takes a prescriptive stance towards mathematics, that he avoids discussing ambiguity by simply inserting extra brackets into mathematical texts (De Bruijn, 1987, p. 935), and that his theory massively overgenerates (see particularly (De Bruijn, 1987, p. 868, §1.10)). Another is that divergences between mathematical practice and the Mathematical Vernacular are often presented without discussion.

In the course of the development of his Mathematical Vernacular, de Bruijn occasionally discusses specific phenomena in the language of mathematics; many of these phenomena will also be considered in this book. As de Bruijn does not base his analysis on any linguistic theory, he tends to organise material according to its surface character, rather than the underlying processes. For example, he makes a detailed taxonomic study of the distinct usages of the indefinite article in Dutch mathematics (De Bruijn, 1982), covering a number of phenomena with analogues in English mathematics. This includes phenomena related to pragmatics (§2.3), variable introduction (§2.4.4, §3.3.4), the treatment of material inside definition blocks (§2.5.1), quantifier scope ambiguity (§4.2.2) and prepositional phrases and genericity (§8.1). In the remainder of the book, we will highlight de Bruijn's observations where they are directly relevant to the phenomena we are analysing.

1.5.3   Computer Languages

There are a number of computer languages for mathematics that have the
stated aim of resembling real mathematical language. Among these, the
language MIZAR (Trybulec, 1978) is considered to be one of the languages
that comes closest to real mathematics (Barendregt and Wiedijk, 2005, p.
14). Figure 1.3 gives an excerpt from this language. Comparing the material
in this excerpt to the corresponding material in a real textbook (Figure 1.2)
shows that there is little resemblance. Accordingly MIZAR, and the majority
of its colleagues, are not relevant to the present discussion; we will not refer
to them again.

Theorem 4.12 (Sylow, 1872).

(i)   If P is a Sylow p-subgroup of a finite group G, then all Sylow p-subgroups
of G are conjugate to P.

(ii)   If there are r Sylow p-subgroups, then r is a divisor of $|G|$ and $r \equiv$
1 (mod p).

Fig. 1.2 Sylow's Theorems in Rotman (1995)

```
theorem  ::  GROUP_10:14
  for G being  finite  Group,
  p being prime (natural  number)  holds
    (for H being  Subgroup  of G st
         H is_p−group_of_prime p holds
      ex P being  Subgroup  of G st
      P is_Sylow_p−subgroup_of_prime p
    & H is Subgroup  of P) &
    (for P1,P2 being  Subgroup  of G
      st P1 is_Sylow_p−subgroup_of_prime p
      & P2 is_Sylow_p−subgroup_of_prime p
      holds P1,P2 are_conjugated );

theorem  ::  GROUP_10:15
  for G being  finite  Group,
    p being prime (natural  number)  holds
    card the_sylow_p−subgroups_of_prime(p,G)
        mod p = 1 &
    card the_sylow_p−subgroups_of_prime(p,G)
        divides  ord G;
```

Fig. 1.3 Sylow's Theorems in MIZAR. From Wiedijk (2009).

A particular exception may be drawn for a recent computer language called
NaProChe, which has the stated intention of expressing mathematics in a way
that is 'nearly natural to human readers' (Koepke, 2009) by utilising techniques from computational linguistics. We will restrict ourselves to considering

NaProChe's contributions towards modelling the language of mathematics, rather than those that relate to computer theorem proving, etc..

When looking for examples which illustrate the NaProChe language, one runs into an immediate difficulty. A key restriction of this NaProChe seems to be that in a given document, one may only refer to mathematical objects of a single type, i.e. only to numbers or only to sets or etc..[3] It is not even possible to talk about numbers and sets of numbers within the same document.[4] Thus we cannot illustrate NaProChe using Sylow's Theorems or any other substantive mathematical results. Nevertheless, mathematically limited examples could potentially be of linguistic interest. One such example is given in Figure 1.4.

Define Trans(x) if and only if $\forall u, v(u \in v \wedge v \in x) \to u \in x$. Define Ord$(x)$ if and only if Trans$(x) \wedge \forall y(y \in x \to $ Trans$(y))$.

Fig. 1.4 Mathematics in NaProChe. From Kuhlwein et al. (2009).

This is certainly easier for a mathematician to read than MIZAR, but at the same time it is at some remove from mathematics as written in textbooks. For example, mathematicians rarely if ever use alphabetical strings to abbreviate assertions, as in 'Trans(x)'; English alternatives such as 'x is transitive' are strongly preferred. Quantifiers and connectives are similarly spelt out in textbooks; symbolic abbreviations such as '$\forall$', '$\wedge$' and '$\to$' are only used in more informal discussions. Further, the bare phrase 'define' is never used to define new assertions, as opposed to new terms; alternatives such as 'we define' or 'we say that' are preferred. The phrase 'if and only if' is not used in definitions. Instead, one invariably uses the word 'if', but this undergoes non-cancellable conditional perfection (Geis and Zwicky, 1971) so that it carries the meaning 'if and only if'.[5] If we were to make these minimally necessary changes, we would be led to the following:

We say that x is transitive if whenever u, v are such that $u \in v$ and $v \in x$, then $u \in x$.

This is acceptable mathematical language, but remains a little stilted. Mathematicians often prefer to use natural language techniques that do not directly correspond to logical operators, in order to state facts more compactly and clearly. For example, one of the authors of NaProChe cites the following textbook excerpt:

A set T is transitive if every element of T is a subset of T.

Koepke (2009), citing Jech (2002).

---

[3] See §3.2 and Chapter 5 for further discussion of types in mathematics.
[4] See Carl et al. (2009).
[5] See §2.3 regarding this phenomenon.

Naproche's authors remark that it is at a prototypical stage, and that the language is currently 'inelegant' (Koepke, 2009, p. 5, p. 10). It seems likely that it will come closer to the actual language of mathematics, but as it stands, NaProChe is sufficiently far removed from that of the language of mathematics that it of limited relevance to the present work. In particular, we will not refer to the syntactic aspects of NaProChe at all. Its main area of relevance is semantic: NaProChe adapts Discourse Representation Theory (or DRT) (Kamp and Reyle, 1993) to provide a semantic representation, on the grounds that it is one of the longest established theories, and that it can analyse a wide range of phenomena (Kolev, 2008, p. 21). We will also adopt a variant of DRT, albeit for very specific reasons.[6] We will provide a comparison of the two DRT-based approaches in §3.5.4.

1.5.4 Other Work

We should note that there are a number of sources which give a linguistic analysis of mathematics in some capacity, but are not comparable to the work in this book. For example, Wolska and Kruijff-Korbayová (2004) describes an experiment that deals with simulated mathematical dialogs, but focuses on subjects with 'little to fair mathematical knowledge' (Wolska and Kruijff-Korbayová, 2004, p. 2). The material produced by these users is not related to the formal dialect of mathematics studied in this book (cf. §1.3). (The paper also treats material in German, whereas we focus exclusively on English.)

---

[6] DRT was developed to handle Geach's 'donkey sentences' (Geach, 1980) and, as we will show in §3.3.1, there are similar sentences in real mathematical texts. We will also be able to adapt DRT to overcome deficiencies noted by Ranta in his own work; see §3.3.2 for details.

2

The Language of Mathematics

We will now give an informal description of the language of mathematics, and highlight some of the major issues that arise to confront a theory of mathematical language. No systematic survey of this kind exists in the literature, and we will therefore for the most part construct our description *ab initio*. Exceptions will be drawn in certain areas where Ranta has discussed similar phenomena, especially in §2.4.

We will start by introducing a basic division of the language of mathematics into 'textual' and 'symbolic' halves (§2.1) and introducing the most important way in which the language of mathematics differs from natural languages (§2.2). We will then examine each of textual and symbolic mathematics in greater detail (§2.3 and §2.4), and finally turn to the macroscopic discourse structure of mathematical language (§2.5).

2.1 Text and Symbol

At first sight, the most striking feature of mathematical language is the way in which it mixes material that looks as if it is drawn from a natural language with material built up out of idiosyncratically mathematical symbols. The distinction is illustrated in Figure 2.1.

There are respects in which the 'natural language' part of mathematics differs from genuine natural languages; for example, as we will discuss below, many pragmatic phenomena are blocked in 'mathematical natural language'. Also, the term 'natural language' carries particular connotations; for example, it suggests that one is dealing with a language that has native speakers. We will therefore use the neutral term 'textual' to refer to the parts of mathematics that resemble natural language. The remaining material will be referred to as 'symbolic', and specific pieces of symbolic mathematics will occasionally be referred to as mathematical 'notation'.

The primary function of symbolic mathematics is to abbreviate material that would be too cumbersome to state with text alone. Thus a sentence

> If $K \leq G$ and there are inclusions $gKg^{-1} \leq K$ for every $g \in G$, then $K \lhd G$: replacing g by g^{-1}, we have the inclusion $g^{-1}Kg \leq K$, and this gives the reverse inclusion $K \leq gKg^{-1}$.
>
> The kernel K of a homomorphism $f : G \to H$ is a normal subgroup: if $a \in K$, then $f(a) = 1$; if $g \in G$, then $f(gag^{-1}) = f(g)f(a)f(g^{-1}) = f(g)f(g^{-1}) = 1$, and so $gag^{-1} \in K$. Hence, $gKg^{-1} \leq K$ for all $g \in G$, and so $K \lhd G$. Conversely, we shall see later that every normal subgroup is the kernel of some homomorphism.

Fig. 2.1 Excerpt from Rotman (1995). Symbolic material highlighted.

The square root of 2 is irrational.

might be expressed more concisely as

$\sqrt{2}$ is irrational.

or even as

$\sqrt{2} \notin \mathbb{Q}$.

Without the capacity of symbolic material to abbreviate text in a remarkably compact way, modern mathematics would quickly become unreadable. For example, the symbolic formula

$$f(gag^{-1}) = f(g)f(a)f(g^{-1})$$

would have to be written as

> The value of f at the product of g and a and the inverse of g is equal to the product of the value of f at g and the value of f at a and the value of f at the inverse of a.

(This last sentence actually contains some residual symbolic material in the form of the variables f, a, and g. Eliminating these would require rewriting the context surrounding the above remark, and the result would be even more unwieldy.)

Because symbolic material functions primarily in an abbreviative capacity, symbolic mathematics tends to occur inside textual mathematics rather than vice versa. Thus mathematical texts are largely composed out of textual sentences, with symbolic material embedded like 'islands' inside text. Most often symbolic terms are embedded in textual contexts that would accept noun phrases, and symbolic formulae are embedded in textual contexts that would accept sentences (i.e. constituents of the category 'S'). For example, in the first sentence of Figure 2.1, the term 'g^{-1}' and the formula '$K \leq G$' appear in contexts that would accept a noun phrase and a sentence respectively. Less frequently, one also find substitutions of symbolic material inside the mathematical equivalents of individual words; for example one might refer to a '$\mathbb{Z}$-module', a '$\mathbb{F}_p$-module', or a '($\mathbb{Z} \times \mathbb{Z}$)-module'.

Ranta states that symbolic material may occur inside textual material, but not vice versa (Ranta, 1997b, pp. 10–11). This remark holds in the fragment he is analysing, which describes only arithmetic and some trigonometry, but is not true of mathematics in general. A counterexample is given by the symbolic term

$$\{(x,y) \in \mathbb{N}^2 \mid x \text{ and } y \text{ are coprime}\}$$

All counterexamples involve symbolic formulae being used in contexts that accept textual sentences. (In fact, formulae and sentences appear to have the same distribution in the register of mathematics we are considering; we know of no context that admits a sentence but not a formula, or vice versa.) When one looks at terms and noun phrases, Ranta's assertion extends to mathematics as a whole; for example, one may not write:

$$\sqrt{\text{the smallest element of } \mathbb{N}}.$$

We will provide a theoretical explanation of this asymmetry of substitutability between terms and noun phrases at the end of §3.3.7.

After discussing another major feature of mathematical language, we will look at each of textual mathematics and symbolic mathematics in more detail (§2.3 and §2.4).

2.2 Adaptivity

When one starts to delve into the language of mathematics, one encounters a phenomenon that is much more remarkable than the use of symbols. Mathematical language *expands* as more mathematics is encountered. The kind of expansion to which we are referring occurs as an individual mathematician reads more and more mathematical texts, and is entirely distinct from the slow change of language over time. All references to 'change' or to 'expansion' in this book will refer to this distinctively mathematical notion, and not to conventional language change. We will call this phenomenon, by which the grammar of an individual mathematician changes as definitions are encountered, *adaptivity*.

Adaptivity occurs when certain mathematical statements, known as definitions, are read. Definitions can change the language of mathematics in two ways. First, they can expand the lexicon of the textual part of mathematics. Second, they can expand the *syntax* of the symbolic part of mathematics. Any given definitions can perform either or both of these functions. For example, consider:

If $\mathfrak{p}$ is a minimal prime of a graded S-module M, we define the *multiplicity* of M at $\mathfrak{p}$, denoted $\mu_{\mathfrak{p}}(M)$, to be the length of $M_{\mathfrak{p}}$ over $S_{\mathfrak{p}}$.

(Hartshorne, 1977, p. 51)

This definition adds the new term 'multiplicity' to the textual part of mathematics and the new notation '$\mu_\bullet(\bullet)$' to the symbolic part of mathematics.[1] As in this example, one always defines new entities in terms of entities that can already be described by the language, such as 'the length of M_p over S_p'. Thus definitions always contain enough information to fully specify the semantics of the material being defined.

Textual adaptivity may be compared to the way in which technical terms are introduced in texts in other fields. There are two differences that are worth emphasising. First, mathematical terms contain no vagueness, and as a result, definitions are perfect specifications of the entities they introduce. For example, the above definition states exactly what (one sense of the word) 'multiplicity' means, leaving no room for disagreement among individual mathematicians as to whether or not the term can be used in a given situation. Second, in advanced mathematics, all mathematical terms are formally introduced by definitions; mathematicians even return to pre-university mathematics and give rigorous definitions for the entities introduced there, such as numbers.[2] Together, these two facts put mathematics on a completely objective basis.

As we will discuss in §2.4, symbolic adaptivity corresponds to the ability to add new syntactic rules to the grammar. This has no correlate in any natural language that we are aware of. As with textual adaptivity, symbolic adaptivity involves no vagueness: the meanings of notations being defined are completely pinned down. Equally, all notations are defined; when mathematicians make pre-university mathematics rigorous, they formally introduce even notations as simple as the addition of numbers used in expressions like '3 + 4'. One point worth emphasising is that just as words may have many senses, any given piece of symbolic mathematics may have many analyses; and just as adding new terms to textual mathematics can increase the degree of word sense ambiguity, adding new notation to symbolic mathematics can increase the degree of ambiguity therein. As we will see in §2.4 and Chapter 4, this includes structural ambiguity; a given piece of symbolic mathematics may be analysed to have many structures.

Finally, it is worth noting that noting that adaptivity in textual material and adaptivity in symbolic material are not as separate as the above discussion may suggest, because textual material can appear inside symbolic constituents and vice versa. For example, as we noted in §2.1, one can refer

---

[1] Note that 'multiplicity' is italicised to emphasise the fact that it is being defined. Some texts use italics for this purpose; others use bold; yet others use both at once, or neither. Because of this last category, i.e. because there exist texts which do not highlight definitions in any way, we will not rely on explicit highlighting to indicate the term being defined at any point in this book.

[2] There are technical problems with the definitions of some elementary objects, which we will discuss in depth in Chapter 7. In that chapter, we will conclude that the problematic definitions can be emended to be completely correct and rigorous; as a result, the technical issues do not affect the current discussion.

to a '$\mathbb{Z}$-module', a '$\mathbb{F}_p$-module', or a '$(\mathbb{Z} \times \mathbb{Z})$-module'. All of these terms are introduced by a definition such as:

> Let A be a ring [...]. An *A-module* is ...
>
> (Atiyah and Macdonald, 1969, p. 17)

As a result, where we come to analyse adaptivity, we will need a unified mechanism to treat the two kinds of adaptivity, rather than two separate mechanisms.

2.3 Textual Mathematics

It is difficult to find examples of textual material with no symbolic material embedded inside them, but there are some. A few such examples may help to convey the general character of textual mathematics:

> The relation of homotopy on paths with fixed endpoints in any space is an equivalence relation.
>
> (Hatcher, 2002, p. 26)

> The set of all rational numbers is countable.
>
> (Rudin, 1964, p. 30)

> Every continuous map from a disk into itself has a fixed point.
>
> (Maehara, 1984, p. 641)

As we noted in §1.3, the language of mathematics consists purely of assertions about mathematical objects. As a result, textual mathematics predominantly uses the third person singular and third person plural, to denote individual mathematical objects (or propositions) and collections of mathematical objects (or propositions) respectively. The first person plural ('we') is also used in a more restricted capacity, with a limited and potentially closed class of verbs, typically to refer to the mutual intent of the author and reader.

Working mathematicians treat mathematical objects *as if* they were Platonic ideals, timeless objects existing independently of the physical world. The interactions and properties of these objects are also seen as frozen, timeless quantities. Mathematical assertions are therefore almost always written as generic (gnomic) sentences in the present simple tense. The only exception is a limited, unproductive, use of the future tense either with passive forms or the first person plural to express intent or to set out conventions which will hold in the remainder of the text. (Cf. 'G will be called the ...' or 'We will call G the ...'.)

The limited variation in person and tense means that inflectional morphology plays only a small part in mathematical language. The only morphological dimensions that exhibit their full range of variation are those of number and mood.

The language of mathematics also utilises a very limited amount of derivational morphology. The most common case is the reification of a property. For example, 'the associativity of $*$' is equivalent to 'the fact that $*$ is associative'. It is also worth noting that the effect of apparent derivations can be unpredictable; for example, to say that a function is 'nonnegative' is not the opposite of saying that it is 'negative'.[3] As a result, careful authors often define derived forms.

The syntax of textual mathematics also exhibits relatively limited variation. A much narrower range of constructions is used than in general natural language, so that mathematical language is formulaic and at first sight repetitive. And in particular, almost no instances of constructions involving long-distance dependencies (topicalisation, etc.) occur in mathematics. Together with the sharply limited range of morphological forms used in mathematical language, this means that textual mathematics can be effectively captured by a context-free grammar (in the sense of (Jurafsky and Martin, 2009, p. 387)).

In contrast to the morphology and syntax of textual mathematics, its lexicon is remarkably varied. As we have noted above, the mechanism of adaptivity is used to expand the lexicon in every significant mathematical text. Even if we were to restrict attention to lexemes which have become reasonably widespread in their respective domains, compiling a full lexicon of mathematical terms would take a lifetime's work. (Fortunately, modelling adaptivity itself means that that step can be avoided.)

However, a subtler distinction can be drawn. As well as the productive mathematical lexemes that comprise the bulk of the lexicon of textual mathematics, there are a small number of non-mathematical or 'extra-mathematical' lexemes used to connect mathematical lexemes and structure mathematical arguments. (Examples are 'hence', 'denote' and 'suppose'.) Mathematical language also uses a number of standard extra-mathematical phrases which are essentially non-existent in general language, such as 'without loss of generality' or 'it remains to prove that'; often such phrases are so standardised as to have standardised abbreviations (such as 'w.l.o.g'). These phrases are sufficiently rigid as to be best regarded as individual (extra-)mathematical lexemes, rather than as compositionally constructed constituents. The extra-mathematical subset of the lexicon is extremely unproductive, resisting even the adoption of general-language synonyms of the words in the phrases it contains; for example, one would never find 'one does not lose any generality by assuming that ...' as a synonym for 'without loss of generality, ...'. Once again, this gives mathematical language a formulaic, repetitive character.

Regarding semantics, there are three points to note. First, textual mathematics is much more restricted than natural language. For example, as noted above, we are dealing with timeless facts and therefore do not need to consider tense or events. There are no propositional attitude reports or similar

---

[3] The proper explanation of what is happening here is that the derivation from 'negative' to 'nonnegative' occurs on the level of adjectives describing numbers, and the two lexical items are then separately 'lifted' to describe functions.

constructs, and therefore no intensionality. Mathematical truths are true in all possible worlds, and therefore there is no modality. (And so on.) There are still presuppositions, anaphors, prepositional phrases, elided constituents and other interesting constructs — but mathematics can be described using a fraction of the semantic machinery used to describe general natural language. This means that it is more feasible to construct total semantic models for mathematics than natural language. Rather than primarily analysing individual phenomena in isolation, we can reasonably attempt to set up a compact semantic framework which assigns a deep semantic analysis to all mathematical sentences.

Second, (the relevant parts of) the standard semantic apparatus are much more effective on textual mathematics than general natural language. For example, while mathematical language can contain (extensive) ambiguity, it is completely free from vagueness. All mathematical assertions are either true or false, with no middle ground.[4] Similarly, mathematical language is not used metaphorically, ironically or in any similar way; the meaning of mathematical language is always its literal meaning. We can sum up effects of this kind by saying that all of the meaning of mathematics can be captured by (nearly) standard semantic representations to a much greater degree than is the case with general natural language.

Third, as noted in §1.2.1, semantic representations for mathematics are anchored with respect to a concretely specified external reference in a way that semantic representations for natural language are not. When applying semantics to a general natural language, we have a great deal of freedom to choose among representations. By contrast, any semantic representation for mathematics should be very similar to a fixed, consensual, standard of 'the content of mathematics', namely assertions in the predicate calculus about the sets of Zermelo-Fraenkel set theory.[5]

Finally, from a pragmatic perspective, textual mathematics is extremely unusual. To a first approximation, mathematics does not exhibit any pragmatic phenomena: the meaning of a mathematical sentence is merely its compositionally determined semantic content, and nothing more. In order to state this point more precisely, we need to remove some of the ambiguity inherent in the term 'pragmatics'. We will do so by adopting the following distinction:

> Near-side pragmatics is concerned with the nature of certain facts that are relevant to determining what is said. Far-side pragmatics is focused on what happens beyond saying: what speech acts are performed in or by saying what is said, or what implicatures are generated by saying what is said.
>
> (Korta and Perry, 2008)

---

[4] Strictly speaking, there are assertions that are logically independent of the axioms being used, and so are neither true nor false. Their status is however completely precise, and they are in no way connected to vagueness.

[5] We will find phenomena which do not fit into this model (see e.g. §3.3.1, §7.2.1). Thus our representation will be *similar* to but not *equal* to the predicate calculus, and will be more nuanced as regards the role of sets.

Most issues relating to near-side pragmatics do not arise in connection with mathematical language. For example, because mathematics is concerned with timeless facts, indexicals and demonstratives never occur in mathematical language.[6]

By contrast, mathematics certainly contains sentences that one would expect to trigger 'far-side' pragmatic phenomena. However, such phenomena simply do not occur. For example, the sentence

The group of symmetries of the cube contains a nontrivial subgroup.

might be expected to trigger an implicature that the group in question contains exactly one nontrivial subgroup. This is not the case; mathematicians would read the above as exactly equivalent to

The group of symmetries of the cube contains **at least one** nontrivial subgroup.

in every respect. Similarly, apparently generic statements such as

A domain is simply connected.

are always read as simple universals when they occur in mathematics; unlike most cases of generics in natural language, they do not admit any exceptions.[7]

There is one important apparent exception to the rule about the absence of pragmatic phenomena.[8] In most definitions, there is an instance of the word 'if' which introduces the conditions under which the defined term or notation applies. For example:

A field K is said to be algebraically closed **if** every polynomial with coefficients in K has a root in K.

(Dummit and Foote, 2003, p. 543; emphasis ours)

This 'if' undergoes conditional perfection (Geis and Zwicky, 1971) to 'if and only if' (sometimes abbreviated 'iff'). Conditional perfection always occurs in definitions and never occurs in other statements. This phenomenon cannot be

---

[6] The primary exception is the pronoun 'we', and this should be read as serving a specific rhetorical function rather than being construed compositionally. One way to see this is by noting that every instance of 'we' in a mathematical text could be rewritten without using indexicals. (Typically one does this by using the passive mood.)

[7] See also the discussion of universals of this kind in Dutch mathematics in (De Bruijn, 1982, p. 85).

[8] The only other possible exception to this rule arises with scalar implicatures of number. The quantifier 'three' might be read as meaning 'at least three' in mathematics. It is very difficult to tell because mathematicians avoid the issue — they almost always write 'at least three' or 'precisely three', or use a circumlocution involving sets.

cancelled. As such, despite its clear roots in pragmatic phenomena in natural language, it may be better analysed as a semantic phenomenon idiosyncratic to mathematics than as a pragmatic phenomenon.

Due to the absence of pragmatic phenomena, phenomena which are sometimes analysed as semantic and sometimes analysed as pragmatic can be treated as being purely semantic where they occur in mathematics, i.e. they can be analysed in purely truth-conditional terms. This applies particularly to presuppositions, which play an important role in mathematics. Because of its restricted subject domain, mathematics does not contain the more exotic kinds of presupposition-related constructs, such as propositional attitude reports. However, definite descriptions like 'the set of natural numbers' abound in mathematical language, and the (mathematically important) presuppositions that they carry can be analysed in purely semantic terms. In the next chapter, we will also analyse certain selectional restrictions as being presuppositional in nature, because this analysis copes with the embedding of symbolic material inside text. For example, as neither 'π is prime' nor 'π is not prime' is felicitous, we will say that 'prime' presupposes that its argument is an integer; this analysis is well-suited to cope with phrases like 'x is prime', in which the properties of x cannot be compositionally determined. (Cf. §2.4.4 on *variables* like 'x').

2.4 Symbolic Mathematics

The general nature of textual mathematics could be compactly conveyed because we were able to reuse the terminology and concepts created in linguistics to describe natural languages. As there is no comparable model to rely on when describing symbolic mathematics, our discussion will be somewhat lengthier, and certain subtler topics that are not suitable for an overview will be deferred to later chapters (as indicated below).

2.4.1 Ranta's Account and Its Limitations

The only substantive survey of symbolic mathematics occurs in the paper Ranta (1997b). This paper is purely concerned with analysing a fragment describing arithmetic and trigonometry. In this section we will summarise the analysis given in that paper and outline the reasons why it cannot be extended to cover symbolic mathematics as a whole.

Although Ranta (1997b) considers mathematics in French, the symbolic material under discussion has exactly the same form that it would take in English, and so the analysis given there is also applicable to arithmetic and trigonometry in English mathematics. The analysis classifies all symbolic material into eight categories which form part of a context-free grammar; the relevant categories can be seen in Figure 2.2. This classification is entirely adequate for the fragment Ranta is considering. However, it cannot be extended to capture the breadth of symbolic material in mathematics as a whole, as is required for our purposes.[9] We will now list some of the more important reasons why this is the case; the list should not be taken as exhaustive.

Category	Example
formula	$x < 2$
term	$\sin(x + 1)$
constant	4
variable	x
2-place predicate	$<$
prefix	sin
postfix	!
infix	+

Fig. 2.2 Categories in Ranta (1997b)

First, there are many notations that cannot be captured in this scheme. For example, if k is a field and K is a field extension of k, one may refer to '$[K : k]$' (Lang, 1993, p. 224); if α and β are ordinal numbers and m and n are natural numbers, one may assert that '$\alpha \to (\beta)_n^m$' (Erdös and Rado, 1956, pp. 429–430); and if (p_n) is a sequence in some metric space, then one may refer to '$\lim_{n \to \infty} p_n$' (Rudin, 1964, p. 47). Schematically, one has:

$$[\bullet : \bullet], \qquad \bullet \to (\bullet)_{\bullet}^{\bullet}, \qquad \lim_{\circ \to \infty} \bullet_\circ$$

(The circle in the third of these notations indicates an arbitrary 'dummy variable'; we will discuss this further in §2.4.4.)

Each of these notations is monolithic, rather than being built up out of simpler notations. So, for example, '$[K : k]$' is not built up using an infix operator ':' — '$K : k$' is meaningless, and cannot even be referred to as an 'expression'.

Second, even if we work within the classification given above, the boundaries between categories are not fixed. For example, consider:

Definition. An operation $*$ on a group G is associative if

$$(a * b) * c = a * (b * c)$$

(Rotman, 1995, p. 10)

When we say that $*$ is associative, we are treating it as a term; but when we write '$a * b$', we are treating it as a infixed operator. Similarly, the putative

---

[9] We should emphasise that Ranta (1997b) does not share this aim; our purpose here is not to criticise the paper, but to show that our analysis will need to run along different lines.

prefix operator 'sin' is treated as a term in statements like 'the function sin is continuous', and any relation R (which is a mathematical object, i.e., a term) functions as a binary predicate in expressions like 'aRb'.

In a similar vein, objects which function as prefixed or infixed operators or as binary predicates under Ranta's classification may themselves have internal structure. For example, if H and N are groups and $\overset{\curvearrowright}{\alpha}$ is a homomorphism from H to the group of automorphisms of N, then one may refer to '$H \rtimes_\alpha N$' (Robinson, 1996, p. 27). Here '$\rtimes_\alpha$' functions like an infixed operator, but has internal structure. Equally, '$\sin^2$' in '$\sin^2 x$' is a prefix operator with internal structure, and the transitive closure 'R^*' of a relation 'R' is a binary predicate with internal structure. This kind of internal structure may be represented in a context-free grammar like Ranta's by adding appropriate rules, but only at the cost of substantial overgeneration.

Third, and most significantly, mathematics is adaptive: new symbolic notations are introduced as new definitions are encountered. Even if we could categorise all the notations we had encountered, there would always be a possibility that fresh definitions would introduce notations that were incompatible with our classification. More generally: whatever theory we give about the range of forms that symbolic material may take, that theory must be compatible with adaptivity; the theory under discussion is not.

For the reasons we have just given, the analysis given for the fragment in Ranta (1997b) is not an appropriate basis for an analysis of symbolic material in mathematics as a whole.

2.4.2 *Surface Phenomena*

Much of the popular mystique of mathematics arises from the fact that symbolic constituents can become quite arcane in appearance. Consider, for example:

$$\left| \delta \int_2^\infty \frac{E(t)}{t^{1+\delta}} \, dt \right| < A\delta \int_2^T \frac{dt}{t} + \frac{A\delta}{\log T} \int_T^\infty \frac{dt}{t^{1+\delta}}$$

(Hardy and Wright, 1960, p. 352)

In reality, the exotic, visually complex, character of such expressions arises mainly from the combination of terms via superscripts, subscripts and other 'positional' operations. The six positions marked in the following diagram encompass all the positional operations we have encountered in symbolic mathematics:

$$\begin{smallmatrix} 6 & & 1 & & 2 \\ 5 & & \bullet & & 3 \\ & & 4 & \end{smallmatrix}$$

Positions 2 and 3, corresponding to superscripts and subscripts, are by far the most common. 'Two-dimensional' visually complex notation (for integrals, sums with conditions, etc.) is built up by combining various positional operations.

There is no obstacle to assimilating this kind of positional notation directly into, say, the context-free grammars typically used to describe formal languages. For example, we could capture superscripts by using a context-free rule:

$$Term \rightarrow Term^{Term}$$

Alternatively, we could linearise positional operations in a reversible way, by writing e.g. '$superscript(x, y)$' in place of 'x^y'. Either way, the 'two-dimensionality' of symbolic mathematics is entirely superficial; for all practical purposes, mathematical notation can be described like more conventional 'linear' material.

One also finds that new symbols are occasionally introduced into mathematical notation. Again we have the option either of encoding these directly into context-free rules or converting them into a more restrictive language, for example by translating them into strings in a fixed alphabet. Whichever option we choose, this mild productivity of the class of mathematical symbols will not have any effect on the phenomena we will discuss, and we will not need to consider it again.

2.4.3 Grammatical Status

Having dispensed with the above technicalities, we can ask what kind of formalism is needed to capture symbolic mathematics. A natural first question is to ask whether mathematical notation is in fact well described by a context-free grammar. The answer is quite complex. The first observation we should make is that the syntax of symbolic mathematics is sensitive to the kinds of mathematical objects that occur in it. For example, the following pieces of notation are defined in various areas of mathematics:[10]

- $M \rightarrow N$
- (e)
- x^y
- x_y

Combining these four syntactic operations allows us to parse

$$\alpha \rightarrow (\beta)_n^m$$

And yet, as we noted in §2.4.1, if α and β are ordinal numbers and m and n are natural numbers, then this notation must be parsed as a *single syntactic operation* on four arguments, namely α, β, m and n. (The operation in question refers to a property of graphs; see Erdös and Rado (1956).) If α, β, m and n are of other types, then this reading is not available.

---

[10] '$M \rightarrow N$' occurs with limits, chained arrow notation or in the lambda calculus. The other three pieces of notation are ubiquitous.

Thus, in some intuitive sense, syntax is dependent on the *types* of expressions in a way that does not occur in existing formal languages. As we will show in §3.2 and Chapter 4, this notion of type is too semantic itself to be formalised in syntactic terms. In other words, the type of an expression is too closely related to what that expression refers to for purely syntactic notions of type to be applicable.

Dealing with this type-dependence of syntax will require a major departure from existing methods for describing formal languages, and will take up a substantial portion of this book. We will introduce the problem in more precise terms in Chapter 4, and resolve it in Chapter 5 and Chapter 6. But for the purposes of the present overview, we need to shove this elephantine issue into a metaphorical drawer, so that we may look at orthogonal issues. One way to do this is to consider ourselves to be looking at maths *locally*: because a relatively limited number of types and syntactic operations occur in each small area of maths, notational clashes are rare and type-independent syntax is sufficient.

If we take this step, symbolic mathematics can be effectively modelled as being context-free. In contrast to nearly all formal languages from mathematics and computer science, it cannot be effectively described by a more restricted syntactic model. For example, a $LR(1)$ model is clearly insufficient. One way to see this is to observe that it is possible to write ambiguous expressions in symbolic mathematics. Suppose that, using an appropriate definition, we introduce the new piece of notation described by

$Term \rightarrow Term \oplus Term$

In essence, we have introduced a new binary operator '$\oplus$'. Now, suppose that immediately after introducing '$\oplus$', we refer to

$1 \oplus 2 \oplus 3$.

This expression has two possible parse trees, corresponding to '$(1 \oplus 2) \oplus 3$' and '$1 \oplus (2 \oplus 3)$'. There is no way to tell which is intended based on the available information — although the first reading would be appropriate for most mathematical operators, there are certainly operators that require the second. Thus the expression is genuinely ambiguous. The example also suggests one reason why many mathematical texts make a point of emphasising that specific operations are associative: associativity allows one to 'drop brackets' and write expressions like '$1 \oplus 2 \oplus 3$' without ambiguity.

Digressing briefly, is worth noting that the example just given only touches on the surface of ambiguity. Ambiguity is absolutely pervasive in both symbolic and textual mathematics, and (as with other phenomena) there are enough examples of ambiguity which intertwine symbolic and textual information that a unified account of textual and symbolic aspects is necessary. The proper description of ambiguity requires so much space that we will dedicate Chapter 4 to it, and will not discuss it further in this section, except to clear up one possible source of misunderstanding. To wit: most ambiguity in mathematics is *not* noticed by mathematicians, just as the extensive ambiguity in natural languages is "simply not noticed by the majority of language users and this testifies to the efficiency and robustness of their mechanisms for disambiguation" (Briscoe, 1988, p. 22). Mathematicians' mechanisms for disambiguating mathematical language are comparably efficient and robust. Replicating them poses a major challenge for a linguistic theory, which we will tackle in Chapter 5 and Chapter 6.

Returning to the main topic, we should also ask whether symbolic mathematics contains phenomena which cannot be modeled by a context free grammar, and require some more powerful formalism. If we set aside the issue of types and also the possibility of including textual material inside symbolic material, as in

$$\{(x,y) \in \mathbb{N}^2 \mid x \text{ and } y \text{ are coprime}\},$$

then we know of no examples where context-free rules cannot capture the syntax of symbolic mathematics. Stronger, there is a good reason why we would expect this to be the case. Symbolic notation is always learnt from definitions. For example, the notation '[● : ●]' denoting the degree of a field extension, can be learnt from the following definition:

If E is an extension of F, we denote by

$$[E : F]$$

the dimension of E as a vector space over F.

(Lang, 1993, p. 224)

Here E and F are variables, which we will discuss in §2.4.4; for present purposes we only need to note that context-free rules can be extracted from definitions by replacing variables with 'slots' accepting other terms. Thus, for example, the phrase '$[E : F]$' in the above definition would result in the creation of a context-free rule:

Term → [Term : Term]

We know of no way in which definitions give rise to rules except by 'replacing variables with slots' in this way; and rules generated thus are necessarily context-free.

2.4.4 *Variables*

As noted in §2.1, symbolic material always abbreviates text, and while replacing symbols by text results in extremely lengthy prose that is difficult to follow, it is nearly always possible. The primary exception relates to *variables*, such as C and T in

Any compact subspace C of a Hausdorff space T is closed in T.

(Sutherland, 1975, p. 82)

Variables in mathematical texts function similarly to variables in the predicate calculus (Hamilton, 1988): they need to be bound (at the logical level) and serve as a mechanism for expressing quantification. Thus the remark above corresponds to

$$\forall T.(topological\_space(T) \land hausdorff(T) \Rightarrow$$
$$(\forall C.(subspace(C,T) \land compact(C) \Rightarrow closed(C,T)))).$$

In most cases, it is not possible to eliminate all variables from mathematical texts while remaining in the formal register. There is a reason for this. Mathematical arguments involve sufficiently many entities that trying to refer unambiguously to those entities by using pronouns or other anaphoric expressions is not viable. Variables allow mathematicians to refer to specific entities in an extremely compact manner. In essence, they serve as a mathematical alternative to anaphor. They cannot be eliminated precisely because anaphor is not powerful enough to replace them. (This said, we should emphasise that anaphors are also used in mathematical texts; cf. §8.1.)

Finally, there are some specific points about variables that we should note. First, the exact rules concerning the binding of variables in mathematical texts are subtly different to those for the predicate calculus; the discussion of this point is lengthy, and will be deferred to §3.3.1. Second, variables may be introduced in one sentence and used in subsequent sentences; we will discuss this usage when we discuss the rhetorical structure of mathematics in §2.5 below. Third, variables may be bound inside a *single* piece of mathematical notation; cf. 'n' in

$$\sum_{n=1}^{N} f(\mathbf{n}).$$

Such 'dummy variables' behave exactly like the variables of the predicate calculus, and do not exhibit any distinctively mathematical properties.

2.4.5 *Presuppositions*

As we noted in §2.1, the primary function of symbolic expressions is to abbreviate textual material. Most symbolic notations actually abbreviate definite descriptions. For example, $\sqrt{2}$ abbreviates 'the square root of 2'; if M is a matrix, 'M^{-1}' abbreviates 'the inverse of M'; and so on. As a result, symbolic terms can themselves carry presuppositions. For example, '$\sqrt{x}$' presupposes that x has a square root, i.e. that x is nonnegative, and 'M^{-1}' presupposes that M has an inverse.

One also finds that symbolic formulae can carry presuppositions, if they abbreviate a phrase that carries presuppositions. For example, if n and m are numbers, then '$n|m$' abbreviates 'n divides m'. Following the approach discussed at the end of §2.3, we analyse 'n divides m' as carrying a presupposition that n and m are integers (cf. the infelicity of 'π divides π^2'); and so this same presupposition is borne by the notation '$n|m$'.

2.4.6 Symbolic Constructions

Symbolic mathematics also contains a range of minor constructions which we do not have space to discuss in detail here. For example:

1. One can compress certain symbolic formulae by writing '$a < b < c$' for '$a < b$ and $b < c$',
2. in some contexts one can use commas to assert that many variables have a particular property by stating, say, that '$\mathbf{n}, \mathbf{m} \in \mathbb{N}$', and
3. in certain contexts one can use certain formulae to stand for terms, as in 'For every real number $\boldsymbol{\epsilon} > \mathbf{0}$, ...'.

Such phenomena will be described in §8.2.

2.5 Rhetorical Structure

When one considers rhetorical relationships between sentences, as described in, say, Asher and Lascarides (2003), mathematical language is extremely simple. This is partly because many of the dimensions involved in rhetorical relations in natural language are not present in mathematical text; for example, the notion of time is inapplicable, and so one cannot present events occurring in a sequence.[11] But above and beyond this, there is a very strong (although not inviolable) convention regarding argument structure in continuous sections of mathematical text. This convention requires that in running prose each sentence in a text is a logical consequence of previous sentences. Thus arguments flow from beginning to end in linear order; it is extremely rare that an author will, for example, state a fact and then elaborate on the reason why it is true. This convention reflects and supports the way in which mathematical texts are normally read; one typically reads a sentence, mentally verifies it, and only then moves to the next sentence. In this respect, stating a fact in one sentence and elaborating it in later sentences is potentially confusing: some readers might attempt to verify the bare fact without looking forwards.

Thus mathematics makes minimal use of the rhetorical mechanisms that are available in natural language. However, this rhetorical simplicity is offset by the existence of two rhetorical mechanisms that are specific to mathematics; we will now consider these in turn.

2.5.1 Blocks

Mathematical texts frequently include *blocks* of mathematics which are explicitly typeset separately from the surrounding text; as a result, such blocks

---

[11] One important explanation to this rule is the relationship of explanation or justification, which we will discuss in §3.5.1.

are much more explicit than the rhetorical constructs available in natural language. Some examples of blocks are

> **Lemma 15.** If $m \geq 2n$, then $\varepsilon(\vec{G}; x, y) = 0$.
>
> (Bollobás, 1979, p. 20)

and

> **Proposition 4.2.** If $r(\mathfrak{a})$ is maximal, then $\mathfrak{a}$ is primary. In particular, the powers of a maximal ideal $\mathfrak{m}$ are $\mathfrak{m}$-primary.
>
> (Atiyah and Macdonald, 1969, p. 51)

These particular blocks are *results*; a result explicitly presents an important mathematical fact without actually proving it. Results serve four purposes. First, they allow an author to explicitly break from the convention that each sentence is the logical consequence of previous sentences. Second, they emphasise particularly important material. Third, they allow a separation between the statement of an important piece of mathematics and the arguments showing that that statement is true. This is accomplished by typesetting a second block, called a 'proof', immediately after the original result. Thus one finds:

> **Proposition 1.5.** The map $\beta_h : \pi_1(X, x1) \to \pi_1(X, x0)$ is an isomorphism.
>
> **Proof:** We see first that β_h is a homomorphism since $\beta_h[f \cdot g] = [h \cdot f \cdot g \cdot \bar{h}] = [h \cdot f \cdot \bar{h} \cdot h \cdot g \cdot \bar{h}] = \beta_h[f]\beta_h[g]$. Further, β_h is an isomorphism with inverse $\beta_{\bar{h}}$ since $\beta_h \beta_{\bar{h}}[f] = \beta_h[\bar{h} \cdot f \cdot h] = [h \cdot \bar{h} \cdot f \cdot h \cdot \bar{h}] = [f]$, and similarly $\beta_{\bar{h}} \beta_h[f] = [f]$. $\qquad\qquad\qquad\qquad\qquad\qquad\qquad\qquad\qquad\qquad\square$
>
> (Hatcher, 2002, p. 28)

(Note the use of a special symbol, '$\square$', to end a proof. This symbol is sometimes called the 'Halmos symbol'.)

Fourth, results facilitate cross referencing. Later mathematical text may refer back to results by number or by name, as in:

> By Lemma 15 each summand is 0 so the sum is also 0.
>
> (Bollobás, 1979, p. 20)

It is standard to number all results, using the chapter number and sometimes the section number as a stem for the result number. Typically, results are named if they are famous or important and are therefore likely to be referred to in other mathematical texts. (An exception is sometimes drawn for results that are short enough to restate compactly.) Named results are often named after their originator.

As well as propositions and lemmas, results include theorems and corollaries to other results. The exact role of each kind of result may vary between texts. After results, the most important kind of block is a *definition*, such as:

> **Definition.** Let V/K be a projective variety and choose $\mathbb{A}^n \subset \mathbb{P}^n$ such that $V \cap \mathbb{A}^n \neq \emptyset$. The *dimension of V* is the dimension of $V \cap \mathbb{A}^n$.
>
> (Silverman, 2009, p. 10)

Unfortunately, the word 'definition' is widely used both to refer to definition blocks like the one just presented, and to definitions of individual concepts, like the the definition of 'the dimension of a vector space' in the sentence

The *dimension of V* is the dimension of $V \cap \mathbb{A}^n$.

(Note that the word 'dimension' is polysemous and occurs in two different senses in this example, so that the definition is not circular. We will discuss examples of this kind in greater detail in Chapter 4.)

This dual usage of 'definition' is potentially confusing, but is so standard among mathematicians that we have no choice but to follow it. We will, however, refer to *definition blocks* and *definition statements* where there is a risk of confusion.

Material that is presented inside definition blocks follows a specific convention. Inside such blocks, usages of the verb 'to be' as the main verb in a sentence are taken to introduce definition statements, rather than being assertions.[12] For example, our statement

The dimension of V **is** the dimension of $V \cap \mathbb{A}^n$.

is only read as a definition statement because it occurs inside a definition block; if we it had expressed the same statement outside a definition block, it would be taken as an assertion about a property of dimensions, rather than a definition.[13]

Notwithstanding this, we should emphasise that not all definition statements occur inside definition blocks; definition statements may be introduced anywhere, as long as they do not involve the verb 'to be' as the main verb. For example, one can write:

We **define** a regular function on Spec R to be simply an element of R.

(Eisenbud and Harris, 2000, p. 10; emphasis ours)

There are also several other kinds of blocks which occur in mathematical texts but which do not exhibit any distinctive behaviour; the most frequent kinds are 'Remarks' and 'Examples'.

2.5.2 *Variables and Assumptions*

In mathematical discourses, it is possible to introduce a variable in one sentence and refer to it in subsequent sentences. For example, one can write,

Let ϵ be any positive real number.

---

[12] A similar observation is made in (De Bruijn, 1987, p. 932).

[13] As noted in §2.2, we will not rely on the italicisation of 'dimension of V', which varies between texts, in formulating our analyses. But when such text-dependent highlighting is present, it invariably marks a definition rather than an assertion.

Following such an assertion, ϵ can be referred to in any subsequent sentence as if it were a concrete quantity; and yet any discourses formed in this way implicitly quantify over many values of ϵ. To be more precise, a discourse

Let *[var]* be a *[N-bar]*. $S_1. S_2. \dots S_n$.

would encode the meaning

$\forall [var].([translation\ of\ 'var\ is\ a\ N\text{-}bar'] \Rightarrow (\hat{S}_1 \wedge \dots \wedge \hat{S}_n))$

where $\hat{S}_i$ is the meaning of S_i. For example, the discourse

Let ϵ be any positive real number. Then there exists a natural number N which is greater than ϵ.

encodes the meaning,

$\forall \epsilon.((real(\epsilon) \wedge positive(\epsilon)) \Rightarrow \exists N.(natural(N) \wedge greater(N, \epsilon)))$

If mathematicians were not able to use variables in this way, they would need to write *extremely* long sentences.

It is also possible to introduce long-term assumptions in a way that parallels the introduction of variables. For example, if one writes

Suppose that 2 is the square of a rational number.

any sentences that follow are taken to be conditional on this fact. More formally, a discourse

Suppose that P. $S_1. S_2. \dots S_n$.

encodes the meaning

$\hat{P} \Rightarrow (\hat{S}_1 \wedge \dots \wedge \hat{S}_n)$

where $\hat{P}$ is the meaning of P and $\hat{S}_i$ is the meaning of S_i.

The main difference between the introduction of variables and the introduction of assumptions is that it is possible to revoke assumptions. This is typical of arguments by contradiction; one supposes that P, deduces a contradiction, and thereby proves that P is false and revokes it; it also occurs when one is showing that some facts hold in several cases, or proving a bidirectional implication.

2.6 Reanalysis

Reanalysis is a phenomenon whereby an individual mathematician's analysis of a mathematical expression can change as more mathematics is learnt. As far as we are aware, this phenomenon has not been commented on before;

the term we have chosen, 'reanalysis', is used to describe a comparable phenomenon in philology. We will introduce it by considering a simple question:[14]

What is a power of a number x?

This question is interesting because the reply will depend on how much mathematics the respondent knows. Here are some typical responses:

Squares.   One can write x^2 to mean $x \times x$.

Squares and Cubes.   One can write x^2 to mean $x \times x$, or x^3 to mean $x \times x \times x$.

Positive Powers.

One can write x^n to mean $\underbrace{x \times x \times \cdots \times x}_{n \text{ copies of } x}$, where n is one of $1, 2, 3, \ldots$.

Non-negative Powers.

A.   One can write x^n just as above when n is one of $1, 2, 3, \ldots$;

B.   if $x \neq 0$, one can write x^0 to mean 1.

Integer Powers.

A.   One can write x^n just as above when n is one of $0, 1, 2, 3, \ldots$;

B.   if $x \neq 0$, one can write x^n to mean $1/x^{-n}$, where n is one of $-1, -2, -3, \ldots$.

Fractional Powers.[a]

If $x > 0$ and $q = a/b$ is a fraction, then one can write x^q to mean $(\sqrt[b]{x})^a$. (Here $\sqrt[b]{x}$ is the largest real number y such that $y^b = x$.)

Real Powers.[b]

If $x > 0$ and y is a real number, then one can write x^y to mean $\exp(y \log x)$.

Complex Powers.[c]

If $x \in (\mathbb{C} \setminus \{x \in \mathbb{R} \mid x \leq 0\})$ and z is a complex number, then one can write x^z to mean $\exp(z \operatorname{Log} x)$.

---

[a] Note that the integer and fractional versions are consistent on fractions that happen to be integers, like '6/2'.

[b] Again, the fractional and real versions are consistent on real numbers that happen to be fractions, although this time it requires a little work to prove.

[c] Again, the real and complex versions are consistent.

Which of the above definitions is correct? Let us consider various possible answers:

---

[14] We deliberately gloss over the type of x, i.e., over whether x is integer or real or complex or etc.. In this otherwise excellent example, we actually face the complication of reanalysis happening in two independent dimensions, corresponding to x and the exponent; presenting this formally only serves to confuse matters. A concerned reader may take x to be real in all but the final definition, in which it should be taken to be complex.

Only the last one is correct.   This is a tempting position, but the problem with it lies in the fact that it is difficult to know when the above list is finished; there is always a possibility that there is some natural generalisation to an even larger class of numbers.[15] In other words, there can always be always a 'better answer' and so we can never be sure that we have the 'best' answer.

None of them are correct.   This is arguably a logically tenable position, but it is hardly practical. So we find ourselves forced towards:

They are all correct.   This seems nearly right; nevertheless, two different definitions of 'power' cannot simultaneously apply. To make sense of this, we need to emend it to:

They are all correct, but at different 'times'.   In other words, the definition of 'power', and the associated symbolic notation, can change over time as a mathematician learns more mathematics.

So we have moved towards a *mutable* notion of notation. Contentious as this may seem, there is ample evidence that it occurs in real mathematics; the key fact which prevent this from causing chaos is that, as in our examples above, the modified definitions are invariably consistent with the old definitions where they overlap — that is, reanalysis is invariably *monotonic*.

There are two points worth noting here. First, reanalysis can sometimes cause the syntactic analysis of a fixed expression to change without affecting its meaning. For example, the '2' in 'x^2' is initially taken to be a fixed symbol, and only later reanalysed as a number. (i.e. we have shifted from '$\bullet^2$' to '$\bullet^{\bullet}$'.) The same may be said of the '0' in '$\aleph_0$'. Another example is given by the fundamental group '$\pi_1(X)$' of a topological space X. There are two distinct dimensions of reanalysis that may occur here. First, after one encounters $\pi_2(X)$, etc., '1' is reanalysed to be considered as a number rather than a

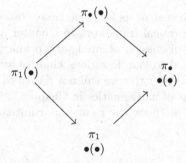

Fig. 2.3 Possible Paths of Reanalysis for '$\pi_1(X)$'

---

[15] And in fact, such a generalisation exists; both complex numbers and cardinal numbers can naturally be regarded as lying inside the algebraic closure of Conway's surreal numbers (Conway, 2001).

fixed token. Second, when one learns some category theory, 'π_1' (or 'π_n', if the first reanalysis has occurred) is reanalysed as a functor, and the entire expression '$\pi_1(X)$' is reanalysed as an example of functor application. Figure 2.3 presents the possible reanalyses in this case schematically. Of course, any given individual mathematician may happen to begin at one of the 'later' positions, for example by encountering the fundamental group after some amount of category theory, and so learning about 'π_1' as a functor *ab initio*.

The second point is that when reanalysis occurs, the overt definition of the 'new' form need not subsume the definition of the 'old' form. For example, the 'fractional powers' definition above did not cover powers of negative numbers, like

$$(-2)^{-2},$$

even though these could be analysed under the previous 'integer powers' rule. The key point here is that the two definitions agree where they overlap. The actual 'complete' definition of power simply becomes the disjunction of every explicit definition. Thus at the end of the main example given above, one has a final definition that is something like:

- One can write x^n to mean $\underbrace{x \times x \times \cdots \times x}_{n \text{ copies of } x}$, where n is one of $1, 2, 3, ...$;
- if $x \neq 0$, you can write x^0 to mean 1;
- if $x \neq 0$, you can write x^n to mean $1/x^{-n}$, where n is one of $-1, -2, -3, ...$;
- if $x \in (\mathbb{C} \setminus \{x \in \mathbb{R} \mid x \leq 0\})$ and z is a complex number, then you can write x^z to mean $\exp(z \operatorname{Log} x)$.

As we emphasised, the process should not be regarded as complete; there is always the possibility that further reanalyses to larger classes of number are just beyond the horizon.

We will not return to reanalysis for some time. Rather than describing it as part of our core theoretical framework in Chapter 3, we will consider it in §4.1.5 as part of our discussion of ambiguity, primarily because the same mechanisms that are used to handle various kinds of ambiguity are effective in describing reanalysis. After this we will not return to the subject until we consider the foundations of mathematics in Chapter 7; but there it will play a crucial role, and will motivate the most important concept introduced in the chapter (cf. §7.2.5).

3

Theoretical Framework

This chapter sets out the basic syntactic and semantic theory needed to describe mathematics.

3.1 Syntax

Our syntactic framework for mathematics will be shaped by two major concerns. First, the framework will need to allow for the introduction of new terms and notation via definitions (§2.2); and we would like to be able to describe the effect of those definitions in an simple, consistent way. It would also be advantageous if the mechanism describing definitions could treat textual and symbolic material in essentially the same fashion. Thus adaptivity leads us to want a syntactic framework that is as simple as possible, and that describes text and symbol in a unified way.

Second, in Chapter 6 we will find ourselves needing to unify parsing, i.e. the operation of determining syntax, with another operation called *type inference*. While there are no theoretical difficulties to unifying complex theories of syntax with this operation, the technical details of such theories could distract from the main focus of Chapter 6. Thus, again, we are led to desire a simple theory of syntax.

In §2.3, we noted that textual mathematics exhibited very limited inflectional morphology and almost no instances of unbounded movement, and therefore that it could be effectively modelled by a context-free grammar. In §2.4, we showed that symbolic mathematics could also be effectively modelled by a context free grammar (subject to caveats concerning type), but that more restrictive models did not suffice. Together, these observations lead us to model both textual and symbolic mathematics using a single context free grammar.

A typical excerpt from the textual side of the grammar would be:

$$
\begin{aligned}
&\text{S} \;\rightarrow\; \underset{0}{\text{NP}_{sg}} \; \underset{1}{\text{VP}_{sg}} \\
&\text{NP}_{sg} \;\rightarrow\; \underset{0}{\text{Det}_{sg}} \; \underset{1}{\text{NBar}}
\end{aligned}
$$

(Each slot on the right-hand side of a rule is numbered in order to facilitate the presentation of compositional semantics in §3.3.)

In keeping with our primary requirement of simplicity, we will not add any formal subcategorial information to the grammar. Thus, from a formal perspective, NP_{sg} and NP_{pl} are unrelated categories.

The division between the textual grammar and lexicon will differ from that in typical general-purpose grammars for two reasons. First, there is a certain granularity of analysis below which mathematical language ceases to have mathematical content. We may illustrate this point with respect to 'topological space', which is a N' which has a formal mathematical meaning. In general English, 'topological space' can be meaningfully broken down into an adjective 'topological' and another N' (or N) 'space'. But this level of analysis is not mathematically meaningful, as 'space' has no formal mathematical meaning. This point is particularly important as the meanings of phrases like 'topological space' will need to be extracted from definitions; we have a way of determining the meaning of 'topological space', but not of 'space'. On a related note, if we allow 'space' to be an N' in our grammar, then that grammar will generate phrases like 'bijective space', which are well formed in general English but meaningless in mathematics. In other words, from a mathematical perspective, allowing 'space' to be an N' would cause our grammar to overgenerate. To avoid both (mathematically) meaningless constituents and overgeneration, we will need to represent phrases like 'topological space' as having no internal structure.

Second, items that would normally be considered to belong to the textual lexicon may contain meaningful symbolic sub-parts. We encountered such an example in §2.2, as a result of the following definition:

Let A be a ring [...]. An A-*module* is ...

(Atiyah and Macdonald, 1969, p. 17)

This definition introduced an N' 'A-module' into the lexicon for each symbolic constituent 'A' denoting a ring. Thus it added '$\mathbb{Z}$-module', '$\mathbb{F}_2$-module', '$(\mathbb{R} \times \mathbb{Z})$-module' and infinitely many other N's to the lexicon.

In order to handle these two phenomena, we will allow our context free rules to contain fixed tokens on their right hand sides. Lexical entries will be encoded as rules, and families of lexical items (such as 'A-module') will be encoded as rules which contain slots for symbolic items. Thus we would encode the lexical items discussed above as follows:[1]

---

[1] Fixed tokens in context free rules will always be typeset in bold, as in this example. Additionally, when presenting such rules, we will consider the presence or absence of a space to be significant on either side of a hyphen, and in no other circumstances. Thus the second of these rules generates '$\mathbb{Z}$-module' but not '$\mathbb{Z}$ -module' or '$\mathbb{Z}$- module'.

> NBar $\rightarrow$ **topological space**
>
> NBar $\rightarrow$ $\text{Term}_{\text{RING}_0}$-**module**

(The subscript in '$\text{Term}_{\text{RING}}$' refers to a *type*, and will be discussed later in this section. For the purposes of the present discussion all subscripts of this kind may be ignored.)

Thus we have obliterated any distinction between the grammar and the lexicon. This will simplify both the mechanism treating definitions and the unification of parsing and type inference. It is also important to note that because all mathematical terms in the lexicon are extracted from definitions rather than being written by hand, the initial grammar (i.e. the grammar as it is before any definitions are encountered) has not become significantly longer.

Once we have allowed fixed tokens to appear on the right-hand side of syntactic rules, it is convenient to allow them to function syncategorematically. Thus we allow textual rules such as:

> NP $\rightarrow$ NP_{sg} **and** NP_{sg}
> $\phantom{\text{NP} \rightarrow } {}_0 \phantom{\text{NP}_{sg} \text{ and }} {}_1$
>
> NP $\rightarrow$ NP_{sg} **or** NP_{sg}
> $\phantom{\text{NP} \rightarrow } {}_0 \phantom{\text{NP}_{sg} \text{ or }} {}_1$

While this approach does not capture the similarities between 'and' and 'or', such similarities are of little relevance to mathematical language; and the gain in simplicity outweighs any loss in insight that might result from adopting cross-categorial generalisations.

Syncategorematic material is also extremely convenient for describing symbolic mathematics. Both constants and fixed material in notations may be represented syncategorematically, as in:

> $\text{Term}_{\text{NUMBER}}$ $\rightarrow$ **1**
>
> $\text{Term}_{\text{NUMBER}}$ $\rightarrow$ $\text{Term}_{\text{NUMBER}_0}$ **+** $\text{Term}_{\text{NUMBER}_1}$

Families of constants, such as the groups SO_n for n a natural number, can also be described in a natural way:

> $\text{Term}_{\text{GROUP}}$ $\rightarrow$ $\mathbf{SO}_{\text{Term}_{\text{NUMBER}_0}}$

The framework allows us to capture the more complex notations that we discussed in §2.4. For example, the degree $[K : k]$ of a field extension K/k corresponds to the following rule:

$$\text{Term}_{\text{NUMBER}} \rightarrow [\underset{0}{\text{Term}_{\text{FIELD}}} : \underset{1}{\text{Term}_{\text{FIELD}}}]$$

The other notations discussed in §2.4 are also straightforwardly handled.

This framework is also effective at describing the interface between textual and symbolic material. The universally available substitutions noted in §2.1 are handled using the following rules:

$$\text{NP} \rightarrow \underset{0}{\text{Term}}$$
$$\text{S} \rightarrow \underset{0}{\text{Formula}}$$

The existence of both of the categories 'S' and 'Formula' is not strictly necessary; as we noted in §2.1, symbolic formulae and textual sentences have the same distribution in the register of mathematics we are considering. However, it is convenient to have an *explicit* representation of the boundary between text and symbol for a number of reasons; for example, preserving the distinction makes it easier to adapt the grammar to other registers of mathematics. The redundancy in the system will be reflected by the fact that the category 'Formula' will never appear on the right-hand side of any rule other than the one above.

Specific notations which cross the interface, for example by allowing the substitution of textual constituents inside symbol, can also be handled within the framework. For example, the set-theoretic notation that allows us to write

$$\{x \in U : x \in X \textbf{ for some } X \in \mathscr{C}\}$$

is captured by a rule which is very similar to:

$$\text{Term}_{\text{SET}} \rightarrow \{ \underset{0}{\text{Var}} \in \underset{1}{\text{Term}_{\text{SET}}} : \underset{2}{\text{S}} \}$$

The actual rule is slightly different because it involves higher order notation, and must account for the function of a dummy variable ('x' in the quoted notation) inside the S constituent. Higher order notation of this kind is discussed in §8.2.

Examples

Figure 3.1 gives the syntactic structure of a textual sentence; Figure 3.2 gives the syntactic structures for a sentence that includes both textual and symbolic mathematics.

The subscript on 'AP$_{dist}$' in Figure 3.1 indicates that we are dealing with an adjective whose effect distributes across plurals: several numbers are prime if and only if each one of them is prime. This contrasts with an adjective like 'disjoint': if some sets are disjoint, that indicates a collective property of those sets. The two kinds of adjective are discussed in §3.3.6.

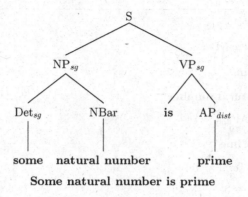

Some natural number is prime

Fig. 3.1 Syntactic structure of a textual sentence

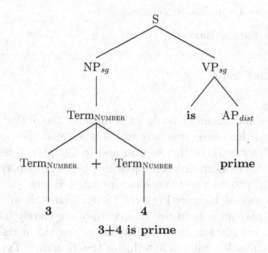

3+4 is prime

Fig. 3.2 Syntactic structure of a mixed sentence

The rules used to parse these trees are given in Figure 3.3. It is important to note that those rules that relate to mathematical concepts (such as 'natural number', '3' and '+') are extracted from definitions in an appropriate document, rather than being built into the language. We will return to this point in §3.4.

3.2 Types

In the previous section, we encountered categories like 'Term$_{\text{NUMBER}}$' and 'Term$_{\text{SET}}$'. The subscripts on these categories are *types*, which we will now discuss. In intuitive sense, types refer to the kinds of mathematical objects that we are dealing with. Eventually, we will come to attach a specific formal

$$S \rightarrow \underset{0}{NP_{sg}} \; \underset{1}{VP_{sg}}$$

$$NP_{sg} \rightarrow \underset{0}{Det_{sg}} \; \underset{1}{NBar}$$

$$Det_{sg} \rightarrow \textbf{some}$$

$$NBar \rightarrow \textbf{natural number}$$

$$VP_{sg} \rightarrow \textbf{is} \; \underset{0}{AP_{dist}}$$

$$AP_{dist} \rightarrow \textbf{prime}$$

$$Formula \rightarrow \underset{0}{Term} = \underset{1}{Term}$$

$$Term_{\text{NUMBER}} \rightarrow \textbf{3}$$

$$Term_{\text{NUMBER}} \rightarrow \textbf{4}$$

$$Term_{\text{NUMBER}} \rightarrow \underset{0}{Term_{\text{NUMBER}}} + \underset{1}{Term_{\text{NUMBER}}}$$

$$Formula \rightarrow \underset{0}{Term} = \underset{1}{Term}$$

Fig. 3.3 Grammar Excerpt

function to types and, in order to do so, will make the notion of type completely formal and determine precisely which types underlie the language of mathematics (Chapter 5). In this section and in Chapter 4, we will lay the groundwork for this by outlining the role which types must play; while doing so, we will continue to interpret types in an intuituve way.

The simplest way of interpreting types is to ignore them. In this interpretation, types play no part in the syntax; they are merely labels (roughly corresponding to certain semantic properties) which aid in reminding us of the functions of rules. We will refer to this as the 'Semantic Types' approach. Under this approach, the underlying context-free grammar consists not of rules like

$$Term_{\text{NUMBER}} \rightarrow [\; \underset{0}{Term_{\text{FIELD}}} : \underset{1}{Term_{\text{FIELD}}} \;],$$

but rather of rules like

$$Term \rightarrow [\; \underset{0}{Term} : \underset{1}{Term} \;].$$

There are a number of problems with this approach. One such problem depends on a fact we noted in §2.4: a particular piece of mathematical notation, such as '$X + Y$', can denote different things, depending on what kinds of objects appear in it. If X and Y are numbers, then '$X + Y$' denotes the sum of those numbers; if X and Y are sets, then '$X + Y$' denotes the symmetric difference of sets (Halmos, 1960, p. 18); and so on. We may now add that there are two distinct reasons for taking each usage of $+$ to correspond to a different syntactic rule. First, the Montagovian approach

(Montague, 1970a,b, 1973) requires us to translate each syntactic rule into exactly one semantic rule. Thus we require one syntactic rule which translates into a semantic notion of 'sum of numbers'; another syntactic rule which translates into 'symmetric difference of sets'; and so on. Second, and more importantly, different usages of '+' may be defined in different mathematical texts, or by different definitions in the same text. It is natural to construct a system in which definitions introduce new syntactic rules rather than modifying existing ones — and so, again, we are led to want different syntactic rules for each usage of '+'.

Thus we have one rule of the form

$$\text{Term} \rightarrow \underset{0}{\text{Term}} + \underset{1}{\text{Term}}$$

for each distinct usage of '+'. There are many such usages. (For example, with numbers, with sets, with vectors, with functions, with matrices, with elements of an abelian group, with ideals of a ring.) Under the Semantic Types approach, all of the rules are formally identical, and so every instance of '+' can be analysed under each rule.[2] Thus every instance of '+ is ambiguous.[3] Additionally, as new kinds of object are introduced over time (cf. §1.2.2), and correspondingly new notations of the form '$X + Y$' are defined, the degree of ambiguity will continue to increase.

This pervasive ambiguity is unsettling. But it is not the worst corollary of the Semantic Types approach. Another problem is exemplified by a very basic piece of mathematical notation, namely the use of '$\#S$' to refer to the size of a set S. An example is as follows:

Frob$_K$ has eigenvalues of the form α, $\alpha\#k(K)$, ...

(Harris et al., 2006, p. 16)

Under the Semantic Types approach, this notation would be captured using a rule:

$$\text{Term} \rightarrow \# \text{Term}$$

This rule could the applied recursively to construct mathematically nonsensical terms such as:

$\#\#\#\#3$

---

[2] We might say that notations for sets, numbers, etc. have *collided*; we will discuss such *notational collision* more extensively in Chapter 5 and Chapter 7.

[3] Certain other notations can exhibit even more extreme ambiguity. For example, the concatenative notation captured by the rule

$$\text{Term} \rightarrow \underset{0}{\text{Term}} \; \underset{1}{\text{Term}}$$

has far more usages than '+', primarily because many usages allow the two arguments to be of different types: one may write 'XY' with X a number and Y a function, and so on.

The situation becomes even worse once one draws on material from other domains. For example, '#' can be used to denote the connected sum of manifolds (Hatcher, 2002, p. 266), as captured by the rule:

$$\text{Term} \rightarrow \text{Term}_0 \,\#\, \text{Term}_1$$

'#' is also sometimes used to denote the sheafification functor (an individual mathematical object). This usage would be captured by the rule:

$$\text{Term} \rightarrow \#$$

Combining these three rules allows us to generate pathologies such as:

$$\#\#0\#\#\#1\#2\#\#\#$$

Thus the Semantic Types approach clearly overgenerates. Again, as new notations involving '#' are introduced over time, the degree of overgeneration will continue to increase.

There is an alternative approach which gives a substantially preferable treatment of all the phenomena we have just discussed. This is the approach under which distinct types correspond to distinct syntactic categories. We will refer to this as the 'Syntactic Types' approach.

Under this approach, $\text{Term}_{\text{NUMBER}}$ and Term_{SET} are distinct syntactic categories. Hence, rather than having many rules of the form

$$\text{Term} \rightarrow \text{Term}_0 + \text{Term}_1,$$

we have distinct syntactic rules such as

$$\text{Term}_{\text{NUMBER}} \rightarrow \text{Term}_{\text{NUMBER}_0} + \text{Term}_{\text{NUMBER}_1}$$

and

$$\text{Term}_{\text{SET}} \rightarrow \text{Term}_{\text{SET}_0} + \text{Term}_{\text{SET}_1}.$$

As a result, usages of '+' are syntactically unambiguous.

In a similar way, rather than having a rule

$$\text{Term} \rightarrow \#\, \text{Term},$$

we have a rule

$$\text{Term}_{\text{NUMBER}} \rightarrow \#\text{Term}_{\text{SET}}.$$

This rule cannot be applied recursively, and thus does not licence '$\#\#\#\#3$'. Additionally, other two rules involving $\#$ are now expressed as

$$\text{Term}_{\text{MANIFOLD}} \rightarrow \text{Term}_{\text{MANIFOLD}_0} \,\#\, \text{Term}_{\text{MANIFOLD}_1}$$

and

$$\text{Term}_{\text{FUNCTOR}} \rightarrow \#.$$

Because each of these three rules involve different categories, they cannot be combined in any way.

Thus the Syntactic Types approach avoids the overgeneration that plagued the Semantic Types approach. Unfortunately, it encounters its own problems. Consider the following sentence:

There is a projective submodule N of M such that $M = N + MB$.

(Tuganbaev, 2000)

In this case, the correct reading of '$N + MB$' is as a sum of submodules, i.e. via a rule:

$$\text{Term}_{\text{SUBMODULE}} \rightarrow \text{Term}_{\text{SUBMODULE}_0} + \text{Term}_{\text{SUBMODULE}_1}$$

But this rule cannot be applied, since the Syntactic Types approach cannot determine that 'N' is an element of the category $\text{Term}_{\text{SUBMODULE}}$. Thus variables create a particular problem for the Syntactic Types approach.

To sum up, neither of these models gives a satisfactory description of mathematics. In fact, the situation is is much more complex than we have indicated; in Chapter 4 we will find that type is intimately connected to disambiguation of both symbolic and textual material. But for the purposes of the present chapter, we wish to focus on developing a simple theory whose treatment of symbolic material improves on that given in Ranta (1997b) (cf. §2.4.1). The analysis in that paper does not need to handle the issues raised above, because it treats only a fragment covering arithmetic, inside which all terms have the type NUMBER.[4] Inside that fragment, 'Term' and '$\text{Term}_{\text{NUMBER}}$' are indistinguishable, so that both of the approaches given above make the same predictions. (In other words, the complications discussed in this section arise from the fact that we are giving a theory covering a large part of mathematics, rather than an individual domain.) For the remainder of this chapter, we will follow the Semantic Types model, and thereby give an analysis comparable to Ranta's.

3.3   Semantics

3.3.1   The Inadequacy of First-Order Logic

In this section, we will take a sentence from a real mathematics text, and show that we cannot construct a compositional semantic representation for that sentence using first order logic. In a very loose sense, the example may be thought of as analogous to Geach's 'donkey sentences' (Geach, 1980). The observation that such sentences exist in mathematics is not novel (cf.

---

[4] We use the word 'type' purely in the technical sense introduced in this section; our types are unrelated to the types of the Constructive Type Theory which Ranta uses. The exact nature of our notion of type will be discussed in Chapter 5.

Ranta (1994)), but to our knowledge this is the first example drawn from a mainstream mathematical text.

The sentence in question, taken from Sutherland's *Introduction to Metric and Topological Spaces*, is:

> Then $V = U \cap H$ for some U in $\mathscr{T}$, by definition of $\mathscr{T}_H$, and $U \cap H = i^{-1}(U)$,
> so $g^{-1}(V) = g^{-1}(i^{-1}(U)) = (i \circ g)^{-1}(U)$.
>
> (Sutherland, 1975, p. 52)

Like most real examples, this sentence contains irrelevant features which obscure the phenomenon we are actually interested in. We will ignore the initial 'then', the relative clause and the final conclusion:

> ~~Then~~ $V = U \cap H$ for some U in $\mathscr{T}$, ~~by definition of $\mathscr{T}_H$,~~ and $U \cap H = i^{-1}(U)$,
> ~~so $g^{-1}(V) = g^{-1}(i^{-1}(U)) = (i \circ g)^{-1}(U)$.~~

This leaves us with a much simpler example, namely:

$$\underbrace{V = U \cap H}_{\alpha[U]} \text{ for some } U \text{ in } \mathscr{T} \text{ and } \underbrace{U \cap H = i^{-1}(U)}_{\beta[U]}.$$

If we label sub-formulae $\alpha[U]$ and $\beta[U]$ as marked above, we can see that the overall sentence has the form:

$(\alpha[U]$ for some U in $\mathscr{T})$ and $\beta[U]$.

(The appearance of 'U' inside square brackets merely serves to emphasise the dependence of the two formulae on the variable U. The notation is not intended to be exhaustive; $\alpha[U]$ happens to also depend on the variables V and H, but those dependencies are irrelevant to the current argument.)

Suppose that we wish to obtain a compositional semantic representation for this sentence in first-order logic. We need to derive a semantic representation for each conjunct, i.e. for '$\alpha[U]$ for some U in $\mathscr{T}$' and '$\beta[U]$', and to combine these two representations in some systematic way. Let us abstract away from the irrelevant details of this specific example by assuming that we have semantic representations $\hat{\alpha}[U]$ and $\hat{\beta}[U]$ for $\alpha[U]$ and $\beta[U]$ respectively. The obvious way to construct semantic representations for the two conjuncts would be as follows:

> **Syntax** $\alpha[U]$ for some U in $\mathscr{T}$ $\beta[U]$,
> $\uparrow$ $\uparrow$
> **Semantics** $\exists U.(in(U, \mathscr{T}) \wedge \hat{\alpha}[U])$ $\hat{\beta}[U]$

And the natural way to combine these to give a semantic representation for the whole sentence would be to join the representations of the conjuncts using '$\wedge$'. (I.e. we would adopt the compositional rule that the semantic representation of a sentence of the form 'ϕ and ψ' was '$\hat{\phi} \wedge \hat{\psi}$'.) Thus we would compositionally obtain a complete semantic representation:

Syntax $\alpha[U]$ for some U in $\mathscr{T}$ and $\beta[U]$

Semantics $\exists U.(in(U, \mathscr{T}) \wedge \hat{\alpha}[U]) \quad \wedge \quad \hat{\beta}[U]$

But this last semantic representation is not meaningful. The variable 'U' is not bound inside the second conjunct!

The argument just given shows that the 'natural' choices for semantic representations inside first-order logic cannot cope with our example sentence. This does leave open the logical possibility that some counterintuitive choices, such as taking the semantic representation of 'ϕ and ψ' to be something other than '$\hat{\phi} \wedge \hat{\psi}$', might yield a functioning representation. This can be ruled out by structural induction over the well-formed formulae of first-order logic. This calculation is lengthy and unilluminating, and so we will not write it out here.

There is one final insight that we can draw out before leaving this example. Preserving the above notation, consider the following variant sentences:

1. $\alpha[U]$ for **some** U in $\mathscr{T}$ and $\beta[U]$.
2. $^{\#}\alpha[U]$ for **every** U in $\mathscr{T}$ and $\beta[U]$.

The first of these sentences is perfectly acceptable, but the second is meaningless. This tells us that *any* theory which correctly predicts the grammaticality of mathematical sentences must treat the quantifiers 'some' and 'every' in an asymmetric fashion with respect to their binding of variables. This observation rules out a large class of theories, and brings Discourse Representation Theory (Kamp and Reyle, 1993) to the forefront of those which remain.

3.3.2   *Discourse Representation Theory*

The examples considered in the previous section are close enough in spirit to donkey sentences to lead us naturally towards Discourse Representation Theory (or 'DRT'; (Kamp and Reyle, 1993)).

DRT is a theory of natural language, never intended for use in describing mathematical phenomena. As a result, we will need to put in some work to develop novel extensions adapting it for our purposes (cf. §3.3.3 through §3.3.7 and §3.5). However, such work would be necessary in any framework other than the Constructive Type Theory (Martin-Löf, 1984) used by Ranta. This work will be repaid by our ability to use DRT to solve various problems that Ranta notes in his analyses of plurals (Ranta, 1994, pp. 11–12) and of variables and quantifiers (Ranta, 1994, p. 13) inside Constructive Type Theory.

Discourse Representation Theory

At heart, DRT is a logic used to describe (the semantic content of) natural language. Its elementary unit is a *Discourse Representation Structure* (or 'DRS'), such as the following:

$x\ y$
$John(x)$
$dog(y)$
$owns(x,y)$

This DRS represents the semantic content of the sentence

   John owns a dog.

and corresponds to the following formula in the first order predicate calculus:

   $\exists x.\exists y.(John(x) \wedge dog(y) \wedge owns(x,y))$

The essential difference between DRSs and formulae in the first order predicate calculus is that elements like x and y in the DRS above are not variables
but discourse referents in the sense of Karttunen (1969); that is, they are
legitimate antecedents for anaphor. Thus the DRS above allows a pronoun
to refer back either to x (John) or y (his dog). This in turn predicts the
grammaticality of the discourses

   John owns a dog. **He** used to own a cat.

and

   John owns a dog. **It** is called Fido.

Logically equivalent sentences do not always expose the same antecedents to
anaphor, and may therefore give rise to DRSs exposing different referents.
Thus, for example, the sentence above is logically equivalent to the sentence

   As for John, it is not the case that he does not own a dog.

The semantic content of the sentence is encoded by the formula

   $\exists x.(John(x) \wedge \neg\neg\exists y.(dog(y) \wedge owns(x,y)))$

in the predicate calculus, which is equivalent to the formula given above. But
this sentence is assigned the DRS

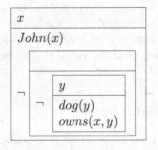

which is *not* equivalent to the DRS given above. (Note, incidentally, that just as formulae of the predicate calculus may contain sub-formulae, this DRS contains an inner 'sub-DRS'.) Discourse Representation Theory states that the only the referents in the outermost DRS are available as antecedents for anaphor. Thus in the DRS quoted above, x (John) is an available antecedent, but y (his dog) is not. This in turn correctly predicts that

> As for John, it is not the case that he does not own a dog. **He** used to own a cat.

is meaningful but

> #As for John, it is not the case that he does not own a dog. **It** is called Fido.

is not.[5]

Thus, in essence, DRT is a variant of the predicate calculus adapted to better cope with pronouns.

More formally, a DRS Δ is recursively defined as an entity of the form

$$
\begin{array}{|l|}
\hline
x_1 \;\ldots\; x_n \\
\hline
\gamma_1 \\
\;\;\vdots \\
\gamma_m \\
\hline
\end{array}
$$

where the x_i are DRS referents and each DRS condition γ_i is one of the following:

1. An atomic predicate evaluated on referents that are accessible from Δ. (*Accessibility* is defined immediately below.)
2. An equation $x = x'$, where x and x' are referents that are accessible from Δ.
3. $\neg \Gamma$, where Γ is a DRS.
4. $\Gamma \Rightarrow \Gamma'$, where Γ and Γ are DRSs.

We will sometimes abbreviate the above DRS as $[x_1 \;\ldots\; x_n | \gamma_1; \gamma_2; \ldots; \gamma_n]$.

A DRS Δ is *immediately accessible* from another DRS Γ precisely when $\Delta = \neg \Gamma$, $\Delta = (\Gamma \Rightarrow \Gamma')$, $\Delta = (\Gamma'' \Rightarrow \Gamma)$ or Δ and Γ occur in a DRS-condition of the form $\Delta \Rightarrow \Gamma$. (Less formally, a DRS can access DRSs that contain it, and also DRSs that entail it using '$\Rightarrow$'.)

The relation of *accessibility* is defined as the transitive reflexive closure of immediate accessibility. We say that a referent x is *accessible from* a DRS Γ if and only if the DRS Δ in which x is introduced is accessible from Γ.

---

[5] We assume that animals are sometimes referred to with gendered pronouns and sometimes with neuter pronouns, but that humans may only be referred to using gendered pronouns.

Discourse Update

As its name suggests, Discourse Representation Theory treats multi-sentence discourses. Each discourse is itself represented by a DRS. This DRS is initially empty. As each new sentence is is encountered, it is converted to a DRS, whose content is then added or *merged* to the end of the discourse-representing DRS in an operation called *discourse update*. For example, consider the discourse:

John owns a dog. Mary owns a cat.

The discourse-representing DRS is initially empty, i.e., has the form

When the sentence 'John owns a dog' is encountered, it is converted into the DRS

$x\ y$
$John(x)$
$dog(y)$
$owns(x, y)$

After discourse update, the discourse-representing DRS has the form

$x\ y$
$John(x)$
$dog(y)$
$owns(x, y)$

When the next sentence, 'Mary owns a cat.', is encountered, it is converted into the DRS

$z\ u$
$Mary(z)$
$cat(u)$
$owns(z, u)$

After discourse update, the discourse-representing DRS contains both the material from the original sentence and the material from the second sentence, and so has the form

$$\begin{array}{|l|}\hline x\ y\ z\ u \\\hline John(x) \\ dog(y) \\ owns(x,y) \\ Mary(z) \\ cat(u) \\ owns(z,u) \\\hline\end{array}$$

Anaphor is handled by the same mechanism. Pronouns are translated into a distinguished class of underlined discourse referents ($\underline{x}$, $\underline{y}$); immediately after merger, one must add to the end of the DRS a condition like '$\underline{x}= u$', asserting that the referent representing the pronoun is equal to some existing (accessible) referent. We may illustrate this using the discourse:

John owns a dog. He is hairy.

As before, after the discourse has been updated with the first sentence, the discourse-representing DRS is

$$\begin{array}{|l|}\hline x\ y \\\hline John(x) \\ dog(y) \\ owns(x,y) \\\hline\end{array}$$

The DRS for the second sentence is

$$\begin{array}{|l|}\hline \underline{u} \\\hline hairy(\underline{u}) \\\hline\end{array}$$

After merger, the discourse-representing DRS is:

$$\begin{array}{|l|}\hline x\ y\ \underline{u} \\\hline John(x) \\ dog(y) \\ owns(x,y) \\ hairy(\underline{u}) \\\hline\end{array}$$

In order to convert this into a legitimate DRS, one must add one of the conditions '$\underline{u}= x$' or '$\underline{u}= y$'. Pragmatic factors tell us that the latter is more likely, leading us to the final discourse-representing DRS:

$$\begin{array}{|l|}\hline x\ y\ \underline{u} \\\hline John(x) \\ dog(y) \\ owns(x,y) \\ hairy(\underline{u}) \\ \underline{u}=y \\\hline\end{array}$$

Note that the definition of accessibility tells us that after merger, pronouns may only be equated to referents defined in the outermost DRS; thus we have recovered the above prediction that 'only the referents in the outermost DRS are available as antecedents for anaphor'.

The example we have just given does not deal with pronouns referring back to material in the same sentence; the treatment is essentially identical, except that the underlined referents may arise in DRSs other than the outermost DRS, and the full definition of accessibility comes into play. We will see a mathematical example of this in §3.3.6 below.

We may present the operation of merger more formally as follows. We define a DRS merging operator $\uplus$ by

$$
\begin{array}{|l|} \hline x_1 \; \ldots \; x_n \\ \hline \gamma_1 \\ \vdots \\ \gamma_m \\ \hline \end{array}
\;\uplus\;
\begin{array}{|l|} \hline x'_1 \; \ldots \; x'_{n'} \\ \hline \gamma'_1 \\ \vdots \\ \gamma'_{m'} \\ \hline \end{array}
\;=\;
\begin{array}{|l|} \hline x_1 \; \ldots \; x_n \; x'_1 \; \ldots \; x'_{n'} \\ \hline \gamma_1 \\ \vdots \\ \gamma_m \\ \gamma'_1 \\ \vdots \\ \gamma'_{m'} \\ \hline \end{array}
$$

If D_n is the DRS for the discourse consisting of sentences $1, 2, \ldots, n$ and S_n is the DRS for sentence n, then the effect of discourse update is captured by the equation

$$D_n = D_{n-1} \uplus S_n$$

together with the requirement that pronouns be equated to existing referents.

3.3.3 Semantic Functions

Our first modification is intended to adapt DRT so that it can describe the symbolic part of mathematics as effectively as it does the textual part. Unlike natural language (or textual mathematics), symbolic mathematics contains many operations which take entities and return other entities. An example can be seen by considering the sentence,

   $3 + 4$ is prime.

Conventional DRT would represent the meaning of the sentence using a Discourse Representation Structure (or DRS)

$$
\begin{array}{|l|} \hline x \; y \; z \\ \hline 3(x) \\ 4(y) \\ sum(z, x, y) \\ prime(z) \\ \hline \end{array}
$$

This representation incorrectly predicts that '3' and '4' are available as antecedents for anaphor. It also makes it very difficult to perceive or verify the structure of the underlying mathematics — and at present we are only considering the simplest of examples. To obtain a satisfactory representation for mathematics, we will augment DRT with functions from entities to entities. (This includes 0-ary functions, which are equivalent to constants.) These functions may be used both inside atomic predicates and inside conditions of the form '$x = y$'. This enables us to write

$$\begin{array}{|l|}
\hline
x \\
\hline
x = sum(3(), 4()) \\
prime(x) \\
\hline
\end{array}$$

This representation correctly predicts that '3 + 4' is an available antecedent for anaphor, but that '3' is not. It also has the virtue of making it considerably easier to verify that the semantic representation of the symbolic constituent is correct.

It is worth noting that general rule about anaphora in mathematics seems to be that terms are never in themselves suitable antecedents for anaphor, but noun phrases are. In the sentence in question, '3 + 4' is (the surface realisation of) both a term and a noun phrase (cf. Figure 3.1), and is therefore an available antecedent. '3' and '4' are only terms, and are therefore not available antecedents.

3.3.4   Representing Variables

Unlike natural language, mathematics contains *variables* such as x and y in:

If x and y are real numbers, then $x^2 - y^2 = (x + y)(x - y)$.

We will need to invent a way of describing variables in our semantic representations. And in particular, we will need to make sure that variables in sentences like

$(\alpha[U]$ for some U in $\mathcal{T})$ and $\beta[U]$.

are treated correctly (cf. §3.3.1).

In order to motivate our actual approach to variables, we will exhibit a pair of sentences which have the same meaning (and therefore ought to have similar semantic representations), but where one sentence is stated using variables and the other is stated without variables. The sentences in question are:

If n is a natural number which is greater than 1, then there is a prime p such that $p|n$.

and

Every natural number which is greater than 1 has a prime divisor.

DRT is quite capable of assigning a semantic representation to the second sentence; our analysis will differ only in that it will use a semantic function to represent '1', for the reasons outlined in §3.3.3 above. The actual semantic representation of the second sentence is:

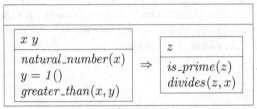

Every natural number which is greater than 1 has a prime divisor.

Now, if we take variables to be *named discourse referents*, then we can assign the second sentence a structurally identical semantic representation:

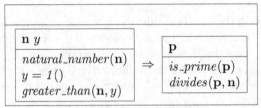

If n is a natural number which is greater than 1, then there is a prime p such that $p|n$.

(We will henceforth distinguish variables in DRSs from other referents by using a bold font, as in this example.)

This approach also treats our donkey-like sentence (§3.3.1) without difficulty. To keep the example simple, we will assume that $\alpha[U]$ and $\beta[U]$ correspond to one-place atomic predicates *alpha* and *beta*. Thus we obtain the following semantic representations for our two contents:

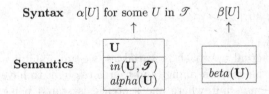

(For now we assume that the referent $\mathscr{I}$, corresponding to the variable $\mathscr{I}$ which is introduced in the previous discourse context, may be accessed from any part of the DRS; we will justify this when we discuss the interaction of variables and discourse structure in §3.5.)

We will also take 'and' to join DRSs using the operator $\uplus$, so that we obtain:

Syntax $\alpha[U]$ for some U in $\mathcal{T}$ and $\beta[U]$

Semantics

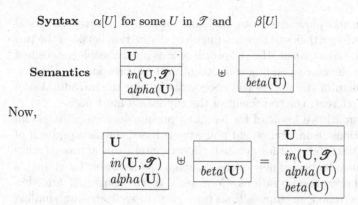

Now,

and the DRS on the right-hand side of this equation is perfectly well formed and, in particular, has **U** bound. Thus our analysis of variables handles their use in 'donkey-like sentences' without difficulty.[6]

Persistence of variables between sentences will be discussed in §3.5 below. When we discuss this, we will also demonstrate that our analysis of variables as discourse referents in DRT is capable of overcoming some of the problems that occur in the type-theoretic analysis of maths given in Ranta (1994).

3.3.5 Localisable Presuppositions

Localisability

As we noted in §2.3 and §2.4.5, both textual and symbolic mathematics contain presuppositions. For example, both the phrase 'the reciprocal of x' and the symbolic expression 'x^{-1}' (for x a number) presuppose that x is nonzero.[7] At first sight, it seems attractive to try to analyse these in the same way, i.e. to use the same mechanism to describe both textual and symbolic presuppositions. This turns out to be inadvisable, for reasons which we will now outline. Consider the phrase

the reciprocal of the reciprocal of x

and the expression

$(x^{-1})^{-1}$.

---

[6] The analysis of variables as named referents is prefigured in (De Bruijn, 1982, pp. 85), although as de Bruijn is not equipped with the notion of a referent, he reverses the observation, stating that certain indefinite phrases (such as 'a X') are very similar to variables.

[7] 'x^{-1}' will be interpreted in different ways depending on the amount of mathematics a reader has encountered; this phenomenon is discussed extensively in §2.6. For simplicity's sake, we will assume in this section that '-1' in 'x^{-1}' is taken to be a fixed part of the notation, rather than a number.

This expression and phrase refer to the same object, and carry the same presuppositions. Nevertheless, there is a linguistic distinction between the two. In the phrase, the constituent 'the reciprocal of x' is an accessible antecedent for anaphor; but the corresponding constituent in the expression, 'x^{-1}' is not. Thus the treatment of the phrase will necessarily involve the introduction of an appropriate referent; the treatment of the expression must not.

The best approach we know of for handling presuppositions arising from definite descriptions in mathematical language is based on the approach of van der Sandt (1992) (cf. §8.1 for details). Unfortunately, this approach relies heavily on the introduction of new referents, and so is unsuitable for giving an analysis of symbolic presuppositions. Conversely, mechanisms that are effective at handling symbolic presuppositions turn out to be ineffective at handling definite descriptions, for reasons that we will outline below. We will therefore give two distinct mechanisms for handling presuppositions. The first mechanism will be given in this section and will handle both symbolic presuppositions and textual presuppositions that do not involve definite descriptions. The second mechanism will be given in §8.1, and will only treat definite descriptions.

The key to the mechanism given in this section will be the attachment of presuppositional information to individual semantic predicates and functions. For example, we will attach the presupposition associated with the expression 'x^{-1}' to the semantic function which represents the meaning of this expression, which we will denote '$reciprocal(\bullet)$'.[8] We should emphasise that the presuppositional information is not attached to the instantiation of the function, i.e. to '$reciprocal(\mathbf{x})$'; it is attached to the function '$reciprocal(\bullet)$' itself. One attractive consequence of this approach is that presuppositions do not need to be explicitly stated as part of the semantic representation. For example, consider the expression '$((x^{-1})^{-1})^{-1}$'. There are three presuppositions associated with this expression, stating that x is nonzero, that x^{-1} is nonzero and that $(x^{-1})^{-1}$ is nonzero respectively. Representing these explicitly in the semantic representation would be unwieldy; but because the presuppositional information is encoded inside '$reciprocal(\bullet)$', one can state relatively compactly that the semantic representation of '$((x^{-1})^{-1})^{-1}$' is:

$$reciprocal(reciprocal(reciprocal(\mathbf{x})))$$

This approach also has the advantage of directly encoding an important generalisation, namely that *every* instance of '$reciprocal$' must carry a presupposition; if we were attaching presuppositions to expressions explicitly, it would be harder to demonstrate that this generalisation held.

Because under this approach all presuppositional information is attached to individual semantic functions and predicates, we will say that the kind of presuppositions described in this section are *localisable*. Conversely, when we

---

[8] Strictly speaking, because in §3.4 below we will determine the name of the predicate representing 'x^{-1}' from the notation itself, we should call the predicate something like '$superscript[-1](\bullet)$' rather than '$reciprocal(\bullet)$'. We choose not to do so for readability's sake.

treat definite descriptions in §8.1, we will find that it is not possible to attach presuppositional information to individual semantic functions and predicates, and so will say that the presuppositions associated with definite descriptions are *non-localisable*. (As we noted in §2.3, mathematics contains very few kinds of textual presupposition; were this not the case, we might find that constructs other than definite descriptions also gave rise to non-localisable presuppositions.)

We will make three final comments before giving the formal treatment of localisable presuppositions. First, it is worth observing that all of the objects which may be introduced in definitions, i.e. textual phrases and symbolic notations, carry localisable presuppositions. By contrast, non-localisable presuppositions almost always arise from definite descriptions, and new ways of forming definite descriptions are never introduced in definitions. Thus we will continually encounter new examples of localisable presuppositions as we learn more mathematics, making them an important phenomenon. By contrast, non-localisable presuppositions are a relatively minor issue.

The second comment relates to a point we raised above, concerning the difficulty of analysing definite descriptions inside a framework suited to handling symbolic presuppositions. It is precisely the difference between localisability and non-localisability that causes this. Symbolic presuppositions are most naturally analysed in a local way, i.e. using information attached to individual functions and predicates; conversely, it is very difficult to analyse definite descriptions in this way.

Our third comment looks ahead, to our discussion of type in Chapters 5 and 6. It is an empirical fact that presuppositions (whether localisable or non-localisable) *never* contribute any information about types. As a result, we will not need to refer to them in Chapters 5 or 6.

Formalism

Every semantic function or predicate has associated with it a DRS called its *defining DRS*. The defining DRS must contain a special DRS-condition, called a *central DRS-condition*. If we are describing a function, the central DRS-condition must have the form:

$$function(\bullet, \bullet, \ldots, \bullet) \stackrel{\mathrm{df}}{=} \textit{[arbitrary term]}$$

If we are describing a predicate, the central DRS-condition must have the form:

$$predicate(\bullet, \bullet, \ldots, \bullet) \stackrel{\mathrm{df}}{\Leftrightarrow} \textit{[arbitrary DRS-condition]}$$

As well as interacting with the mechanisms we will describe below, '$\stackrel{\mathrm{df}}{=}$' and '$\stackrel{\mathrm{df}}{\Leftrightarrow}$' carry the force of '$=$' and '$\Leftrightarrow$' respectively. Thus, for example,

$$reciprocal(x) \stackrel{\mathrm{df}}{=} a$$

expresses the same fact as

$$reciprocal(x) = a,$$

but also carries additional information about presuppositions.

In order to actually relate the defining DRSs and central DRS-conditions to the presuppositions they encode, we will need a technical notion associated with the structure of DRSs.

We define the relation of *command* between two DRS-conditions to be the smallest relation such that:[9]

- In a DRS of the form $[x_1 \ \ldots \ x_n | \gamma_1; \gamma_2; \ldots; \gamma_n]$, each γ_k commands each of $\gamma_{k+1}, \ldots, \gamma_n$.
- In a DRS-condition of the form $[\ldots | \gamma_1; \gamma_2; \ldots; \gamma_n] \Rightarrow [\ldots | \gamma_1'; \gamma_2'; \ldots; \gamma_m']$, each γ_i commands every γ_j'.
- If γ commands γ', then γ commands any DRS-condition contained within γ' (at any depth).

We may illustrate this notion using the sentence:

We can write $\sqrt{2} = a/b$, where $a, b \in \mathbb{N}$ and a and b are relatively prime.

The compositionally constructed DRS for this sentence is:

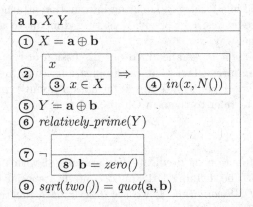

① commands ② – ⑨; ② commands ⑤ – ⑨; ③ commands ④; ④ commands nothing; ⑤ commands ⑥ – ⑨; ⑥ commands ⑦ – ⑨; ⑦ commands ⑨; ⑧ commands nothing; ⑨ commands nothing.

Presuppositions are determined from the defining DRS in the following way. A semantic predicate or function presupposes all the DRS-conditions that command the central DRS-condition in its defining DRS. Any referents which do not appear in the predicate or function itself are existentially quantified over. Any variables appearing in the defining DRS are treated exactly like other referents.

For example, the defining DRS for the semantic predicate '$reciprocal(x)$' associated with the notation 'x^{-1}' (where x is a number) is:

---

[9] The terminology has been chosen to bring out a parallel with the notion of c-command in syntax (Reinhart, 1981).

$$
\begin{array}{|l|}
\hline
x\ a \\
\hline
number(x) \\
number(a) \\
times(x,a) = 1() \\
reciprocal(x) \overset{\text{df}}{=} a \\
\hline
\end{array}
$$

The first three DRS-conditions in this DRS command the central DRS-condition '$reciprocal(x) \overset{\text{df}}{=} a$'. Thus '$reciprocal(x)$', which is the semantic representation of 'x^{-1}', presupposes that

$$number(x) \land \exists a.(number(a) \land times(x,a) = 1())$$

Because the notation '$reciprocal(x)$' refers to the reciprocal of a number, $number(x)$ holds vacuously. The remainder of the presupposition asserts that there is a number a such that $xa = 1$, i.e. that the reciprocal of x exists. (This is, of course, equivalent to asserting that x is nonzero.)

We can also give a slight variant of this example to illustrate the effect of command. Suppose that the defining DRS for the semantic predicate $reciprocal(x)$ had been

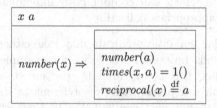

Despite the difference in the structure of the DRS, the command relationships are unchanged; in particular, '$number(x)$' still commands the central DRS-condition, and so the same predictions about presuppositions are obtained.

Examples involving semantic predicates proceed in exactly the same way as those involving semantic functions. For example, the defining DRS for the semantic predicate '$prime\_ofnumber(x)$' associated with the adjective 'prime' (as applied to numbers) is:

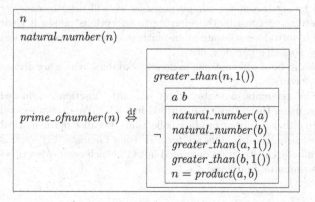

Here only '*natural_number(n)*' commands the central DRS-condition; as a result, '*prime_ofnumber(n)*' always presupposes that n is a natural number. Because '*prime_ofnumber*(**a**)' is the semantic representation of 'a is prime', this correctly predicts that statements like '3/2 is prime' result in a presupposition failure.

3.3.6   Plurals

Plurals are presented as an extension to Discourse Representation Theory in Kamp and Reyle (1993). Our approach follows the one given there; it essentially consists of:[10]

1. The introduction of a class of plural discourse referents (conventionally denoted by capital letters), denoting collections of objects.[11]
2. The addition of a DRS-condition '$x \in X$', where (as the convention suggests) x is a singular discourse referent, X is a plural discourse referent and the condition '$x \in X$' asserts that x is an element of the collection denoted by X.
3. The introduction of an operator $\oplus$ which can conjoin both individual entities and collections to form an appropriate collection.

Crucially, any given slot of a particular semantic predicate may take either a singular referent, or a plural referent, but not both.[12] So, for example, when we assert that lines are parallel, this is captured by the use of a unary predicate '*parallel*' which requires a plural discourse referent as its argument; one may write '*parallel*(X)', but not '*parallel*(x)'. By contrast, the adjective 'prime' (relating to numbers) is translated into a predicate '*prime_ofnumber*', which may be applied to a single discourse referent, but not to a plural discourse referent. Thus, for example, 'a and b are parallel' may be represented by a DRS:

---

[10] Often treatments of DRT speak of 'sets' rather than 'collections'. We will not do so as the collections involved cannot themselves contain collections; rather they are extensions of predicates applied to some fixed universe of objects. The distinction will be significant for our purposes as we will need to consider collections of sets, etc., and consistently referring to collections makes it clear that we do not need to introduce separate meta-mathematical and mathematical levels of sets, discuss Russell's paradox, etc..

[11] Capital letters typeset in bold will continue to denote variables, which are always *singular* discourse referents.

[12] Slots allowing singular referents may also admit semantic functions evaluated on singular referents, using the extension described in §3.3.3. We do not extend semantic functions to either accept or produce collections, because mathematical terms denote individual entities; plurals are formed using linguistic expressions or by a dedicated symbolic construction described in §8.2, which can be described without reference to semantic functions.

$$\boxed{\begin{array}{l} \mathbf{a}\ \mathbf{b}\ X \\ \hline X = \mathbf{a} \oplus \mathbf{b} \\ parallel(X) \end{array}}$$

By contrast, if we were able to form a sentence '*a is parallel', this would correspond to a DRS

$$\boxed{\begin{array}{l} \mathbf{a} \\ \hline parallel(\mathbf{a}) \end{array}}$$

which is ill formed as '*parallel*' has an inappropriate argument.

In fact, we preclude the formation of such sentences at the syntactic level: adjectives like 'parallel' are assigned to the syntactic category AP_{coll}, and may only be used with plural noun phrases. By contrast adjectives like 'prime' are assigned to a distinct syntactic category AP_{dist}. Such adjectives may be used with either singular or plural noun phrases; but when such an adjective is used with plural noun phrases (which correspond to plural discourse referents), the underlying semantic predicate is *lifted* to apply 'element-wise' to the plural argument. Thus

> 3 is prime.

is mapped to a DRS

$$\boxed{\begin{array}{l} x \\ \hline x = 3() \\ prime\_ofnumber(x) \end{array}}$$

By contrast,

> 3 and 5 are prime.

is mapped to a DRS

$$\boxed{\begin{array}{l} x\ y\ X \\ \hline x = 3() \\ y = 5() \\ X = x \oplus y \\ \hline \overline{prime\_ofnumber}(X) \end{array}}$$

where $\overline{prime\_ofnumber}(X)$ is a shorthand for the lifted DRS-condition

$$\boxed{\begin{array}{l} x \\ \hline x \in X \end{array}} \Rightarrow \boxed{\begin{array}{l} \\ \hline prime\_ofnumber(x) \end{array}}$$

Similar distinctions between distributive and collective readings are maintained for parts of speech other than adjectives; again, the distinctions exist both at the syntactic level and in the underlying semantic predicates.

Our approach also correctly handles an area which Ranta highlights as a deficiency of his own analysis. He notes that the plural pronoun 'they' is sometimes given a distributive reading and sometimes a collective reading; cf.

> Nor do we quite understand the use of the plural pronoun *they*, which is sometimes distributive, paraphrasable by the term conjunction e.g.
>
> > *if A and B do not lie outside the line a, they are incident on it*
>
> but sometimes used on the place of the "surface term conjunction", so that it fuses together the arguments of the predicate, e.g.
>
> > *if a and b do not converge, they are parallel.*

(Ranta, 1994, p. 12)

Our analysis correctly distinguishes distributive and collective readings. 'they' is always taken to be a pronoun introducing an underlined plural discourse referent, requiring a plural antecedent. The difference in the readings of the two sentences given above is accounted for by the fact that 'incident on it' is distributive (as a single point is incident on a single line) and the adjective 'parallel' is collective (a single line cannot be parallel, but a collection of lines can). Correspondingly, the underlying semantic predicates are '$incident(x, y)$' (requiring singular arguments) and '$parallel(X)$' (requiring a plural argument). If 'incident on ...' is used with a plural noun phrase like 'they', the underlying semantic predicate '$incident(x, y)$' is lifted so that it can accept a plural argument.

Abbreviating '$lies\_outside$' to 'lo' and '$incident$' to 'i' to save space, the DRS for

If A and B do not lie outside the line a, they are incident on it.

is:

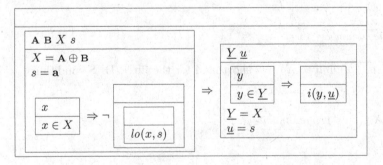

(Here we have used 'A' and 'B' instead of '**A**' and '**B**' to emphasise that the variables A and B behave like *singular* discourse referents.)

Since we have the DRS-conditions '$X = \text{A} \oplus \text{B}$', '$\underline{Y} = X$', '$\underline{u} = s$' and '$s = \text{a}$' in appropriate parts of the DRS, the DRS-condition

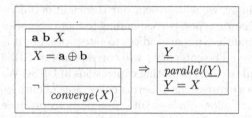

asserts that A is incident on a and that B is incident on a, as required.

We should note that the DRS for the complete sentence also illustrates a subtlety concerning lifting. The predicate '*incident*' has been lifted with respect to the argument corresponding to the plural noun phrase 'they', but not with respect to the argument corresponding to the singular noun phrase 'it'. Similarly, the predicate '*lies_outside*' has been lifted with respect to the argument corresponding to the plural noun phrase 'α and β', but not with respect to the argument corresponding to the singular noun phrase 'the line a'. (We will make some additional remarks on lifting, and on this specific point, in §3.4.)

The DRS for the sentence

If a and b do not converge, they are parallel.

is simpler as no lifting is required:

$$
\boxed{
\begin{array}{l}
\boxed{
\begin{array}{l}
\textbf{a b } X \\
\hline
X = \textbf{a} \oplus \textbf{b} \\
\neg \boxed{converge(X)}
\end{array}
}
\Rightarrow
\boxed{
\begin{array}{l}
\underline{Y} \\
\hline
parallel(\underline{Y}) \\
\underline{Y} = X
\end{array}
}
\end{array}
}
$$

Since we have the DRS-conditions '$X = \textbf{a} \oplus \textbf{b}$' and '$\underline{Y} = X$' in appropriate parts of the DRS, '$parallel(\underline{Y})$' asserts that a and b are jointly parallel, as required.

3.3.7 Compositionality

In order to be able to systematically determine the meanings of sentences, we need to attach *compositional* semantic representations to our syntactic rules. We will proceed using two stages. First, we will construct a 'compositionalised' variant of Discourse Representation Theory that can attach semantic representations not only to complete sentences, but also to terms, noun phrases, and all other syntactic constituents. Second, we will annotate our syntactic rules so that they can combine the semantic representations of their syntactic parts to compositionally construct semantic representations for the entire constituents they describe.

The standard approach for giving compositional semantic representations to noun phrases and all other textual categories derives from Montague (1970b,a, 1973). This approach essentially involves constructing the collection of typed λ-terms over the type t of formulae in the predicate calculus and the type e of entity-denoting expressions in the predicate calculus.[13] Thus, for example, proper names like 'John' correspond to individual entities, and so are given semantic representations of the category e; verb phrases, like 'sleeps' map individual entities to propositions, and so are represented by λ-terms of the category $e \rightarrow t$; and noun phrases, like 'every man' and 'some woman' may be regarded as mapping verb phrases to propositions (the *Generalised Quantifier* analysis), and so may be represented by λ-terms of the category $(e \rightarrow t) \rightarrow t$.

For our purposes, we need to construct a semantic theory that is to DRT as non-intensional Montague Grammar is to the First-Order Predicate Calculus. This essentially involves using DRSs instead of propositions of the predicate calculus. Thus, for example, the semantic representation of a verb phrase like 'sleeps', of category $e \rightarrow t$, will need to map individual entities to DRSs. Theories of this kind have been constructed previously; see, for example, Blackburn and Bos (2009). However, our version of λ-DRT will differ from standard accounts in certain ways that are needed to describe mathematical phenomena; for example, we will need to distinguish variables from other entity-denoting entities. Accordingly, we will present our theory in detail.

We will take four primitive semantic types, corresponding to four categories of objects. (Strictly speaking, semantic types are indices to categories, but it is convenient to blur this distinction.) The category t will corresponds to DRSs and the category e will correspond to entity-denoting expressions in DRSs. We will add a category E that denotes expressions denoting collections of entities in DRSs (cf. §3.3.6); as we do not allow our semantic functions to produce such collections, E will only contain plural referents and sums (via $\oplus$) of elements of e and E. Finally, we will add a category *var* to denote the named referents that correspond to variables; this will be a proper subcategory of the category e. This will be necessary because we will sometimes form terms like

$$\lambda v. \;\boxed{\begin{array}{c} v \\ \hline \cdots \end{array}}$$

Allowing v to be of the category e in this example would allow the creation of ill-formed DRSs. (An example illustrating this point will be given in §3.4.) As *var* is a subcategory of e, it follows that elements of $e \rightarrow t$ may be converted

---

[13] Montague's own analysis involved an extra type s introduced to handle intensionality; we will not need to make use of this type.

to elements of $var \rightarrow t$ by restriction, and so on. We also allow the use of the DRS-joining operator $\uplus$ in our compositional DRT representations.

The resulting version of λ-DRT will be capable of giving semantic representations to objects of symbolic categories as well as those of textual categories. For example, the Term '0' can be represented by the expression '$\theta()$' of the category e, and the Formula '$0 < 1$' can be represented by the DRS

$$\boxed{\begin{array}{l} \\ \hline less\_than(0(), 1()) \end{array}}$$

which belongs to the category t.

Terms of this version of λ-DRT will be directly attached as semantic representations of terminal rules. (Semantic representations attached to rules will always be enclosed inside curly braces, as below). Thus we will write, for example:[14]

$$
\begin{array}{ll}
\text{Term} \rightarrow \mathbf{3} & \{three()\} \\[2ex]
\text{AP}_{dist} \rightarrow \mathbf{prime} & \left\{ \lambda x._{:e} \boxed{\begin{array}{l} \\ \hline prime\_ofnumber(x) \end{array}} \right\} \\[3ex]
\text{NBar} \rightarrow \mathbf{natural\ number} & \left\{ \lambda x._{:e} \boxed{\begin{array}{l} \\ \hline natural\_number(x) \end{array}} \right\} \\[3ex]
\text{Det}_{sg} \rightarrow \mathbf{some} & \left\{ \lambda\, \underset{:e\rightarrow t}{n}\, .\, \lambda\, \underset{:e\rightarrow t}{v}\, . \left(\boxed{\begin{array}{l} r \\ \hline \end{array}} \uplus n\,(r) \uplus v\,(r) \right) \right\}
\end{array}
$$

For non-terminal rules, such as

$$\text{NP}_{sg} \rightarrow \underset{0}{\text{Det}_{sg}}\ \underset{1}{\text{NBar}}$$

we will attach semantic representations as above, but allow the use of numbered 'slots' in the semantic representation. These slots are compositionally filled with the semantic representations of the corresponding arguments to the rule. So, for example,

$$\text{NP}_{sg} \rightarrow \underset{0}{\text{Det}_{sg}}\ \underset{1}{\text{NBar}} \qquad \{0(1)\}$$

indicates that the semantic representation of the noun phrase is computed by evaluating the semantic representation of the determiner (argument 0) on the semantic representation of the NBar (argument 1).

We can give a complete example using the following grammar fragment:

---

[14] In the first of these rules, we refer to the semantic function as '*three*' rather than '3' to avoid confusion with the numbers we will introduce in the next paragraph to refer to slots in rules.

$$S \;\rightarrow\; \underset{0}{\text{NP}_{sg}}\; \underset{1}{\text{VP}_{sg}} \qquad \{0\,(1)\}$$

$$\text{NP}_{sg} \;\rightarrow\; \underset{0}{\text{Det}_{sg}}\; \underset{1}{\text{NBar}} \qquad \{0(1)\}$$

$$\text{Det}_{sg} \;\rightarrow\; \textbf{some} \qquad \left\{ \lambda \underset{:e\rightarrow t}{n} . \lambda \underset{:e\rightarrow t}{v} . \left(\boxed{\begin{array}{|c|} \hline r \\ \hline \\ \hline \end{array}} \uplus n\,(r) \uplus v\,(r) \right) \right\}$$

$$\text{NBar} \;\rightarrow\; \textbf{natural number}$$

$$\left\{ \lambda \underset{:e}{x} . \boxed{\begin{array}{|c|} \hline \\ \hline natural\_number\,(x) \\ \hline \end{array}} \right\}$$

$$\text{VP}_{sg} \;\rightarrow\; \textbf{is}\; \underset{0}{\text{AP}_{dist}} \qquad \{0\}$$

$$\text{AP}_{dist} \;\rightarrow\; \textbf{prime} \qquad \left\{ \lambda \underset{:e}{x} . \boxed{\begin{array}{|c|} \hline \\ \hline prime\_ofnumber(x) \\ \hline \end{array}} \right\}$$

As we saw in §3.1, these syntactic rules can generate the sentence

Some natural number is prime.

It will be useful to convenient to have the relevant parse tree to hand:

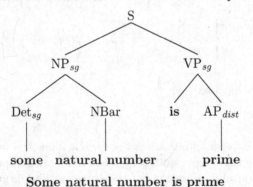

Some natural number is prime

We will work up this parse tree from the leaves to the root and compositionally construct semantic representations for each node. We will start with the VP$_{sg}$, as its derivation is somewhat simpler than that of the NP$_{sg}$. The relevant rules are:

$$\text{VP}_{sg} \;\rightarrow\; \textbf{is}\; \underset{0}{\text{AP}_{dist}} \qquad \{0\}$$

$$\text{AP}_{dist} \;\rightarrow\; \textbf{prime} \qquad \left\{ \lambda \underset{:e}{x} . \boxed{\begin{array}{|c|} \hline \\ \hline prime\_ofnumber(x) \\ \hline \end{array}} \right\}$$

In order to construct the semantic representation for 'is prime', we substitute the semantic representation for 'prime' as argument 0 of the first rule to obtain:

$$\lambda x. \quad \boxed{\;prime\_ofnumber(x)\;}$$
$$_{:e}$$

The treatment of the NP_{sg} 'some natural number' proceeds in the same way. We have the rules:

$$\text{NP}_{sg} \;\rightarrow\; \underset{0}{\text{Det}_{sg}} \; \underset{1}{\text{NBar}} \qquad \{0(1)\}$$

$$\text{Det}_{sg} \;\rightarrow\; \textbf{some} \qquad \left\{ \lambda \underset{:e\to t}{n} . \lambda \underset{:e\to t}{v} . \left(\boxed{\begin{array}{c} r \\ \hline \end{array}} \uplus n(r) \uplus v(r) \right) \right\}$$

$$\text{NBar} \;\rightarrow\; \textbf{natural number}$$

$$\left\{ \lambda x. \quad \boxed{\; natural\_number(x) \;} \right\}$$
$$\phantom{\left\{ \lambda \right.}_{:e}$$

We substitute into the rule for NP_{sg} the semantic representation for 'some' as argument 0 and the semantic representation for 'natural number' as argument 1. The result is:

$$\left(\lambda \underset{:e\to t}{n} . \lambda \underset{:e\to t}{v} . \left(\boxed{\begin{array}{c} r \\ \hline \end{array}} \uplus n(r) \uplus v(r) \right) \right) \left(\lambda x. \boxed{\; natural\_number(x) \;} \right)$$
$$_{:e}$$

$$= \lambda \underset{:e\to t}{v} . \left(\boxed{\begin{array}{c} r \\ \hline \end{array}} \uplus \boxed{\; natural\_number(r) \;} \uplus v(r) \right)$$

$$= \lambda \underset{:e\to t}{v} . \left(\boxed{\begin{array}{c} r \\ \hline natural\_number(r) \end{array}} \uplus v(r) \right)$$

Finally, we can construct the semantic representation for the entire sentence by combining the semantic representations for the noun phrase and the verb phrase. The relevant grammar rule is:

$$\text{S} \;\rightarrow\; \underset{0}{\text{NP}_{sg}} \; \underset{1}{\text{VP}_{sg}} \qquad \{0(1)\}$$

Substituting the semantic representations for the noun phrase and verb phrase into this rule gives:

$$\left(\lambda \underset{:e \to t}{v} . \left(\boxed{\begin{array}{c} r \\ \hline natural\_number\,(r) \end{array}} \uplus v\,(r) \right) \right) \left(\lambda \underset{:e}{x} . \boxed{\begin{array}{c} \\ \hline prime\_ofnumber(x) \end{array}} \right)$$

$$= \boxed{\begin{array}{c} r \\ \hline natural\_number\,(r) \end{array}} \uplus \boxed{\begin{array}{c} \\ \hline prime\_ofnumber(r) \end{array}}$$

$$= \boxed{\begin{array}{c} r \\ \hline natural\_number(r) \\ prime\_ofnumber(r) \end{array}}$$

This asserts that there is an entity r such that r is a natural number and r is prime, which is exactly what we need. It is also worth noting that this analysis correctly predicts that r is an available antecedent for an anaphor in a subsequent sentence.

Finally, we may note that our compositional semantic framework allows us to explain why terms may be used as singular noun phrases, but not vice versa (§2.1). The semantic representations of terms are of type e, whereas the semantic representations of singular noun phrases need to be of type $((e \to t) \to t)$ in order to handle the generalised quantifier analysis of noun phrases like 'some man'. There is a canonical injection from e to $((e \to t) \to t)$ which maps an entity x to the second-order function θ defined by $\theta(f) = f(x)$, but there is no injection in the opposite direction.[15] Thus there is a natural way of treating terms as noun phrases, but not vice versa.

3.3.8 Ambiguity and Type

A word such as 'prime' may be used to refer to prime numbers, prime ideals, and so on. Inside the theory developed above, we can represent this by adding separate lexical items to the grammar, encoded as rules with identical syntax but distinct semantics:[16]

---

[15] We in fact encode this injection as part of our compositional semantics, in the form of the rule:

$$\text{NP} \; \to \; \underset{0}{\text{Term}} \qquad \left\{ \lambda \underset{:e \to t}{v} . v(0) \right\}$$

[16] In fact, the names of all the semantic predicates and functions given in this chapter should include type information, just as these examples do. We have suppressed such information for readability's sake.

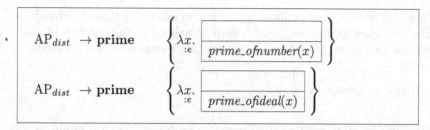

But to give a proper description of mathematics, we need to determine which of these rules applies to any given instance of 'prime'. As with the issues given in §3.2 on types, this is an issue which does not apply when describing small domains, but only when one is treating large bodies of mathematics. For the same reasons that we gave in §3.2, we will defer discussion of this issue to Chapter 4 and subsequent chapters; and, in fact, we will find there that the resolution of this ambiguity is intimately tied to the notion of type itself.

3.4 Adaptivity

3.4.1 Definitions in Mathematics

As noted above (§2.2), one of the remarkable features of mathematics, as a language, is adaptivity: the phenomenon where nearly every mathematical term or piece of notation is formally *defined*. For example, the NBar 'group' could be introduced by the following definition:

> **Definition.** A **group** *is a semigroup G containing an element e such that:*
>
> *(i) $e * a = a * e$ for all $g \in G$;*
> *(ii) for every $a \in G$, there is an element $b \in G$ with*
>
> $$a * b = e = b * a.$$

(Rotman, 1995, p. 12)

We will rely on this convention in our formalisation. All mathematical concepts, with their syntactic and semantic details, will be extracted from definitions. Our mechanism for handling adaptivity is built into the grammar itself. Definitions like the ones above are captured by syntactic rules which are themselves part of the grammar; thus we might have the rule

$$\text{Def} \to \text{a new-NBar}_{0} \text{ is a NBar}_{sg\,1} \quad \left\{ \begin{array}{|c|} \hline x \\ \hline 0(x) \overset{df}{\Leftrightarrow} 1(x) \\ \hline \end{array} \right\}$$

capturing the above definition. Note that the occurrence of 'new-X' in a syntactic rule does not refer to a genuine category, but to a 'pseudo-category' which may match against most words and symbols. In this example, 'new-NBar' matches against the word 'group', resulting in the creation of a new semantic predicate '*group*' and a rule relating lexical item and predicate,

$$\text{NBar}_{sg} \ \to \ \textbf{group} \qquad \left\{ \lambda x. \begin{array}{|c|} \hline \\ \hline group(x) \\ \hline \end{array} \right\}$$

Following this, the newly created semantic representation for 'group' is substituted as argument 0 of

$$\begin{array}{|l|} \hline x \\ \hline 0(x) \stackrel{\text{df}}{\Leftrightarrow} 1(x) \\ \hline \end{array} .$$

Together with argument 1 ('semigroup G containing ...'), which is treated in the usual way, this gives us

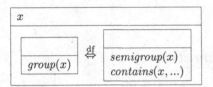

which specifies exactly what it means to satisfy the predicate *group*. This DRS is also the defining DRS for '*group*(•)' in the sense of §3.3.5, i.e. it determines the presuppositions attached to '*group*(•)'. (In this example, the central DRS-condition is not commanded by any other DRS-conditions and so '*group*(•)' has no presuppositions attached to it. We will see an example of a definition introducing a presupposition below.)

At this point, we need to recall a crucial fact about mathematics. The symbolic part of mathematics is *syntactically productive* (§2.2). Definitions can introduce not only new linguistic lexical items, but new symbolic notation — and that notation can be described by arbitrary grammar rules. For example, consider the following definition:

If E is an extension of F, we denote by

$$[E : F]$$

the dimension of E as vector space over F.

(Lang, 1993, p. 224)

This definition adds the following rule to the language:

$$\text{Term}_{\text{NUMBER}} \ \to \ [\ \text{Term}_{\text{FIELD}}_{0} \ : \ \text{Term}_{\text{FIELD}}_{1} \ ]$$

Note that variables in the term been defined have been turned into 'slots' in the rule. This is a general phenomenon, and applies to variables in textual items like 'k-linear' as well. In most cases, slots created by definitions accept elements of the category Term. In a few instances, such as in definitions of (potentially transitive) verb phrases, i.e. definitions of new elements of the category VP_{sg}, certain slots may need to accept noun phrases. (See §2.1 and §3.1 for the relationship between terms and noun phrases.) This difference in behaviour is encoded in two ways. First, we express as part of the grammar a list of textual categories that behave like 'VP_{sg}'; second, we state in the theory certain universal rules about when slots in instances of such categories correspond to noun phrases and when they correspond to terms. Whenever a slot accepting a noun phrase is introduced, both unlifted and lifted variants of the rule are introduced, accepting singular and plural noun phrases respectively (cf. §3.3.6). If two noun phrases are present (as with a ditransitive verb), four variants are created, and so on.

(Prepositional phrases are also treated in a special way whenever they occur as part of *any* term being defined; cf. §8.1.)

We should emphasise that we may end up adding to the language rules like the one for '$[E : F]$', but with *arbitrary* tokens and constituents on the right-hand side. In other words, there are no hard boundaries delimiting the kind of notation that may be introduced. Certain symbols tend to be used to convey certain kinds of concepts, but such tendencies are just that: tendencies, not rules. As we shall see in Chapter 4, when one looks at enough mathematics, one sees notation used in some very surprising ways.

All of the mechanisms discussed in this book will have to be compatible with adaptivity; and in particular, they will need to extract any required information about mathematical objects from definitions in a systematic way. For example, consider the distinction between adjectives like 'prime' (of the category 'AP_{dist}') and adjectives like 'parallel' (of the category 'AP_{coll}') that we introduced in §3.3.6. This distinction is only admissible because we can find a systematic way of distinguishing definitions of these two kinds of adjective. It is an empirical fact that adjectives like 'prime' are invariably introduced using the singular 'is', as in

We say that a natural number n **is** prime if ... .

Adjectives like 'parallel' are necessarily introduced using the plural 'are', as in

We say that lines X and Y **are** parallel if ... .

This distinction is reflected in our treatment of adaptivity, as we have both of the following rules (among many other variants):

$$\text{Def} \to \mathbf{a} \underset{0}{\text{NBar}} \underset{1}{\text{Var}} \mathbf{is} \underset{2}{\text{new-AP}_{dist}} \mathbf{if} \underset{3}{\text{S}} \left\{ \begin{array}{|l|} \hline 1 \\ \hline 0(1) \\ 2(1) \overset{\text{df}}{\Leftrightarrow} 3 \\ \hline \end{array} \right\}$$

$$\mathrm{Def} \rightarrow \underset{0}{\mathrm{NP}_{pl}} \text{ } \mathbf{are} \text{ } \underset{1}{\text{new-AP}_{coll}} \text{ } \mathbf{if} \text{ } \underset{2}{\mathrm{S}} \quad \left\{ \boxed{\begin{array}{|c|} \hline \\ \hline 0(1) \overset{\mathrm{df}}{\Leftrightarrow} 2 \\ \hline \end{array}} \right\}$$

The first of these rules also serves to illustrate two minor points brought up earlier in this chapter. First, the occurrence of '1' in the rule needs to be restricted so that it can only admit (semantic representations of) variables, and not arbitrary entities. This illustrates the necessity for our compositional version of DRT (§3.3.7) to contain a category *var* in addition to the usual category *e*. Second, if we look at the use of the rule in the example,

We say that a natural number n **is** prime if ... .

we find that the defining DRS (§3.3.5) for '*prime_ofnumber*($\bullet$)' is

$$\boxed{\begin{array}{l} \hline \mathbf{n} \\ \hline natural\_number(\mathbf{n}) \\ prime\_ofnumber(\mathbf{n}) \overset{\mathrm{df}}{\Leftrightarrow} \cdots \\ \hline \end{array}}$$

Here '*natural_number*($\mathbf{n}$)' commands the central DRS-condition (cf. §3.3.5), and so this defining DRS correctly predicts that '*prime_ofnumber*(x)' presupposes '*natural_number*(x)'.[17]

3.4.2   Real Definitions and Functional Categories

The general framework for definitions is as presented above, but the rules in the real grammar can sometimes be considerably more complicated than the examples given above. In this section we will consider one complicated sentence and illustrate the requirements which it places upon the grammar. The sentence in question is:

If x is an element of a set S, we write $x \in S$ and say that x is in S or that S contains x.

This example has two distinctive features:

1. The defining phrase (or *definiens*) 'x is an element of a set S' appears before the item(s) to be defined (the *definiendum*).
2. Several items are being defined simultaneously with the same definiens.

In order to handle the second point, we first need to separate the definiens and definiendum in the semantic representation, so that each is represented by a separate semantic object. We then combine these objects by function

---

[17] As noted in §3.3.5, the variable '$\mathbf{n}$' is treated exactly like any other referent for the purpose of determining presuppositions.

application.[18] We may either apply the definiens to the definiendum, or apply the definiendum to the definiens; either choice is valid, so long as we are consistent.

Since we have to handle the situation with one definiens and several definienda, but (as it happens) one never finds more than one definiens, it is easiest to evaluate the definiendum on the definiens. We encode this choice in the grammar by writing

$$\underset{:\,t}{S} \rightarrow \textbf{If}\ \underset{0\,:\,t}{S}\ ,\ \underset{1\,:\,t\rightarrow t}{\text{WeDefiniendum}} \qquad \{1(0)\}$$

We then need to consider how to build up the definienda in the grammar. We will start with some simplified examples, namely:

- we write $x \in S$
- we say that x is in S
- we say that S contains x

Each of these needs to have as its semantic representation a function that takes a definens (from the semantic category t) and returns an appropriate definition. More precisely, we need the following *composite rules*, i.e., rules which may be formed by compositional combination of grammar rules:[19]

$$\underset{:\,t\rightarrow t}{\text{WeDefiniendum}} \rightarrow \textbf{we write}\ \underset{0}{\text{new-Formula}} \qquad \left\{ \underset{:t}{\lambda p.\,(0 \overset{\text{df}}{\Leftrightarrow} p)} \right\}$$

$$\underset{:\,t\rightarrow t}{\text{WeDefiniendum}} \rightarrow \textbf{we say that}\ \underset{0}{\text{Variable}}\ \textbf{is}\ \underset{1}{\text{new-PP}}$$

$$\left\{ \underset{:t}{\lambda p.\,(1(0) \overset{\text{df}}{\Leftrightarrow} p)} \right\}$$

$$\underset{:\,t\rightarrow t}{\text{WeDefiniendum}} \rightarrow \textbf{we say that}\ \underset{0}{\text{Variable}}\ \underset{1}{\text{new-VPsg}}$$

$$\left\{ \underset{:t}{\lambda p.\,(1(0) \overset{\text{df}}{\Leftrightarrow} p)} \right\}$$

Direct conjunction of these rules is easy to define:[20]

$$\underset{:\,t\rightarrow t}{\text{WeDefiniendum}} \rightarrow \underset{0\,:\,t\rightarrow t}{\text{WeDefiniendum}}\ \textbf{and}\ \underset{1\,:\,t\rightarrow t}{\text{WeDefiniendum}}$$

$$\left\{ \underset{:t}{\lambda p.\,(0(p) \uplus 1(p))} \right\}$$

---

[18] This is the first example in which we are introducing new syntactic and semantic categories in order to support compositionality, rather than to directly model the entities in the language. These 'functional' categories are akin to the categories created by type raising in Montague Grammar.

[19] The treatment of prepositional phrases and 'new-PP' is described in §8.1; for present purposes it suffices to note that 'new-PP' matches against 'in S'.

[20] This rule only handles the conjunction of two items, i.e. 'A and B'. Handling the idiomatic conjunction of several items, as in 'A, B, C and D' requires some minor modifications to the theory. We will not discuss these as they contain no interesting ideas.

I.e. we evaluate each of the conjoined items to be defined on the definens separately, obtaining two separate definitions ('0(p)' and '1(p)'); we then join these definitions using ⊎.

So we have now set up rules that can handle, for example,

> If x is an element of a set S, we write $x \in S$ and we say that x is in S and we say that S contains x.

But our actual example, repeated here, was a little subtler:

> If x is an element of a set S, we write $x \in S$ and say that x is in S or that S contains x.

In order to handle this, we need to break down the above composite rules and introduce some subtler forms of conjunction. First, we want to be able to say 'we VP$_1$ and VP$_2$' rather than having to write 'we VP$_1$ and we VP$_2$'. To do this we introduce another functional category, as follows:

$$\underset{: \, t \to t}{\text{WeDefiniendum}} \to \textbf{we} \; \underset{0 \, : \, t \to t}{\text{WeDefVP}} \qquad \{0\}$$

We then rewrite our composite rules in terms of this category:

$$\underset{: \, t \to t}{\text{WeDefVP}} \to \textbf{write} \; \underset{0}{\text{new-Formula}} \qquad \left\{ \lambda p. \, \underset{:t}{(0 \overset{\text{df}}{\Leftrightarrow} p)} \right\}$$

$$\underset{: \, t \to t}{\text{WeDefVP}} \to \textbf{say that} \; \underset{0}{\text{Variable}} \; \textbf{is} \; \underset{1}{\text{new-PP}} \qquad \left\{ \lambda p. \, \underset{:t}{(1(0) \overset{\text{df}}{\Leftrightarrow} p)} \right\}$$

$$\underset{: \, t \to t}{\text{WeDefVP}} \to \textbf{say that} \; \underset{0}{\text{Variable}} \; \underset{1}{\text{new-VPsg}} \qquad \left\{ \lambda p. \, \underset{:t}{(1(0) \overset{\text{df}}{\Leftrightarrow} p)} \right\}$$

And finally we allow conjunction of these new VPs (in addition to conjunction of elements of the category 'WeDefVP'):

$$\underset{: \, t \to t}{\text{WeDefVP}} \to \underset{0 \, : \, t \to t}{\text{WeDefVP}} \; \textbf{and} \; \underset{1 \, : \, t \to t}{\text{WeDefVP}}$$
$$\left\{ \lambda p. \, \underset{:t}{(0(p) \uplus 1(p))} \right\}$$

Finally, coping with 'say that x is in S or that S contains x' requires us to introduce yet another functional category:

$$\underset{: \, t \to t}{\text{WeDefVP}} \to \textbf{say} \; \underset{: \, t \to t}{\text{WeDefSay}} \qquad \{0\}$$

With this new category available, we can break down the rules involving 'say' yet further:

$$\underset{: \, t \to t}{\text{WeDefSay}} \to \textbf{that} \; \underset{0}{\text{Variable}} \; \textbf{is} \; \underset{1}{\text{new-PP}} \qquad \left\{ \lambda p. \, \underset{:t}{(1(0) \overset{\text{df}}{\Leftrightarrow} p)} \right\}$$

$$\underset{: \, t \to t}{\text{WeDefSay}} \to \textbf{that} \; \underset{0}{\text{Variable}} \; \underset{1}{\text{new-VPsg}} \qquad \left\{ \lambda p. \, \underset{:t}{(1(0) \overset{\text{df}}{\Leftrightarrow} p)} \right\}$$

Having broken down these rules it is straightforward to introduce conjunction, either with 'and' or with 'or':

WeDefSay → WeDefSay **and** WeDefSay
: $t{\to}t$ 0 : $t{\to}t$ 1 : $t{\to}t$

$$\left\{ \lambda p.\, (0(p) \uplus 1(p)) \right\}_{:t}$$

WeDefSay → WeDefSay **or** WeDefSay
: $t{\to}t$ 0 : $t{\to}t$ 1 : $t{\to}t$

$$\left\{ \lambda p.\, (0(p) \uplus 1(p)) \right\}_{:t}$$

Finally, in order to cope with examples like 'we say **that** X and Y' (rather than 'we say **that** X and **that** Y'), we introduce yet another level of intermediate categories and associated rules. The necessary changes are essentially identical to those we have made above.

3.5 Rhetorical Structure

In this section, we will cover the formal treatment of the phenomena discussed in §2.5, including rhetorical relations, blocks and the treatment of variables and assumptions.

3.5.1 *Explanation*

As noted in §2.5, the vast majority of the rhetorical relations found in natural language are not present in mathematical language, due to its restricted subject matter and also to the convention requiring that each sentence in a mathematical text is a logical consequence of previous sentences. The one important exception to this rule is the relationship of explanation or justification, i.e. the relationship telling us why a given fact is true. For example, consider

Since (x_n) is Cauchy, there exists N such that $d(x_m, x_n) < \epsilon$ for all $m, n \geqslant N$.

(Sutherland, 1975, p. 124)

Here '(x_n) is Cauchy' explains why 'there exists N such that $d(x_m, x_n) < \epsilon$ for all $m, n \geqslant N$' is true. Similarly, many constituents of category S begin with a word like 'so', 'thus', 'hence', indicating that they are justified by the assertion immediately preceding them; for example, we have:

If $Sa = Sb$, then $a = 1a \in Sa = Sb$, and so there is $s \in S$ with $a = sb$.

(Rotman, 1995, p. 25)

We will encode these relationships by introducing two new DRS-conditions. The first is of the form $\Gamma \vdash \Gamma'$, and indicates that Γ explains why Γ' is true.

The second is of the form $\vdash \Gamma'$, and indicates that the previous DRS-condition (in the immediately enclosing DRS) explains why Γ' is true.

In order to illustrate these relationships using the above examples, we will label constituents as follows:

Since $\underbrace{(x_n) \text{ is Cauchy}}_{\text{P}}$, $\underbrace{\text{there exists } N \text{ such that}}_{\text{Q}}$ ....

If $\underbrace{Sa = Sb}_{\text{X}}$, then $\underbrace{a = 1a \in Sa = Sb}_{\text{Y}}$, and so $\underbrace{\text{there is } s \in S \text{ with } a = sb}_{\text{Z}}$.

Using these abbreviations, the appropriate DRSs are

and

where $\hat{P}$ is the semantic representation of P, etc..

3.5.2   *Blocks*

The super-sentential structure of a mathematical text, including blocks, is straightforward and may be directly captured by a context free grammar containing rules such as:[21]

    ResultStatement → **Lemma** Number Name ⊃ SentenceList ⊃

    Proof → **Proof** SentenceList ⊃

The main grammar can change after a sentence is processed, but the super-sentential grammar cannot; that is, we cannot introduce new ways of structuring mathematical documents in definitions. In consequence, we will regard the super-sentential grammar as being entirely separate from the main grammar.[22]

---

[21] Here the symbol '⊃' indicates an obligatory end-of-line. Mathematics language is only sensitive to typesetting information of this kind at the super-sentential level.

[22] In mathematical texts, the nesting of blocks is extremely limited; only claims may appear inside other blocks, and claims cannot appear inside claims. As a consequence, the super-sentential grammar actually turns out to be regular.

In terms of semantics, there is relatively little to say about blocks; they may essentially be preserved at the semantic level, so that the complete semantic representation consists of theorems whose statements consist of a DRS, etc.. The DRSs for distinct blocks do not interact with each other, with two exceptions. First, any material in a proof DRS may access referents defined in (the outermost scope of) the corresponding result DRS. This ensures that variables introduced in the statement of a result may be referred to in the corresponding proof. Second, where a claim is enclosed inside the proof of another result, both the statement and proof of the claim may access referents previously introduced in the result or the proof.

There are two subtleties worth noting. The first concerns the numbers and names of results, such as 'Theorem 4.10' and 'Cauchy's Theorem' in

Theorem 4.10 "Cauchy's Theorem"

   ...

These may be referenced in text, as in

By Theorem 4.10, ...

By Cauchy's Theorem, ...

In order to allow this, we add a category 'ResultName' to the main grammar, and then stipulate that whenever a result is encountered, appropriate rules are added to the main grammar. For example, after the above result is encountered, we would add the following rules to the main grammar:

ResultName → **Theorem 4.10**

ResultName → **Cauchy's Theorem**

Then at the semantic level, we introduce a construction allowing the use of references to results as elements of the semantic category t (as defined in §3.3.7), i.e. as elements that may be used wherever DRSs may be used. We will simply denote these as '[Theorem 4.10]', etc.. In combination with the rhetorical relationship of explanation (§3.5.1), this allows us to encode, say, 'By Theorem 4.10, P' as

$$[\text{Theorem 4.10}] \vdash \hat{P}$$

where $\hat{P}$ is the semantic representation of P.

The second subtlety relates to the distinctive behaviour of 'to be' inside definition blocks (§2.5). We handle this by introducing a new category S_{def} which is used to capture sentences inside definitions. A rule

$S \to S_{def}$

ensures that normal sentences can be used inside definitions, but we also
add specific rules which treat 'to be' as specifying a definition, as well as
appropriate rules for conjunctions of S_{def} s, etc.. Finally, we will add a
disambiguation convention stating that a reading involving any of these other
rules to be preferred to a reading which factors through the category S.[23]

3.5.3 Variables and Assumptions

We will first describe a mechanism for handling variable introduction in
DRT. As we noted above, discourse update is conventionally performed by
merging new material to the end of the discourse DRS. We may rephrase this
by stating that new material is inserted at the '•' symbol in the following
diagram:

$$\begin{array}{|l|}
\hline
x_1 \; x_2 \; \ldots x_n \\
\hline
\gamma_1 \\
\gamma_2 \\
\ldots \\
\gamma_m \\
\bullet \\
\hline
\end{array}$$

To handle the introduction of variable in a statement like

   Let ϵ be positive real number.

we perform two operations. First, we introduce the variable in the antecedent
of a conditional statement; as noted in §3.3.4, the variable itself is precisely
a named referent. Second, we 'move' the *insertion point* '•' so that all subsequent material appears in the consequent of the conditional.[24] Thus the last
example sentence would yield:

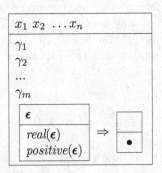

---

[23] Such conventions are discussed in §4.2.3.

[24] The movement of the insertion point is compositionally encoded as part of the
semantics of the grammar rule for the 'let' statement.

The standard rules about accessibility (§3.3.2) then correctly predict that subsequent material, which will be introduced at the insertion point, may access ϵ, but that $\gamma_1, \ldots, \gamma_m$ cannot do so.

A similar operation can be used to handle long-term assumptions, such as:

Suppose that there exist finitely many prime numbers.

The only difference is that such assumptions can be discharged (for example, on deduction of a contradiction); in such cases the insertion point is restored to its previous position. Crucially, the treatment using DRT correctly predicts that when an assumption is discharged, all the variables introduced since the assumption was made become inaccessible.

Note that once merger is completed, the insertion point is irrelevant; thus from the point of view of the completed discourse, or any intermediate discourse, we have encoded the above rhetorical operations inside DRT without introducing any additional machinery. This will be significant when we come to consider ambiguity and type flow within DRSs, in Chapter 6; it will allow us to give a unified treatment of intra-sentential and discourse phenomena.

Implicit Variable Introduction

In some cases, a variable ϵ can be introduced by a statement like

If ϵ is a positive real number, then ... .[25]

or

Given a positive real number ϵ, ...

Such examples are handled by moving the insertion point exactly as in the examples given earlier in this section.[26] This approach is capable of overcoming some of the problems that occur in the type-theoretic analysis of maths given in Ranta (1994). The analysis given there is unable to cope with kinds of variable introduction that cannot be formalised as quantifiers. For example, consider the variable-introducing sentence:

If a point A lies outside a line a, A determines a parallel to a.

---

[25] If this sentence is used in a context in which ϵ is already bound, it is read as an assertion about ϵ rather than as an instance of implicit variable introduction. Note that a simple constraint stating that every referent must be bound and that no referent maybe bound twice selects correctly between the two readings. We will see another use of this constraint in §4.3.2, and discuss the constraint further in §6.3.2.

[26] de Bruijn considers that it is 'bad manners' to introduce a variable in this way (De Bruijn, 1987, p. 928). However, this usage is ubiquitous in actual mathematical texts.

Ranta notes that his theory is unable to cope with this sentence because it would need to analyse 'if a point A lies outside a line a' as a quantifier, and the variable names would not be usable outside the scope of this quantifier (Ranta, 1994, p. 13).

Our own approach assigns this sentence the DRS:[27]

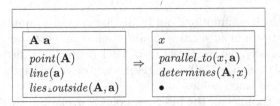

The standard rules about accessibility of referents tell us that A and a may be accessed by any material inserted at the '•'. Consequently, A and a may be freely referred to in the subsequent discourse.

3.5.4 Related Work: DRT in NaProChe

In §1.5.3 we referred to NaProChe, a computer language for mathematics which uses a variant of DRT as a semantic representation. As we have now described our own usage and modification of DRT, we are in a position to contrast our approach with that of NaProChe, as described in Kolev (2008).

We should first note that NaProChe converts an entire mathematical document, including all super-sentential structure, into a single DRS. Results, proofs and other blocks are converted into sub-DRSs. This is largely a stylistic difference, making no substantive difference to the predictions of the theory.[28] We ourselves prefer not to represent blocks inside DRSs for two reasons. First, this approach results in extraordinarily large DRSs; an entire mathematical document is represented by a single DRS, and that DRS will normally be too large to actually display. Second, in order for DRSs to represent general blocks, one has to modify DRSs to encode the names of results, etc.. The presence of such additional material would complicate and obscure the more important DRS-related definitions that we will present when discussing typed parsing in Chapter 6.

The primary modification of DRT in NaProChe is the addition of a collection of 'mathematical referents' to every DRS. See Figure 3.4.

---

[27] There is a strong argument that 'determines' should be treated as a semantically higher-order construct. (Such constructs will be discussed briefly in §8.2.) This issue is orthogonal to the current discussion of variables and quantification; accordingly, for the purpose of the present example, we will analyse 'determines' as a simple two-place predicate.

[28] Indeed, the authors of NaProChe note that their original approach represented blocks separately, and that they shifted approach because it allowed the use of one parsing program, rather than two (Kolev, 2008, p. 31).

Discourse Referents	Mathematical Referents
DRS-Conditions

Fig. 3.4 Structure of Modified DRSs in NaProChe

Turning to the mathematical referents, we find that each symbolic constituent in a mathematical text, including both terms and formulae, is converted into such a mathematical referent. Mathematical referents are then placed in correspondence with discourse referents by a DRS-condition of the form

$math\_id$(discourse referent, mathematical referent)

If the same symbolic constituent occurs twice, two mathematical referents are generated but these are assigned the same discourse referent. If a given mathematical referent is a formula, the corresponding discourse referent is asserted to be true by use of a DRS-condition

$holds$(discourse referent)

The approach is illustrated using the following sentence:[29]

Hence $\forall u(u \in x \leftrightarrow \mathrm{Ord}(u))$.

The DRS assigned to this sentence is:

$1 \mid \forall u(u \in x \leftrightarrow \mathrm{Ord}(u))$
$math\text{-}id(1, \forall u(u \in x \leftrightarrow \mathrm{Ord}(u)))$ $holds(1)$

We are unable to follow the motivation for this approach in several respects. First, it is unclear what function the mathematical referents play. Where they represent formulae, those formulae could be directly inserted into the '$holds$' condition, as in:

$holds(\forall u(u \in x \leftrightarrow \mathrm{Ord}(u)))$

For that matter, the '$holds$' condition itself seems redundant; one could simply write:

$\forall u(u \in x \leftrightarrow \mathrm{Ord}(u))$

---

[29] See §1.5.3 for a discussion of the respects in which the sentence differs from those found in mathematical texts.

It is *a priori* conceivable that the formula has been made into a referent so that one may refer back to it in later text, although the need for references of this kind is not apparent. But since an exact textual equivalent to the formula ('every element u of x is an ordinal') will not be assigned a referent, this motivation seems improbable.

Whether or not one has the levels of indirection provided by '*math-id*' and '*holds*', the fact remains that the semantic representation of formulae is just their syntactic representation. Conversely, the range of syntactic notation allowed in a language using this approach is just the (presumably fixed) range which is permitted inside semantic representations. Thus any approach of this kind must have a limited capacity to cope with the range of symbolic notation found in mathematics, and little if any ability to deal with the productive character thereof.

Turning to terms, it seems that the function of mathematical referents is to ensure that two instances of the same term ('x' and 'x', or '$\cup S$' and '$\cup S$') are assigned the same discourse referent. In the case where the term is simply a variable, this can be achieved by simply using the variable as a discourse referent, as we do in §3.3.4. In the case where the term is complex, two instances of the corresponding textual phrase ('the union of the elements of S') would be assigned distinct discourse referents, and so it is unclear why the symbolic equivalents should be assigned the same discourse referent.

3.6 Conclusion

The analysis given above is comparable to that given for the fragments covered in (Ranta, 1994, 1995, 1996, 1997a,b), but handles a much wider range of mathematics. Additionally, and more significantly, it extracts all mathematical material from definitions, rather than requiring it to be manually specified. A number of self-contained minor topics, including some discussed by Ranta, are deferred to Chapter 8; but excepting these, this chapter concludes the material for which there is a precedent in the literature.

In subsequent chapters we will move on to more advanced topics. A broad indication of the nature of those topics arose in §3.2, discussing types. As we saw, an approach which took types to be semantic resulted in extensive overgeneration and ambiguity; an approach which too them to be syntactic categories was effective in avoiding extensive overgeneration, but encountered problems when handling sentences like

There is a projective submodule N of M such that $M = N + MB$.

(Tuganbaev, 2000)

In order to develop a theory which can handle a large amount of mathematics, rather than a single domain, we need to unify these perspectives: we will need to construct types which resemble both grammatical categories (such as Term$_{\text{SUBMODULE}}$) and extensional properties (such as 'being a submodule of

M') in different respects. The heart of the difficulty here is worth underlining. In the example just given, a variable is used in one place and effectively assigned a syntactic category in another. This has no direct analogue in natural language: we cannot introduce a word in one part of a sentence, and declare that it is a noun in another. As a result, we have no exemplar which we can adapt to describe the nature of type; we will need to create techniques ab initio. In addition, the actual information about types needed to correctly interpret the symbolic constituent '$N + MB$' derives from a piece of text, namely 'submodule'. Thus type information flows from textual mathematics into symbolic, and (as we will show in §4.3.2) vice versa. Handling this requires us to unify standard linguistic techniques for analysing language and fresh techniques for handling symbolic mathematics. The dissimilarity of these two classes of technique makes this problem substantive.

The next three chapters are concerned with determining the functions which type needs to serve in order to support a theory that can describe a wide range of mathematics, and with formalising it to do precisely that. In Chapter 4 we will find that type is intimately connected to disambiguation of both symbolic and textual material, and that it therefore needs to handle a range of examples which are harder than the one given above. In Chapter 5 we will clarify the exact nature and function of types, as well as determining precisely which types are needed in order to describe mathematics. Chapter 6 will then show how one can use this formal notion to formulate a theory which does not overgenerate, which handles variables and which correctly resolves the wide range of ambiguity which we will discuss in Chapter 4.

4

Ambiguity

Ambiguity and the resolution of ambiguity will occupy us for the next three chapters. Before we delve into specifics, it is worth setting out the particular points that make the disambiguation of mathematics difficult. Some of these points can be compactly conveyed; others will be sketched here and substantiated in the remainder of this chapter, which surveys ambiguity in mathematics. All of the points will be addressed in the course of Chapter 5 and Chapter 6.

The first point of difficulty is the one we encountered at the very end of the previous chapter, relating to the introduction and use of variables within one sentence. As we noted, in

There is a projective submodule N of M such that $M = N + MB$.

(Tuganbaev, 2000)

the variable N is introduced in one part of the sentence, and used in another. Given that, as we noted in §3.2, variables of distinct types can behave like objects of different categories in the underlying grammar, there is no analogue to this in natural language: one cannot introduce a word in one part of a sentence and state that it behaves like an adjective in another.

The second point of difficulty also relates to symbolic mathematics. As we saw in §2.4, symbolic mathematics is much richer than any of the formal languages that are studied in mathematics and computer science. We will find in §4.1 below that the disambiguation mechanisms associated with these formal languages are radically insufficient for removing structural ambiguity in symbolic mathematics.

The third point relates to textual mathematics. A sentence like

Some natural number is prime.

is *a priori* ambiguous because the adjective 'prime' has many senses. Yet the sentence clearly contains enough information to determine the sense in use. In order to give an adequate theory of mathematical language, we need to give some formal theory that can track information flow inside this sentence and determine which sense of the adjective is needed. Statistical methods are of no use; we need something that *guarantees* the correct answer. We know of no existing method that can resolve ambiguity in textual mathematics.

The fourth point relates to the interaction between symbolic and textual mathematics. It is not hard to see that information needed to resolve ambiguities may need to flow over the boundary between text and symbol. For example, to distinguish the senses of 'prime' in

3 is prime.

and

$G_{n,3}(\mathbb{C})$ is prime.[1]

we need to examine the symbolic material. A priori, it is entirely unclear how to transmit information between these dissimilar kinds of language, consisting of words and symbols respectively.

The fifth and final point, which will prove the hardest to tackle, relates to the way in which one can analyse sentences which mix textual and symbolic content. In §4.3, we will exhibit specific sentences which demonstrate two points about the order of analysis. The first kind of sentence will show that in general, symbolic material cannot be interpreted without knowing the textual structure of a sentence. The second kind of sentence will exhibit that in general, the textual structure of a sentence cannot be determined without interpreting symbolic material. Together, these sentences will show that neither ambiguity in symbolic material nor ambiguity in textual material can be resolved before the other: we are faced with the linguistic equivalent of simultaneous equations. To predict the meanings of sentences, some unified mechanism for simultaneously disambiguating both symbolic material and textual material will be needed.

Several of these issues will have ramifications for our treatment of type, and its relation to both disambiguation and parsing. We will discuss these ramifications as they arise in the chapter below, and then summarise them at the end of this chapter (§4.4).

Chapter Structure

We have previously noted that ambiguity is a major issue for any theory of the language of mathematics and, using the benefit of hindsight, intimated that type is the key to resolving those issues. This chapter will expand upon these points. It will survey the range of ambiguity in mathematical language and discuss its relation to type in much greater detail than in our previous discussion; it will also present the promised evidence supporting the points listed above, and discuss those disambiguation mechanisms that can be formulated independently of type. The end aim of the chapter is to leave

---

[1] '$G_{n,3}(\mathbb{C})$ is prime' is part of the title of (Ferdinands, 1998); $G_{n,3}(\mathbb{C})$ is a manifold.

us in a position where we know exactly what we require of type if it is to disambiguate mathematics. The next two chapters will then discuss type in greater detail and explain how it may be unified with the parsing process in order to simultaneously disambiguate both textual and symbolic material, and resolve all of the points listed above.

The chapter is broken into three main parts. §4.1 discusses ambiguity in symbolic material. It begins by surveying disambiguation mechanisms in existing formal languages and goes on to prove that such mechanisms are not adequate for handling symbolic mathematics, as noted in the second point above. It then discusses the way in which we should handle adaptivity in a syntactically productive language, and finally presents certain disambiguation mechanisms which are unrelated to type.

§4.2 surveys kinds of ambiguity in natural language, indicates which of these kinds occur in mathematics, and then presents disambiguation mechanisms that can remove certain of those kinds without recourse to type.

§4.3 surveys ambiguity in mathematics as a whole, when textual and symbolic material are mixed. Its main purpose is to present the evidence underlying the final point above, i.e. to show that neither textual or symbolic material can be disambiguated prior to or independently of the other.

Finally, §4.4 recapitulates the kinds of ambiguity that the mechanism of type will need to deal with, and lists the main questions that we will have to answer when considering types, leading into our actual discussion of types in Chapter 5. It also summarises the argument showing that parsing and the determination of type cannot be independent processes, which motivates our eventual presentation of a joint 'typed parsing' algorithm in Chapter 6.

All of the examples, analyses, arguments and other material in this chapter are novel, expect where it is explicitly stated otherwise.

4.1 Ambiguity in Symbolic Mathematics

We will start this section by recalling the examples of ambiguity in symbolic mathematics that we have already encountered (§4.1.1). We will then give a quick survey of ambiguity and disambiguation mechanisms in formal languages (§4.1.2) before showing that the ambiguity in symbolic mathematics cannot be handled by such mechanisms (§4.1.3). Finally, we will then present those disambiguation mechanisms for symbolic mathematics which are largely orthogonal to type (§4.1.5); the use of type for disambiguation will be described in Chapter 6.

4.1.1 Ambiguity in Symbolic Material

We have already seen some examples of ambiguity in symbolic material, in §2.4 and in §3.2. It is worth briefly summarising these examples here, and

briefly discussing their significance to a discussion of ambiguity, before moving
on to broader but related topics.

The first example we saw (in §2.4) was

$$\alpha \to (\beta)_n^m$$

The significance of this example was that this expression could either be
interpreted as a single piece of notation, referring to a property of graphs,
or as a combination of four different pieces of notation ('• → •', '(•)', '••'
and '•.'). Which of the two was indicated depended, in an intuitive sense, on
the *types* of α, β, m and n. So this example gave us our first indication that
the syntactic structure of a fixed expression in symbolic mathematics might
depend on the types of the entities it referred to.

We took up the discussion of types in much greater depth in §3.2. We
started by briefly considering the piece of notation '$X + Y$', and noting
that this needed to be parsed with a different syntactic rules for each distinct usage of '+' (with numbers, vectors, functions, and many other kinds
of mathematical object). So this example showed that a very simple piece
of notation could have many readings if we did not use some formal notion of
type for disambiguation. One point worth noting about this example is that
all of the different readings have essentially the same structure; even though
different syntactic rules must be for used each reading of '$X + Y$', the parse
tree that is obtained always has the same structure. Thus, unlike the first
example, this is not an example of structural ambiguity.

After this, we moved on to clear examples of structural ambiguity. We took
three different notations involving the character '#', and showed that if these
were not made subordinate to some notion of type, then we could generate
pathological and nonsensical expressions such as:

$$\#\#0\#\#\#1\#2\#\#\#$$

At this point, it is worth adding that the rules given in §3.2 generate not one
but *many* readings for this expression, with a variety of structures; in other
words, we have not just a pathological example but a pathological and highly
ambiguous example.

Thus we have considered three examples in which ambiguity occurs unless
some notion of type is used for disambiguation purposes. In the first, we found
that a standard mathematical expression was given two structurally different
readings in the absence of any notion of type. In the second, we found that
a ubiquitous expression could be given many readings in the absence of type,
albeit structurally similar readings. In the third, we noted that pathological
expressions which should not be parsed at all were given a variety of structures
in the absence of type.

All of these examples indicate that some notion of type is highly necessary
for disambiguation purposes. And, in particular, the first and third examples
strongly suggest that it is not in general possible to determine the structure
of a piece of symbolic mathematics without knowing the types of the entities

involved in it. They do not demonstrate this conclusively. If we were playing devil's advocate, we could argue that the graph-theoretic notation in the first example could be somehow 'built up' out of the four simpler notations in a way that was invisible to mathematicians, and that the third example was not a genuine example of ambiguity precisely because it was pathological. We will address these concerns in §4.1.3 below. More specifically, we will give an example of a simple mathematical expression, taken from a textbook, which *must* be assigned different syntactic structures depending on the types of the entities that refers to; and in this case it will be transparently clear that neither structure can be built up out of the other. This example will also serve to show that the standard disambiguation mechanisms for formal languages cannot cope with mathematics. Accordingly, it will be useful to give a survey of those mechanisms before presenting the example; we will turn to this task now.

4.1.2 Survey: Ambiguity in Formal Languages

Formal languages are generally designed to be unambiguous; cf.:

> When we are using a grammar to help define a programming language we would like that grammar to be unambiguous. Otherwise, a programmer and a compiler may have differing opinions as to the meaning of some sentences.
>
> (Aho and Ullman, 1972, p. 202)

Linguists occasionally remark on the sharp contrast with natural language, as in:

> [...] all formal languages have been designed to be unambiguous. Where ambiguity might arise (for example, in the order of arithmetic or logical operations), either parentheses (or some similar notation) are employed, or an exceptionless convention is built into the syntax of the language (as in the case of Polish notation).
>
> (Wasow et al., 2005)

We can be a little more precise. To begin with, virtually all current formal languages exclude all syntactic ambiguity at the syntactic level. Given a string in almost any formal language, it is possible to determine the parse tree of that string without any reference to semantics.

So, for example, given an expression

$$p \Rightarrow q \land r$$

in a typical formulation of the propositional calculus, it is possible to determine that this expression has the structure

$$p \Rightarrow (q \land r)$$

rather than the structure

$$(p \Rightarrow q) \land r.$$

The primary mechanism used to avoid ambiguity in such cases is that of *precedence*.[2] Most formal languages distinguish a class of operators, such as '+' or '×', and specify that some of these have higher precedences than others. When an expression with two or more operators is to be evaluated, one evaluates operators in order of decreasing precedence. The example above is accounted for by giving '∧' a higher precedence than '⇒'. In addition, each individual operator is said to be either *left associative* or *right associative*. If an operator ∘ is left associative, then '$x \circ y \circ z$' means '$(x \circ y) \circ z$'; if it is right associative, then '$x \circ y \circ z$' means '$x \circ (y \circ z)$'. Together, precedence and associativity preclude most syntactic ambiguity; residual ambiguity is typically dealt with by language-specific mechanisms.

Precluding syntactic ambiguity still leaves room for other kinds of ambiguity. For example, in the language of the theorem prover HOL (Gordon and Melham, 1993), the expression

    x + y

may refer to the sum of two natural numbers or to the sum of two integers (or to other kinds of addition); the two kinds of sum are distinguished in the underlying logic.[3] Such ambiguities are resolved by stages subsequent to and separate from the syntax.

Resolution procedures in such post-syntactic stages do not reason generally about the semantic content of the expressions they consider, but restrict themselves to mechanically computable properties. Such properties are often called 'types', and in most cases they correspond to the intuitive kind that an object has. (The history of the notion of 'type' is discussed in introduction to Chapter 5.) In the example above, if x and y both have the type 'num', then the expression unambiguously refers to the sum of natural numbers; if both have the type 'int', then the expression unambiguously refers to the sum of integers. (If they have different types, the expression is invalid. This usage of type for both disambiguation and legitimacy testing is found in many formal languages; see §5.1 for further discussion of this point.)

In some cases, determination of types is not a straightforward process; and in particular, types are not explicitly assigned to entities but are deduced in some way. In such cases one speaks of a *type inference algorithm* which deduces types; the classic example of such an algorithm is given in Milner (1978).

For our purposes, the salient properties of formal languages are these: syntactic ambiguities are resolved with reference to syntax alone, then residual ambiguities are *fully* removed, typically by assigning types to entities.

---

[2] Ad hoc versions of precedence can be found as far back as in Principia Mathematica (Whitehead and Russell, 1910); the term 'precedence', and the formalisation of the notion, seem to date from Floyd (1963).

[3] This is in contrast to the language of mathematics; in §7.2.2 we will see that attempts to draw type distinctions between different kinds of numbers yield predictions that conflict with the observed usage of mathematics.

4.1.3 Failure of Standard Mechanisms

In §2.4, we saw that a given surface string might have different parse trees depending on the kind of entities it referred to. A similar but more striking example can be found in the lambda calculus. The example is just

$$\lambda + \mathbf{K} = \mathbf{S}$$

(Barendregt, 1984, p. 33)

In structure, this is identical to an assertion about the sum of two numbers, or vectors, or matrices, or even the symmetric difference of two sets, as in

$$X + Y = Z.$$

But it is parsed in quite a different way. In its original setting, $\lambda + \mathbf{K} = \mathbf{S}$ is not read as $(\lambda + \mathbf{K}) = \mathbf{S}$; that is, it is not an assertion that $\lambda + \mathbf{K}$ is equal to $\mathbf{S}$. Rather it refers to a mathematical term, $\lambda + (\mathbf{K} = \mathbf{S})$. λ is a set of 'equations' about the lambda calculus, and $\lambda + (\mathbf{K} = \mathbf{S})$ is the result of adding '$\mathbf{K} = \mathbf{S}$' to this set. So we have disparate structures for two expressions whose surface forms are essentially identical:

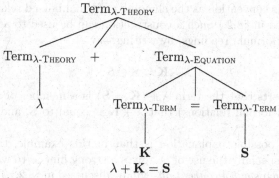

$$\lambda + \mathbf{K} = \mathbf{S}$$
(In the example taken from Barendregt (1984).)

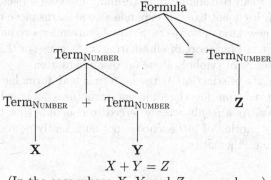

$$X + Y = Z$$
(In the case where X, Y and Z are numbers.)

This would seem to suggest that we cannot state that '$=$' has a higher precedence than '$+$' or vice versa, and so that the mechanism of precedence is not sufficiently powerful to disambiguate symbolic mathematics. A priori, there are two distinct ways in which we could try and avoid this conclusion, by giving an alternative explanation for the different structures assigned to '$\lambda + (\mathbf{K} = \mathbf{S})$' and '$X + Y = Z$'. We will consider these in turn.

The first possible explanation is that the distinction between a term (like '3', or '$\lambda + (\mathbf{K} = \mathbf{S})$' in the above context) and a formula (like '$3 = 4 - 1$', or '$X = Y + Z$' when referring to numbers) could appear to be a means of distinguishing the two structures. There are, however, contexts which neutralise this distinction. One such context uses a widespread notational convention of symbolic mathematics whereby two or more 'overlapping' formulae in mathematics can be fused together in a single assertion. The simplest example is the use of

$$a_0 < a_1 < a_2 < a_3$$

as an abbreviation for

$$a_0 < a_1 \text{ and } a_1 < a_2 \text{ and } a_2 < a_3.$$

(We refer to this convention as the chaining of formal infixed relations, and it will be discussed in §8.2.) Such a construction can be used to accommodate both term and formula readings, by writing, say

$$\lambda + \mathbf{K} = \mathbf{S} \in S.$$

This either asserts that the term $\lambda + (\mathbf{K} = \mathbf{S})$ is a member of S, or (using chained infixed formal relations) that $\lambda + \mathbf{K}$ is equal to $\mathbf{S}$, and that $\mathbf{S}$ is a member of S.

The second possible explanation is that in this example, the choice of symbols, and especially the use of 'λ', gives a strong hint as to which reading is intended. (Such *symbol conventions* will be discussed in §8.2.) The difficulty with relying on such cues is that in mathematics as a whole, there is a severe scarcity of distinct symbols. As a result, any given mathematical symbol (such as, say, 'R') can reasonably refer to many kinds of object. Worse, this range of possibilities is not fixed; it expands as one learns more mathematics, and encounters new kinds of objects. Symbol conventions reduce the extent of this effect, but fall far short of eliminating it. Because of this, we cannot safely rely on choices of symbols alone for disambiguation.

Thus neither the distinction between terms and formulae nor symbol conventions can account for the different structures assigned to the two expressions above. As a result, we are forced to conclude that the standard, type-independent, notion of precedence is not sufficiently powerful to disambiguate symbolic mathematics.

4.1.4   Discussion

Expecting the Unexpected

As well as showing the inadequacy of the standard disambiguation model for formal languages, the example just given highlights a critical point about mathematics as a whole. Mathematics does unexpected things. Had we not seen it happen, there was no way in which we could have guessed that '=' might bind more tightly than '+'. And because the language of mathematics is exceptionally productive in every aspect, including its syntax, a corollary is this: mathematics will keep doing unexpected things.

Thus, as we encounter more mathematics, we will keep seeing surprising syntactic phenomena; correspondingly, as our theory adaptively assimilates more mathematics, it will need to handle those surprising syntactic phenomena. We have a two pronged strategy for giving it the best possible chance of handling these. First, we will allow type-dependent syntax; just because, say, '+' is associative on numbers, sets, vectors, etc., we will not require it to be associative on all types. (And, indeed, nonassociative addition exists in the literature; cf. Chernoff (1972). Notions like 'addition' are family resemblances in the sense of Wittgenstein (1953), not sharply delineated categories.) This sharply limits the degree to which the notation in one area of mathematics can conflict with that in another.

Second, our parsing methods will only ever rely on *positive information*. So if we know that 'a' and 'b' are both numbers, or both sets, or etc., we will parse '$a + b$' in the usual way; but if they are not known to be objects of some type for which addition has been defined (or even if one is a number and the other a set), we will not parse '$a + b$' at all. This leaves open the possibility of (monotonically) defining '$a + b$' to have some unexpected syntactic structure for these new types.

Asymptotic Frequency of Notational Collision

We should emphasise one final point about ambiguity in symbolic mathematics before moving onwards. If we concentrate too much on the particular examples of ambiguity given in §2.4, §3.2 and in this chapter, we risk missing the forest for the trees. There is a much more abstract argument which is more significant than our individual, domain-specific, examples. The argument rests on the asymptotic frequency of instances of *notational collision* (§3.2), as occurs in the ambiguous expressions '$\alpha \to (\beta)_n^m$' (in §2.4) and '$X + Y = Z$' (above).

We will start with three observations. First, symbolic mathematics has essentially unrestricted productive syntax: arbitrary new notation may be defined in mathematical texts. Second, the probability of collision between notations grows faster than linearly in the amount of notation defined. (We would hesitate to say that it is at least quadratic, because notation is not chosen at random, and the space of symbols used is mildly productive; but growth is certainly faster than linear.) Third, mathematics is monolithic: for reasons discussed in §2.2, we need to consider all of mathematics as if it were a single discourse. Thus very large amounts of notation will eventually be defined.

Putting together these observations makes it clear that notational collision will become an increasingly severe problem as we consider more and more mathematics. For a language that aims to describe all of mathematics, rather than small parts at the time, some mechanism for preventing notational collision is a *sine qua non*. Our own approach, hinted at in §3.2 above and earlier in this section, will be to make notation subordinate to a notion of type; effectively we cut up the space of notations into many cells labelled by types, so that notations defined for one type cannot clash with notations defined for another.[4] We will present this approach in full in Chapters 5 and 6.

4.1.5 Disambiguation without Type

The main burden of disambiguating symbolic mathematics will fall on the concept of type, which will be the topic of the next chapter. Nevertheless, there are some mechanisms that are relatively orthogonal to type; we will present these here.

The easiest way to diagnose whether a given mechanism is essentially orthogonal to type is to determine whether it would be needed even in a domain with one type. Thus any kind of mechanism that would be needed to disambiguate, say, numbers alone belongs in this section. So, for example, we need a mechanism to account for the fact that if a, b and c are numbers then '$a + bc$' means '$a + (bc)$', not '$(a + b)c$'.

When we state such mechanisms, we will need to make them subordinate to type; for example, we will only want to set up the convention about '$a + bc$' to apply to numbers, not objects of all types. Nevertheless, these disambiguation mechanisms are very different from those that relate to type as such; they are subordinate to type rather than being concerned with its internal workings. Thus references to types below may be ignored, or taken to refer to 'NUMBER', on a first reading; the precise technical type-related details should only be assigned significance after Chapter 5 has been assimilated.

The two key examples motivating the mechanisms we will now introduce have already been mentioned. In §2.4, we noted that expressions like '$1 \oplus 2 \oplus 3$' are ambiguous until and unless one observes that $\oplus$ is an associative operator when applied to numbers, i.e. objects having the type NUMBER. (For the reasons described in previous sections, we must not assume that $\oplus$ is associative, or even an operator, when applied to objects other than

---

[4] A computer scientist might say that the significance of our method lies not its effectiveness on mathematics, but its ability to allow productive syntax without inter-library clashes becoming a problem; loosely speaking, the mechanism is to productive syntax as namespaces are to variable names.

numbers.) Further, as noted above, we need to account for the fact that when 'a', 'b' and 'c' refer to numbers, '$a + bc$' means '$a + (bc)$', not '$(a + b)c$'.

Replacing Precedence

Conventions like the one about '$a + bc$' are usually not explicitly stated; that is, they constitute instances of an informational gap (§1.2.3). There are in fact few conventions of this kind, and the examples we have seen are all closely related to arithmetic. For example, if v_1, v_2 and w are vectors, then '$v_1 \otimes w + v_2 \otimes w$' means '$(v_1 \otimes w) + (v_2 \otimes w)$' rather than '$v_1 \otimes (w + v_2) \otimes w$'. The underlying point here is that $\otimes$ is *like* multiplication, and so mathematical readers can deduce the appropriate convention by analogy with the well-known convention for addition and multiplication.

We noted in §1.2.3 that whenever we encountered an informational gap, it would be possible to insert into texts sentences that would 'fill' the gap, i.e. sentences from which one could systematically derive the missing information. Thus we now need to describe a way in which one might describe conventions like the one just discussed.

Before giving an actual convention of the kind required, we will take a brief detour and discuss the inadequacy of the corresponding mechanism used in formal languages, namely precedence (cf. §4.1.2). While considering this, we will shelve the orthogonal type-related issues by imagining that we are only dealing with objects of a single type.

Precedence mechanisms require us to assign a numerical 'precedence level' to every operator; for example, we might say that $+$ has precedence 30 and that the (invisible) concatenative operator used for multiplication in mathematics has precedence 40. There are a number of problems with this approach. First, mathematicians simply do not think in this way; no mathematician 'knows' what the precedence of $+$ is. The second problem relates to the notion of time discussed in §1.2.2. Two mathematicians might introduce operators, say '$\circ$' and '$\bullet$', in different textbooks, with neither author being aware of the work of the other; in this situation, neither author is in a position to know how '$a \circ b \bullet c$' should be interpreted — that is, neither individual author is in a position to know whether $\circ$ should be given a higher 'precedence' than $\bullet$ or vice versa. The third point is closely related: precedence mechanisms predict that all expressions like '$a \circ b \bullet c$' are unambiguous. In reality, in the situation we have just described, '$a \circ b \bullet c$' is genuinely ambiguous and our theory should predict this. It should also allow a third author, aware of the work of both original authors, to introduce a disambiguation convention specifying the true parsing of '$a \circ b \bullet c$'.

In addition to the criticisms just described, precedence is narrowly targeted at a single kind of ambiguity, namely the kind that arises when one has two or more infixed operators. But, as the discussion in §4.3.1 showed, ambiguity in symbolic mathematics is much more general. As a result, we will not use a precedence-based method to 'fill in' the informational gap. Instead, we observe that the required information could be extracted from a statement like the following:[5]

If M, N and K are matrices, then '$M + NK$' means '$M + (NK)$'.

More generally, we allow statements of the form

If *[variables]* are *[descriptions corresponding to types]*, then '*[expression]*' means '*[unambiguous expression]*'.

The '*[unambiguous expression]*' must have exactly the same content as the '*[expression]*', except that it must have brackets added to yield a single parse tree.

Collectively, a group of statements of this kind have the same effect as precedence declarations. However, they are very local assertions, which make no claim about operators (or other mathematics) which an author has not seen; they can be made by the third author in the situation described above, where the authors introducing the individual operators are not in a position to compare them; they make no claims about 'global precedence hierarchies'; and they allow disambiguation of cases other than 'two or more infixed operators'. They are also subordinate to type; each statement of the above form only applies to objects of particular types.[6]

We should comment briefly on the efficiency of this approach to disambiguation. It is the case that if one has n infixed operators, each pair of which may be used together in an unambiguous way, then the number of statements of this kind that are needed is quadratic in n, as each operator needs to be compared with every other operator. However, we know of no case where $n > 3$ in mathematics (as opposed to computer science); the only triple of operators with this property which we know of are '$+$', '$-$' and concatenative multiplication. Note in particular that in mathematics, division and exponentiation are both expressed in ways that do not allow ambiguity of the kind we are discussing.

Associativity

In real mathematics, associativity of operators is normally stated explicitly, although this is usually done in informal language. Thus in this case, we do

---

[5] Strictly speaking, as '$M + (NK)$' does not refer to a fixed string but to something into which material can be substituted, one should use Quine's corner quotes here (Quine, 1940, p. 36). I.e., one should write $\ulcorner M + (NK) \urcorner$ rather than '$M + (NK)$'. However, as this is not a subtlety which the working mathematician should have to worry about, we will not follow that approach here.

[6] Note that variables must be quantified over entire types: one cannot introduce a disambiguation convention for, say, positive definite matrices only. This requirement interacts with certain details of the type system in interesting ways, which we do not have space to describe properly here; referring forward to §7.4.2, we will only note that before two types can be collapsed into one by identification, disambiguation conventions for those types must match.

not have an informational gap; we simply need to specify how the theory deals with the assertion that a given operator is associative.

The relevant treatment is in fact relatively simple. Suppose that we see an assertion that, say, $+$ as applied to matrices is associative. In order for our theory to be fully adaptive, it must construct the appropriate disambiguation convention when it sees such a statement. Our task here is therefore to describe how that convention functions.

We may start by noting that the content of the assertion just mentioned is as follows:

If M_1, M_2 and M_3 are matrices, then '$M_1 + M_2 + M_3$' is unambiguous.

It is important to note that this restated assertion implies that '$M_1 + M_2 + M_3 + M_4$', etc. are also unambiguous.

Now, in the absence of any conventions, '$M_1 + M_2 + M_3$' has two parses; one is as '$M_1 + (M_2 + M_3)$' and the other is as '$(M_1 + M_2) + M_3$'. For the purposes of disambiguation, we can simply have our convention state that the first reading is illegal. To be more precise, the convention states that no tree may contain a subtree with the following form:

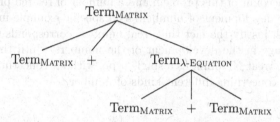

Note that we have broken symmetry here; we could equally well have ruled out the other configuration.

The fusion of such disambiguation conventions into the parsing process is described in §6.3.

Reanalysis

In §2.6 we discussed reanalysis, the phenomenon where old notation is reinterpreted in terms of new, more general syntactic rules. Authors do not usually explicitly state that they are generalising notation, but simply present the new notation and rely on a reader using common sense to determine that the new notation should replace the old, rather than conflicting with it. Unfortunately, a formal theory has no basis on which to draw a comparable conclusion.

We may illustrate these remarks by returning to the main example discussed in §2.6. The 'positive integer powers' version of power and the 'real powers' version of power generate the following (indistinguishable) syntactic rules:

$\text{Term}_{\text{NUMBER}} \rightarrow \text{Term}_{\text{NUMBER}}{}^{\text{Term}_{\text{NUMBER}}}$

$\text{Term}_{\text{NUMBER}} \rightarrow \text{Term}_{\text{NUMBER}}{}^{\text{Term}_{\text{NUMBER}}}$

From a formal viewpoint, the existence of both of these rules causes expressions like 'π^2' to be ambiguous; the formal theory has no way of knowing that the second rule is meant to make the first obsolete.

We have therefore encountered an example of an informational gap (§1.2.3). It is therefore incumbent upon us to show that the necessary information could be extracted from a statement that could be inserted into the text, rather than being obtained in some more mysterious fashion. In fact, the mechanisms given above suffice; all one needs to do is to use a 'X is unambiguous' statement may be used to show that this ambiguity may be ignored. For example, the statement

Observe that if n is a real number, then 'n^2' is unambiguous.

removes the ambiguity in the example given above.

The only subtlety in this example arises with respect to the phrase 'a real number'; in order for the above statement to set up a disambiguation convention, 'real number' must correspond to an entire type. This is a subtle issue. We will find in §5.3.2 that the standard foundational account of numbers exhibits technical problems, and we will devote Chapter 7 to providing a satisfactory account of this problem and a number of related problems. We will discuss the development of numbers as a specific example in §7.5; while doing so we will justify the fact that 'real number' corresponds to a type at a particular stage in the development of the numbers. Until that time, we will continue to treat NUMBER as a single type, without concerning ourselves with subtleties concerning different kinds of number.

Subsumption

The language of mathematics exhibits a phenomenon whereby more specific syntactic usages can 'hide' or 'override' less specific ones. This can be illustrated by considering the expressions 'f^n', '$\sin^n$' and '$\sin^{-1}$' (where f is a function and n is an integer). '$\sin^2$' is never treated like the less specific 'f^2' applied to 'sin', and '$\sin^{-1}$' is always interpreted as 'arcsin' rather than as an instance of the less specific '$\sin^n$'. Note that these remarks relate to intension rather than extension, i.e. they deal with the occurrence of the sequence of characters 'sin' rather than with functions which happen to be (extensionally) equal to the function sin.

Formally, this phenomenon is not difficult to capture; one simply adds a principle specifying that whenever one typed syntactic rule strictly subsumes another, in the sense that every expression matching the second matches the first, but not vice versa, instances of ambiguity are automatically resolved towards the more specific construction. So, for example, consider the rules:

$$\text{Term}_{\text{FUNCTION}} \rightarrow \text{Term}_{\text{FUNCTION}}{}^{\text{Term}_{\text{NUMBER}}}$$

$$\text{Term}_{\text{FUNCTION}} \rightarrow \sin{}^{\text{Term}_{\text{NUMBER}}}$$

$$\text{Term}_{\text{FUNCTION}} \rightarrow \sin^{-1}$$

The first of these rules strictly subsumes the second and the third (at the level of typed syntax), and the second strictly subsumes the third. Thus the principle correctly predicts the readings of 'f^n', '$\sin^n$' and '$\sin^{-1}$'.

Unfortunately, this approach conflicts with our treatment of other phenomena. Often one finds that the presuppositions (§3.3.5) on a definition are relaxed, to give a more general definition. In some cases, the generalised definition may syntactically subsume the original one. For example, when one reanalyses 'x^2' as a special case of 'x^n' (§2.6), one passes from the rule

$$\text{Term}_{\text{NUMBER}} \rightarrow \text{Term}_{\text{NUMBER}}{}^2$$

to the rule

$$\text{Term}_{\text{NUMBER}} \rightarrow \text{Term}_{\text{NUMBER}}{}^{\text{Term}_{\text{NUMBER}}}$$

The latter strictly subsumes the former. Nevertheless, we do not want the more specific rule to 'hide' the less specific one. Instead, as discussed in the previous section, we need the two to collide to obtain the correct treatment of reanalysis.

Thus there seems to be no principled way of characterising the case where a distinct notation 'overrides' a more specific one, as opposed to the case where a notation is being generalised in a consistent manner. Without such a characterisation, we are precluded from adopting the 'subsumption' principle. This is therefore another instance of an informational gap (§1.2.3); we cannot make the correct predictions without some additional material being added to texts. The 'means' statements discussed earlier in this section are suitable for this task. More specifically, we will handle examples like the one involving 'f^n' and '$\sin^n$' by allowing the relevant rules to collide and requiring an explicit 'means' statements to disambiguate them. Thus one needs to define both 'f^n' and '$\sin^n$' (in, say, Definitions 4.1 and 4.2 respectively), and then to state that:

If n is a real number, then '$\sin^n$' means '$\sin^n$' in the sense of Definition 4.2.

(Note the introduction of the formula 'in the sense of' to refer to notation as introduced in a particular definition; this is one of the few places where such a qualification is necessary.)

4.2 Ambiguity in Textual Mathematics

In this section we will give a quick survey of the kinds of ambiguity that occur in natural language (§4.2.1), indicate which of these kinds of ambiguity occur in textual mathematics (§4.2.2) and then present disambiguation mechanisms that can remove certain of these kinds of ambiguity without recourse to type (§4.2.3). Type-related disambiguation mechanisms will be discussed in Chapter 6.

4.2.1 Survey: Ambiguity in Natural Languages

Early attempts at broad-coverage computer parsing led to the realisation
that natural languages contained a remarkable amount of ambiguity. Based
on their experiences with a parser, Church and Patil write that "there may be
hundreds, perhaps thousands, of syntactic parse trees for certain very natural
sentences of English" (Church and Patil, 1982, p. 1). Most of this ambiguity is
"simply not noticed by the majority of language users and this testifies to the
efficiency and robustness of their mechanisms for disambiguation" (Briscoe,
1988, p. 22).

There has been extensive research into effective techniques to disambiguate
natural language on computer. We do not know of any linguistic methods
that can disambiguate even purely textual sentences in mathematics. We
will not enumerate and demonstrate the inadequacy of individual methods
of this kind, partly because this would consume a large amount of space, but
primarily because such a case-by-case demonstration is superseded by a more
powerful argument: as we will show in §4.3, the interlocking nature of text and
symbols in mathematics precludes application of *any* linguistic techniques:
information from the symbolic side is needed to resolve natural language-like
ambiguities in the textual part of mathematics. We will therefore need to
develop our own techniques to disambiguate textual and symbolic material
simultaneously (Chapter 6). The purpose of this section, then, is not to
survey disambiguation techniques but to outline the more important kinds
of ambiguity that occur in natural language. We will confine ourselves to the
kinds of ambiguity that occur in text, as opposed to speech.

The kind of ambiguity that is most easily presented to native speakers is
word sense ambiguity, as occurs in:

> Canberra is the **seat** of government.
> He finished the speech and took his **seat**.

The relevant word (here 'seat') is said to exhibit *polysemy*. In the example
just given, the two senses of the word are related; this is not always the case,
as the following example shows:

> I took all of my savings out of the **bank**.
> He sat on the **bank**, fishing.

In such cases the word in question is said to exhibit *homonymy*.

Often ambiguity does not arise from single words, but because sentences
or other constituents have more than one possible syntactic structure. This
is referred to as *structural ambiguity*, and the best-known kind, called *attachment ambiguity*, arises in the presence of sequences of prepositional phrases.
Church and Patil (1982) observed that a sentence like

> Put the block in the box on the table.

can be interpreted either as

Put the block [in the box on the table].

or as

Put [the block in the box] on the table.

When more prepositional phrases are added, the number of possible interpretations rises rapidly: when there are n prepositional phrases, the number of interpretations is given by the nth Catalan number (Church and Patil, 1982),

$$C_n = \frac{(2n)!}{n!(n+1)!}.$$

It follows (from Stirling's approximation to $n!$) that the number of interpretations is asymptotically exponential in the number of prepositional phrases present.

Another kind of structural ambiguity is exhibited in the sentence

Old men and women were left behind.

This can either be read as stating that

Old men were left behind and women were left behind.

or as stating that

Old men and old women were left behind.

This kind of ambiguity, arising in the presence of a 'coordinating' word like 'and' or 'or', is referred to as *coordination ambiguity*.

Even when words and syntax are unambiguous, ambiguities can arise at the semantic level. A classic example occurs in sentences with more than one quantifier, such as

Every man loves a woman.

This may mean that

For each man, there is some woman who he loves.

or that

There is some woman who is loved by every man.

This kind of ambiguity is referred to as *quantifier scope ambiguity*. Since quantifier scope ambiguities are never included in the figures giving the number of parses of sentences, the number of readings of a sentence can be far greater than the actual number of parses.

Finally, it is worth noting that when there are multiple ambiguities in a sentence, and each can be resolved independently of the others, the number of available readings compounds multiplicatively. This can yield a very large number of readings for relatively short sentences.

The above falls far short of being an extensive discussion of ambiguity in natural language, but covers the material we need for our discussion below.

4.2.2   Ambiguity in Textual Mathematics

Textual mathematics contains several kinds of ambiguity, but two are of particular concern to us. The first is word sense ambiguity. Polysemy abounds in mathematics; for example, we have 'prime ideals', 'prime numbers', 'prime fields', 'prime knots', 'prime manifolds', and so on. (Although there is an intuitive connection between these different notions of the adjective 'prime', they are formally unrelated, and so need to be treated as distinct senses; cf. §3.1 on 'topological space'.) Homonymy also occurs: 'normal subgroups', 'normal polynomials' and 'normal planes' have nothing in common. From the perspective of the formal content of mathematics, homonymy is no different from any other kind of polysemy; we will not draw a distinction between them again.

The second significant kind of ambiguity is structural ambiguity, and in particular attachment ambiguity. Given a sentence like

ρ is normal if ρ generates the splitting field of some polynomial over $\mathbf{F}_0$.

(Grigoriev et al., 1995)

we need to determine whether 'over $\mathbf{F}_0$' refers to 'generation over $\mathbf{F}_0$', a 'splitting field over $\mathbf{F}_0$' or a 'polynomial over $\mathbf{F}_0$'.[7] Such disambiguation can be complicated by interactions between attachment ambiguity and word sense ambiguity; for example, one can have a plane normal 'to' another mathematical object, but a polynomial cannot be normal 'to' anything.

The language of mathematics also contains quantifier scope ambiguity and coordination ambiguity. These tend to be governed by strong disambiguation conventions implicit in mathematics texts themselves. As Ranta (1994) notes, quantifier scope ambiguity is not present in mathematical texts because there is a convention that quantifiers are read in order, even when this results in a false statement. Ranta supports this remark with the example of 'some point lies on every line', which is read to mean

$\exists x.(point(x) \wedge \forall y.(line(y) \Rightarrow lies\_on(x, y)))$

despite the fact that this reading is false and the other reading is true. We may add that this convention is violated in sentences involving 'of' and certain similar cases; for example, consider:

Every element of some set of natural numbers is prime.

This is certainly read with the existential quantifier outscoping the universal quantifier, despite the fact that 'every' precedes 'some'. This phenomenon is discussed in greater detail in Kurtzman and MacDonald (1993).

---

[7] Note, incidentally, that in this example 'ρ is normal' does not refer to normality qua polynomial, even though the sentence contains the word 'polynomial'. Mathematics cannot be disambiguated by shallow examination of the local context.

Turning to coordination ambiguity, we find similar strong conventions. For example, 'P and Q or R' means '(P and Q) or R', and 'P and Q if and only if R and S' means '(P and Q) if and only if (R and S)'. However, not all cases of coordination ambiguity can be resolved by such conventions; we shall see a counterexample in §4.3.2 below.

4.2.3 Disambiguation without Type

Most examples of textual ambiguity in mathematics need some notion of type to resolve. For example, to determine which sense of the word 'prime' is in use in a given example, we need to know whether 'prime' is applied to number(s), or ideal(s), or etc.; in an intuitive sense, we need to know whether we are dealing with objects of type NUMBER, or type IDEAL, or etc.. In fact, without reference to type, the only kind of disambiguation we can perform is to apply the aforementioned conventions governing scope ambiguity and coordination ambiguity.

Coordination ambiguity can be handled using the same mechanisms we introduced in §4.1.5. In effect, we will handle expressions like 'P and Q or R' as if we had seen a appropriate 'means' assertion stating that:

... then 'P and Q or R' means '(P and Q) or R'.

The only difference is that conventions governing coordination ambiguity are part of our theoretical description of mathematical language, and so are present *ab initio*. As with the conventions generated by the 'means' assertions of §4.1.5, the use of these conventions during the parsing process is covered by the mechanisms described in §6.3.

Turning to scope ambiguity, we find that virtually no work is needed to assimilate the appropriate conventions into our theory. In fact, one tends to require special linguistic machinery such as Cooper storage (Cooper, 1983) to support scope ambiguity; to avoid ambiguity, one just uses a semantic theory without any machinery of this kind. The actual resolution of scope is encoded into the particular rules for compositionally constructed semantic representations. For example, when a sentence consists of a noun phrase followed by a verb phrase, a quantifier that appears in the noun phrase needs to outscope any quantifiers that appear inside the verb phrase. We can illustrate that our compositional semantic representation of §3.3.7 does indeed predict that this is the case. We will continue with Ranta's example,

Some point lies on every line.

The grammar rules that are needed in this example given in Figure 4.1.

Substituting 'some' and 'point' into the rule for noun phrases gives us:

$$\text{NP}_{sg} \rightarrow \textbf{some point} \quad \left\{ \lambda \underset{:e \to t}{v} . \left(\boxed{\begin{array}{c} r \\ \hline point(r) \end{array}} \uplus v(r) \right) \right\}$$

$$S \rightarrow \underset{0}{NP_{sg}} \ \underset{1}{VP_{sg}} \qquad \{0\,(1)\}$$

$$NP_{sg} \rightarrow \underset{0}{Det_{sg}} \ \underset{1}{NBar} \qquad \{0(1)\}$$

$$Det_{sg} \rightarrow \textbf{some} \qquad \left\{ \underset{:e \rightarrow t}{\lambda\, n} . \underset{:e \rightarrow t}{\lambda\, v} . \left(\boxed{\begin{array}{|c|} \hline r \\ \hline \\ \hline \end{array}} \uplus n\,(r) \uplus v\,(r) \right) \right\}$$

$$NBar \rightarrow \textbf{point} \qquad \left\{ \underset{:e}{\lambda x}. \boxed{\begin{array}{c} \\ \hline point\,(x) \end{array}} \right\}$$

$$Det_{sg} \rightarrow \textbf{every}$$

$$\left\{ \underset{:e \rightarrow t}{\lambda\, n} . \underset{:e \rightarrow t}{\lambda\, v} . \left(\boxed{\begin{array}{c} \\ \boxed{\begin{array}{|c|} \hline r \\ \hline \\ \hline \end{array}} \uplus n(r) \Rightarrow v(r) \\ \end{array}} \right) \right\}$$

$$NBar \rightarrow \textbf{line} \qquad \left\{ \underset{:e}{\lambda x}. \boxed{\begin{array}{c} \\ \hline line\,(x) \end{array}} \right\}$$

$$VP_{sg} \rightarrow \textbf{lies on} \ \underset{0}{NP_{sg}} \qquad \left\{ \underset{:e}{\lambda x}.0 \left(\underset{:e}{\lambda y}. \boxed{\begin{array}{c} \\ \hline lies\_on(x,y) \end{array}} \right) \right\}$$

Fig. 4.1 Grammar Rules for Scope Ambiguity Example

Similarly, substituting 'every' and 'line' into the same rule gives us:

$$Det_{sg} \rightarrow \textbf{every line} \qquad \left\{ \underset{:e \rightarrow t}{\lambda\, v} . \left(\boxed{\begin{array}{c} \\ \boxed{\begin{array}{|c|} \hline r \\ \hline line(r) \\ \hline \end{array}} \Rightarrow v(r) \\ \end{array}} \right) \right\}$$

Substituting this semantic representation into the rule for 'lies on' tells us that the semantic representation for the verb phrase 'lies on every line' is:

$$\underset{:e}{\lambda x}. \left(\left(\underset{:e \rightarrow t}{\lambda\, v} . \boxed{\begin{array}{c} \\ \boxed{\begin{array}{|c|} \hline r \\ \hline line(r) \\ \hline \end{array}} \Rightarrow v(r) \\ \end{array}} \right) \left(\underset{:e}{\lambda y}. \boxed{\begin{array}{c} \\ \hline lies\_on(x,y) \end{array}} \right) \right)$$

This expression β-reduces to

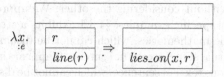

To finish our analysis of the example, we need to substitute the semantic representations of the verb phrase and the noun phrase 'some point' into the rule for the sentence. Doing so and applying α-conversion to keep variables distinct gives us:

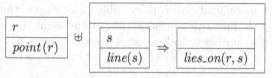

This β-reduces to

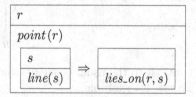

Rewriting this according to the definition of $\uplus$ (§3.3.2) shows that the semantic representation for the entire sentence is:

Here the point r is determined independently of the line s; the DRS is equivalent to

$$\exists r.(point(r) \land \forall s.(line(s) \Rightarrow lies\_on(r, s)))$$

Thus our semantic framework has correctly predicted that the existential quantifier outscopes the universal quantifier, so that the convention is observed. Ensuring that this happens in general is simply a matter of choosing semantic representations in grammar rules carefully.

4.3 Text and Symbol

The purpose of this section is to show how tightly textual and symbolic mathematics are bound together, and more specifically to show that neither can be disambiguated without considering the other. We approach this task by considering two very specific examples. §4.3.1 exhibits a structurally ambiguous piece of symbolic mathematics, which cannot be disambiguated without knowledge of the textual structure of the sentence it appears in. §4.3.2 exhibits a structurally ambiguous textual sentence, which cannot be disambiguated without examining the symbolic material it contains. Finally, §4.3.3 discusses the ramifications of these examples for any method that attempts to disambiguate mathematics as a whole.

4.3.1 Dependence of Symbol on Text

Consider the following excerpt from (Weisstein et al., 2009):

> Two elements x and y of a set S are said to be commutative under a binary operation $*$ if they satisfy $x * y = y * x$.

In this example, $*$ is a mathematical object in its own right; the sentence uses '$*$' in order to quantify over all possible binary operations (on S). So the string '$x * y$' is just the concatenation of the symbols 'x', '$*$' and 'y', each referring to a mathematical object. Syntactically, it has the following structure:

This usage is in sharp contrast to the usual usage of concatenation to denote multiplication. When we see, for example,

$2\pi r$

in a typical context, we parse it as '$(2\pi)r$', i.e. as follows:

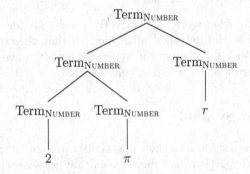

(Other analyses of multiplication are possible, but all of them yield different parses for '$x * y$' and '$(2\pi)r$' in their respective contexts, which is all that we need for the present argument.)

So, as in the previous example, to determine the correct parse tree for the sentence, we need to know the types of the objects it refers to. But in this case, there is a twist. In our sentence,

> Two elements x and y of a set S are said to be commutative under a binary operation $*$ if they satisfy $x * y = y * x$.

all of the variables ('S', 'x', 'y' and '$*$') are introduced *within the sentence itself*. And, in particular, the fact that '$*$' is a binary operation can only be determined by analysing the sentence. So we need to parse the sentence in order to obtain the types of the variables, and we need the types of the variables in order to parse the symbolic material. The natural conclusion to draw here is that we need to analyse the textual structure of the sentence before looking at the symbolic structure; i.e. that we should analyse the textual structure of the sentence while treating constituents like 'S' and '$x * y = y * x$' as 'black boxes', and later determine the content of the black boxes. As we will see in the next section, this view is too simplistic.

4.3.2 Dependence of Text on Symbol

In the previous examples, ambiguity has been confined to the symbolic part of mathematics. This is not always the case. There are kinds of ambiguity that span both textual and symbolic material, as can be seen by comparing the following two sentences:

> Whenever aRb and bRc for some a, b, c then aRc.

> So $f(x) > 0$ for $x > 0$ and $f(x) < 0$ for $x < 0$.

Both of these sentences have the structure 'P and Q for X':[8]

> Whenever $\underbrace{aRb}_{P}$ and $\underbrace{bRc}_{Q}$ for $\underbrace{\text{some } a, b, c}_{X}$ then aRc.

> So $\underbrace{f(x) > 0 \text{ for } x > 0}_{P}$ and $\underbrace{f(x) < 0}_{Q}$ for $\underbrace{x < 0}_{X}$.

Yet these sentences are parsed in different ways:

> Whenever $(\underbrace{aRb}_{P}$ and $\underbrace{bRc}_{Q})$ for $\underbrace{\text{some } a, b, c}_{X}$ then aRc.

> So $\underbrace{f(x) > 0 \text{ for } x > 0}_{P}$ and $(\underbrace{f(x) < 0}_{Q}$ for $\underbrace{x < 0}_{X})$.

---

[8] The first instance of 'for' in the second sentence is not pertinent; we will not refer to it again.

This example could be taken as another point about the inapplicability of (some textual analogue of) precedence to 'for' and 'and'. The idea which we want to draw out is, however, more significant. It is as follows: in both cases, we can determine the correct structure by looking at the symbolic content. If we take 'for' to attach low in the first sentence, then we obtain

$^\#$Whenever aRb **and** (bRc **for** some a, b, c) then aRc.

Here 'a' and 'b' are not bound variables in 'aRb', and so this is meaningless. By contrast, if we take 'for' to attach high, then in the resulting reading all variables are bound, and the reading is acceptable.

Moving to the second sentence, if we were to take 'for' to attach high, then we would obtain

$^\#$So ($f(x) > 0$ for $x > 0$ **and** $f(x) < 0$) **for** $x < 0$.

This sentence is syntactically valid, but again contains a semantic problem: the variable x is bound twice in nested contexts. Schematically, we have an analogue to '$\forall x.\forall x.\phi(x)$'. Although such expressions are valid in some logics, examining the language of mathematics shows that such 'double binding' invariably indicates an error. By contrast, if we take 'for' to attach low, then in the resulting reading no variables are doubly bound, and the reading is acceptable.

Thus, looking at the two sentences together, we see that information from the symbolic side of mathematics can be needed to resolve structural ambiguity in its textual side. We cannot determine the textual structure of a sentence without looking inside the symbolic material inside. One point in this example bears particular emphasis. In general, to resolve examples of textual ambiguity like the one discussed above, we rely on symbolic type information in an *irreducible* way. The point is easier to bring out if we consider the variant sentence,

Whenever $a \in b$ **and** $b \in c$ **for** some ordinal numbers a, b, c then $a \in c$.

This is ambiguous in precisely the same way as the first sentence above, and can be disambiguated in just the same way. But in this case, in order to determine that one particular reading was in fact correct, we needed to parse '$a \in b$'; and in order to do that, we needed to know that b was a set (cf. our remarks about monotonicity at the end of §4.1.3). In this case that information was easy to extract, but in a more complex proof we might have encountered something like

Whenever $a \in b \cup \{b\}$, ...

In such a case we would have bring type information across from the right-hand side of the sentence to find the type of 'b', then make inferences about the symbolic portions to determine the type of '$b \cup \{b\}$', and finally use this information to check that '$a \in b \cup \{b\}$' parsed correctly.

4.3.3 Text and Symbol: Conclusion

Together, the two examples we have considered show that our theory cannot treat either textual material and symbolic material in isolation; if it is to correctly predict the structures and meanings of sentences, we need to consider text and symbol simultaneously. We should emphasise that this is not a problem relating to computation, but a purely linguistic one; leaving aside all computational concerns, we do not have a way of specifying the structure and meaning of either textual mathematics or symbolic mathematics without reference to the other. Thus we need a unified approach to disambiguating textual and symbolic mathematics, which must somehow overcome the fact that the two are very different in character.

There is one particular corollary of this fact which is worth underlining here. As we saw in §4.1.3, the structure of symbolic material cannot be determined without some analysis of types. But, as we have just seen, the structure of textual material cannot in general be determined without knowing the structure of the symbolic material embedded in it. The corollary, then, is that the structure of textual material cannot in general be determined without some analysis of types. This point is worth underlining because, as we shall see in Chapter 5, the actual types we need to work with are distinctively mathematical, and do not resemble any theoretical constructs that arise in the analysis of natural language. As a result, we can safely assert that no method from linguistics or computational linguistics, however obscure, will be able to disambiguate even the textual part of mathematics.

4.4 Conclusion

In §2.4 and §3.2, the examples we considered strongly suggested that type had a key role to play in disambiguating symbolic material. The example from §4.1.3 demonstrated this conclusively: it showed that it is not in general possible to determine the structure of a piece of symbolic mathematics without knowing the types of the entities involved in it. Together with more general arguments, this example led us to want all of our disambiguation mechanisms for symbolic material to be subordinate to a notion of type. Subsequently, §4.3 showed that textual and symbolic material were so interdependent that it is not in general possible to disambiguate one without considering the other; and this in turn proved that the notion of type had to be considered while analysing textual material.

This last constraint suggests that we attempt to use the notion of type to directly disambiguate textual material as well as symbolic. In some sense, we want to look at sentences like

Some natural number is prime.

and

> An ideal I in a commutative ring R is prime if and only if the factor ring R/I is an integral domain.

and use the distinction between types such as NUMBER and IDEAL to determine the correct reading of the textual constituent 'prime' as well as the symbolic constituent 'R/I'. To do so, we will not only have to apply some notion of type to the textual material, but understand how type information flows between textual and symbolic material, and how the type information in variables like I interacts with the textual structure of the sentence.

This leaves us with two broad areas to study. The first relates to types, which we have up to now used in an extremely informal way; these need to put on a sound footing. We need to answer questions like, what *are* types? How do the types we use to describe mathematical language relate to the types in computer science? What types do we need to describe mathematical language? Are natural numbers of the same type as real numbers? What is the *basis* for saying that particular types exist or do not exist, i.e. what is the right methodology for determining the set of types? How does the methodology relate to the utility of types for disambiguation? These questions, and others, will be answered in Chapter 5.

The second area we need to study is how types may be used to actually parse and disambiguate both symbolic and textual mathematics. This raises a number of difficult problems. What does it mean to assign a type to a textual entity, such as a noun phrase? How do we make type information flow from textual constructs to symbolic constructs, and vice versa? How do variables, which are symbolic, gain type information from textual constituents, as when I is given the type IDEAL by the phrase 'an ideal I' in the example above? And how do we deal with the fact that the type given to a variable in this way in one part of a sentence can affect the syntactic structure of a completely different part of the sentence? We will answer all of these questions, and others, in Chapter 6.

5
Type

In this chapter, following on from our discussion of ambiguity (Chapter 4), we will introduce the types which are necessary to disambiguate mathematical language. As noted in §4.4, the actual inference of types will need to be fused into the parsing process; this will be the subject of the next chapter (Chapter 6). Additionally, in the course of this chapter, we will encounter a number of issues relating to the foundations of mathematics; these issues will be discussed extensively in Chapter 7.

There are two major difficulties that arise when one is trying to find the types necessary to describe mathematics. First, a great many type systems seem reasonable until a key counterexample is discovered; and, more specifically, these counterexamples are difficult to find because they are *mathematically counterintuitive*. There is a real disparity between what the rules of mathematics itself allow, and the way in which we think about mathematical objects. Each of the counterexamples we will present below reflects this disparity in a different way.

In our experience, one starts with a type system that is very close to the intuitive notion of type, and then steadily moves away from this as more and more pathological but mathematically valid examples are discovered. Eventually, this leads us to the second difficulty. The disparity become so great that certain required types become *non-extensional*. For example, we will find that a type like 'SET OF NUMBERS' needs to be present in order the type system to adequate the describe mathematical language, but that this type does not correspond to the property of 'being a set of numbers', or any other property. There is no precedent for dealing with such non-extensional types; one cannot simply look up what they are or how they behave, or even find a reasonable analogue in the literature. Stronger, *a priori* it is not even clear that the notion of a non-extensional type is coherent.

In order to keep our discussion precise, we will discuss these two problems in reverse order. §5.1 will discuss the amorphous concept of 'type' as it is used with formal languages, and tease out two different conceptual strands which are not normally distinguished. §5.2 will then use these two distinct notions to analyse what types are needed to model mathematics; by doing so it will specifically make sense of the notion of a 'non-extensional type'.

After this, we will return to the first problem. As we do not have space to present the many plausible but ultimately flawed type systems that might be encountered, we will concentrate on the key counterexamples that invalidate them. More specifically, in §5.3, we will repeatedly present atypical but mathematically legitimate examples which force any adequate type system to have certain properties. The later examples will concentrate on the phenomenon of non-extensionality, and will also briefly note how non-extensional types might be used in practice. §5.4 then presents the actual types needed to model mathematics faithfully. Finally, §5.5 briefly discusses the relationship between this system and the more conventional systems studied formally in *type theory*.

All of the examples, analyses, arguments and other material in this chapter are novel, expect where it is explicitly stated otherwise.

5.1 Distinguishing Notions of Type

As we noted in §4.1.2, the concept of 'type' has had a complex history. The earliest notion of type is a formal notion used in *Principia Mathematica* (Whitehead and Russell, 1910) to avoid Russell's Paradox; in time this notion led to the mathematical study of numerous varieties of type theory, the most famous of which is Simple Type Theory (Church, 1940). 'Types' were then adapted for computer programming languages, and in that context the term came to denote a family resemblance spanning several largely unrelated properties; an overview of different kinds of 'type' in programming languages can be found in Cardelli (1997).

Due to this complex history, 'type' has come to denote several distinct but related notions, which have not (to our knowledge) been clearly separated in the literature. In typical applications several of these notions coincide, so that one can gain an intuitive notion of what a type is without separating its distinct functions. As we noted in the introduction to this chapter, careful study of the language of mathematics will force us out of this zone of typical behaviour: some of the types we consider will necessarily behave in unusual ways. It is therefore worth carefully unthreading the distinct functions of 'type' which we will encounter in the language of mathematics, in order to build up a conceptual inventory to handle the situations which we will discuss in the remainder of the chapter.

In this section we will tease out two independent notions of type out of the usual amorphous picture: that of types as tags that discriminate among syntactic readings (§5.1.1) and that of types as properties which we may reason about (§5.1.2). In §5.2, we will use these notions to analyse type in the language of mathematics.

5.1.1 Types as Formal Tags

The first notion of type which we will consider arises primarily in computer languages. (This discussion is, however, self-contained, and requires no knowledge of computer science.) In such languages, 'types' serve two essentially syntactic functions: they exclude certain 'illegitimate' operations at the syntactic level (*type checking*), and they allows the ascription of different meanings to a given syntactic string (*type overloading*). Thus, for example, typical computer languages disallow expressions like

   1 + "this is a string"

via type checking. Many computer languages also use type overloading to allow a fixed expression like '$x + y$' to refer to, for example, either the addition of numbers or the addition of vectors, depending on the types of x and y. In the remainder of this section, we will formulate a unified account of both type checking and type overloading within a linguistic framework.

In an untyped language, the meaning of a syntactic constituent may be computed directly from the constituent. We will only consider the case where the language has a context-free grammar and is given compositional semantics; these assumptions are not strictly necessary, but they make the ideas in this discussion more transparent. Under these assumptions, our language will have combined syntactic/semantic rules such as

   Term → Term + Term $\{plus(0, 1)\}$

Collectively, these rules induce a map from the space of syntactic constituents to the space of semantic representations. Schematically, we have a 'meaning' map

$$\mu : \text{Syntax} \to \text{Semantics}$$
$$\text{constituent } C \mapsto \text{meaning of } C$$

A typed language tags certain syntactic constituents (typically those representing expressions) with formal tags, known as *types*. In such a language, the 'meaning' map has as its domain the set of type-annotated constituents. That is, we have shifted to:

$$\mu : \text{Typed Syntax} \to \text{Semantics}$$
$$\text{type-annotated constituent } C \mapsto \text{meaning of } C$$

Thus we have might have

$$\mu(\text{`}x_{\text{NUMBER}} + y_{\text{NUMBER}}\text{'}) = plus\_number(\mu(\text{`}x\text{'}), \mu(\text{`}y\text{'}))$$

but

$$\mu(\text{`}x_{\text{SET}} + y_{\text{SET}}\text{'}) = symmetric\_difference\_of\_sets(\mu(\text{`}x\text{'}), \mu(\text{`}y\text{'}))$$

Now, the very act of tagging constituents with formal tags has expanded the space of distinct entities that maybe assigned meanings. This expanded space may be utilised in two different ways.

First, one can choose not to assign meanings to the entire expanded space. (Effectively, μ will be reinterpreted as a partial function.) Thus one might choose to, for example, refuse to assign any meaning to the tagged constituent '$x_{\text{NUMBER}} + y_{\text{FUNCTION}}$'. Any attempt to form this expression would then constitute an error. If types are judiciously chosen and are used in this way, they can collectively exclude a class of unwanted operations at the syntactic level. Thus we have recovered the notion of type checking. The smaller the fraction of the expanded space that we assign meanings to, the more effective type checking is.

Second, one can choose to assign distinct meanings to typed constituents that have the same underlying untyped constituent. One might choose to, for example, define

$$\mu(`x_{\text{NUMBER}} + y_{\text{FUNCTION}}') = plus\_function(coerce\_function(\mu(`x')), \mu(`y')).$$

(Here we are converting x from a number into a function so that it can be added to y; this kind of implicit change of type is sometimes called *type coercion* by computer scientists.) Using types in this second way allows the contextual assignment of different meanings to a fixed syntactic string. Thus we have recovered the notion of type overloading.[1] The larger the fraction of the expanded space that we assign meanings to, the more expressive type overloading is.

Note that this unified account of type checking and type overloading within a single framework explicitly demonstrates that there is a trade-off between them; that is, there is a trade-off between detecting 'errors' (using a small fraction of the space) and increasing expressivity (using a large fraction of the space).

It is worth emphasising that in the sense described here, type is a *purely formal* mechanism to expand the space of things that we can say. In particular, any tags whatsoever may be used as types, and the types assigned to a given constituent may be computed in any way using any information. This includes information from the context and information from the concrete presentation of the syntactic constituent. Thus one could, for example, have two types, a type TYPEA which tagged expressions written using an even number of characters and a type TYPEB, which tagged all other expressions. Then, say, '12 − 3' would have type TYPEA but '9' would have type TYPEB. The system containing these two types is clearly useless, but it remains perfectly

---

[1] Computer scientists should note that under this formulation, *type polymorphism* is not related to overloading. Type polymorphism consists of a particular way of structuring the set of types and an associated method for computing them. Types computed in this way may be used *either* for type checking *or* for type overloading.

legitimate under the definitions given in this section. The formal character of (this notion of) type may also be illustrated by noting that there is no sharp boundary between syntax and type: anything that one framework encodes as a difference in syntactic category, another may encode as a difference in type. The latter option is unparsimonious, but it remains perfectly legal.

In practice, most useful type systems mix the notion of type given here with the more semantic notion introduced in the next section, to the extent that the two notions are difficult to distinguish. However, in §5.2 below, we will discuss the divergence of the two notions in mathematics.

Interpretations

There is one final point to make before we leave this notion of type. The discussion above may make it seem that this notion of type is purely syntactic. This is not the only interpretation.

In a very rough sense, we have been treating μ as a map:[2]

$$\mu \ : \ \underbrace{\text{Parse Trees} \times \text{Type}}_{\text{Syntax}} \to \underbrace{\text{Semantic Representations}}_{\text{Semantics}}$$

(constituent, type annotations) $\mapsto$ meaning

Under this interpretation, type is a part of syntax; syntax consists of pure syntax (parse trees) together with associated type information. But we are not forced to regard μ in this way. Currying allows us to reinterpret it as

$$\mu \ : \ \text{Parse Trees} \to (\text{Type} \to \text{Semantic Representations}).$$

At this point, we may note that what we label 'Semantics' is largely a matter of convention. We could shift terminology to think of the situation as

$$\mu \ : \ \underbrace{\text{Parse Trees}}_{\text{Syntax}} \to \underbrace{(\text{Type} \to \text{Semantic Representations})}_{\text{Semantics}}.$$

Under this interpretation, the true semantic representation (i.e. meaning) of a constituent is itself a map from types (i.e. formal tags) to some secondary semantic representation. Thus the conception of (this notion of) type as part of syntax or semantics is somewhat arbitrary.

The choice of interpretation is not purely a philosophical matter. It affects the predictions that the theory makes about 'incorrectly typed' cases, such as '$a + b$' in a context where a is a vector and b is a matrix. If type is interpreted as part of syntax, then '$a + b$' is actually ungrammatical. If type is interpreted as part of semantics, then '$a+b$' is grammatical but meaningless.

---

[2] This formulation is not technically correct, because types may not be chosen independently of the syntactic constituent which they annotate. We actually have not a product but a fibered product here — but the key idea to be presented remains valid under this simplification, and is obscured by the full, technical version.

The latter interpretation essentially implies that there is a notion of syntactic well-formedness which is independent of type; this interpretation is standard in all formal languages which we are aware of.

The existence of these two interpretations will be significant when we consider the actual language of mathematics in §5.2 below.

5.1.2   Types as Properties

Our second notion of type is more closely connected to mathematical logic.[3] It is irreducibly semantic, and only applies to languages whose semantic representations contain notions of individual objects and of predicates applying to those objects. It treats types as being *distinguished properties*. More formally:

> For every type T, there exists a unary predicate P_T such that for all x, x has type T if and only if $P_T(x)$ holds.

Thus, for example, one might define a type INTEGER corresponding to a predicate 'is an integer'; then an object x would have type INTEGER if and only if it was an integer.

Typically, the set of types is chosen so as to support *reasoning*. More specifically, the set of types is often chosen so that it is possible to compute the type(s) of a complex expression based on the types of its parts alone. So, for example, one could consider the system in which the following properties were types:

1. Being an integer.
2. Being a set of objects of type T.
3. Being a function from objects of type T_1 to objects of type T_2.

In this system, 3 would have type INTEGER; $\{3, 4\}$ would have type SET OF INTEGERS; and the identity function on $\mathbb{Z}$ would have type FUNCTION FROM INTEGERS TO INTEGERS. The key point about this system is that it supports the following kind of inference:

> If x has type T_1 and f has type FUNCTION FROM T_1S TO T_2S, then the complex expression $f(x)$ has type T_2.

This inference rule is able to deduce the type of $f(x)$ based on the types of f and x, without having to examine any details about f or x other than their types. It operates at the granularity of type, and abstracts away from sub-type information. Note that we have effectively partitioned the space of objects in a way that is compatible with inference: if we know which cells certain

---

[3] It is not, however, the primary notion of type discussed in mathematical logic. *Type theory* introduces a freestanding notion of type which can itself serve as the semantic underpinning of a formal language. The relationship between the material described in this chapter and type theory is addressed in §5.5.

objects lie in, we (often) know which cells combinations of those objects lie in. In this sense, this notion of types as properties is a *quotient* of semantics.

In an ideal world, type inference would be *complete*. In such a system, it would always be possible to compute the type(s) of a complex expression from the types of its parts. Thus type would form a perfect abstraction from semantics: it would always be possible to consider the system at the granularity of type, without ever delving into sub-type semantics. In practice, this is not always achievable. As we will now show, there is a three-way trade-off between this property of complete inference, the amount of information carried by types, and the richness of the objects being described.

An example of an 'overly informative type' is NONNEGATIVE REAL NUMBER. Common operations on real numbers are typically closed, i.e. they yield real numbers as answers. Thus type inference about the type REAL NUMBER can often be complete. But some common operations on nonnegative real numbers do not yield nonnegative real numbers as answers; for example, $3 - 4 = -1$. Thus it is difficult to construct a complete type inference system in which NONNEGATIVE REAL NUMBER is a type.

To illustrate the situation in which the richness of the underlying objects interferes with complete type inference, we may return to our example with integers, sets and functions. Consider the function

$$f : \{0, \{0\}\} \to \{0, \{0\}\} \qquad 0 \mapsto \{0\} \qquad \{0\} \mapsto 0$$

Neither the set $\{0, \{0\}\}$ nor the function f have a type under the system described above. This means that although $f(0)$ has exactly one type (SET OF INTEGERS), no type inference rule could deduce that type from complete information about the types of 0 and of f. Thus any type inference system based on the particular types described above is necessarily incomplete.

This naturally raises the question of whether one could deduce the types of $f(0)$ and similar expressions in some system containing more types. As phrased, that is the wrong question: introducing a type for each possible property would trivially answer the question in an uninteresting way. The right question is harder to phrase precisely — but if one is dealing with a sufficiently rich collection of objects, there is typically no 'sensible' type system allowing complete inference about interesting properties.

5.2 Notions of Type in Mathematics

In typical formal languages, the notions of type introduced in (§5.1.1) and (§5.1.2) completely coincide. Types function both as formal tags affecting the meaning of constituents and as extensional properties. So:

1. As in §5.1.2, an expression e would have type VECTOR if and only if it denoted a vector, and

2. as in §5.1.1, possessing the type VECTOR would affect the interpretation of e as a subexpression of a more complex expression, such as $\ulcorner (e) + (e') \urcorner$.[4]

The situation in mathematics is more complex. We will need a version of type that has as aspects both of the notions above, but with considerable adjustments to reflect subtleties that do not occur in formal languages. The aspect considering types as formal tags will be largely preserved, with some care concerning interpretation. The aspect considering types as properties will require considerable adjustments. We will consider each of these in turn.

5.2.1 Aspect as Formal Tags

We have already seen that there are many examples in mathematics in which a given sequence of symbols may have different meanings. At the simplest level, '$a + b$' should be assigned different semantic representations when a and b are, say, vectors and when they are, say, matrices.

This phenomenon forces us to introduce types in the sense of §5.1.1 above (or some equivalent notion). Further, individual examples of overloading force the existence of certain tags. For example, the '$a+b$' case just mentioned forces us to have types 'VECTOR' and 'MATRIX', and to overload based on these so that '$a_{\text{VECTOR}} + b_{\text{VECTOR}}$' and '$a_{\text{MATRIX}} + b_{\text{MATRIX}}$' have different interpretations. In order to determine which types underlie mathematical language, we need to consider a wide range of examples. This will be the main focus of §5.3.

The mere existence of appropriate types is far from all that is required: we need to add additional constraints to make sure that sequences of symbols have the type 'VECTOR' (resp. 'MATRIX') precisely when a human mathematician would analyse them as vectors (resp. matrices) in a mathematical text. Such constraints are clearly related to the semantics of the elements in question — being analysed as being a vector must bear some close relation to *being* a vector. Thus these constraints are properly discussed with the aspect of types as properties, which we turn to below.

Interpretation

Before we conclude this section, we need to discuss the issue of interpretation brought up in §5.1.1 with respect to the language of mathematics. The key question is whether an 'erroneously typed' expression is ungrammatical, or grammatical but meaningless. Equivalently, we need to ask whether a mathematician fails comprehend the structure of such a sentence, or is able to comprehend it but not to assign meanings.

---

[4] Note that we cannot speak of subexpressions of '$(e) + (e')$': '$(e) + (e')$' is a fixed string, in which 'e' is a single fixed character. As we noted in §4.1.5, the appropriate kind of quotation to use here is corner quotation, introduced in Quine (1940).

The answer to this question seems to vary depending on the example being considered. Frequent expressions such as '$a + b$' seem to be assigned the 'obvious' structure even if they are technically ill-typed; but more exotic expressions such as '$\#\#a\#b\#$' are clearly not assigned any structure. As a result, we will not worry overly over whether type is part of syntax or semantics; our main concern will be to produce a theory that correctly predicts the available (and meaningful) readings of real mathematical sentences. Equivalently, we will not choose one of the two interpretations given above; we will simply say that the distinction between the two is neutralised in mathematics. That said, there is a substantive point worth emphasising here: in existing formal languages, there is a clear notion of syntax prior to and entirely distinct from type; by contrast, as we saw in Chapter 4, mathematics admits no such notion.

Henceforth, we will refer to an expression as 'ambiguous' if it is ambiguous with respect to a combined notion of type and syntax. In other words, the expressions which we describe as 'ambiguous' will be those that cannot be disambiguated based on syntax or on type information. This leads to a notion of ambiguity that closely corresponds to what a human mathematician will actually find ambiguous.

5.2.2   Aspect as Properties

The notion of types as properties runs into two problems. The first of these is relatively straightforward to describe and handle. The second will require a serious change in approach, and will lead into the discussion in §5.3. We will consider these in turn.

Halting Equivalence of Type Inference

The first problem is one which we introduced briefly at the end of §5.1.2: if one has sufficiently rich objects floating around, type inference ceases to be complete. Consider, for example, the function $f : \mathbb{R} \to \mathbb{R} \cup \{\{\}\}$ defined by

$$f(x) = \begin{cases} x & \text{if the Goldbach conjecture holds,} \\ \{\} & \text{otherwise.} \end{cases}$$

Although this function is clearly pathological, it is entirely legitimate under the standard formal definitions. Determining whether f(0) is a number or a set is equivalent to deciding the Goldbach conjecture. Now, the choice of numbers, sets and the Goldbach conjecture in the example was arbitrary; we could have substituted arbitrary types and an arbitrary statement. This makes it clear that if types are taken to be extensional properties then, in general, determining the type(s) of a mathematical object is arbitrarily hard, i.e. halting equivalent.

We should emphasise that the potential issue with the situation does not arise from the halting equivalence in itself. Our aim in this book is to give a theory of mathematical language, which has nothing to do with a computer; as such, the computability or otherwise of types is not a direct problem.[5]

The potential issue with the situation is more indirect: the theory is psychologically implausible, in that it suggests that mathematicians can and do decide arbitrary problems while interpreting mathematics. This is not in fact a genuine issue, and the reason is as follows. Although f and its relatives are formally legitimate, they would never occur in any real mathematical text. There is a large gap between what is allowed in theory, and what is used in practice. In practice, mathematics contains an *intuitive* notion of type and the sets that occur in mathematics are homogenously typed, relative to that notion. One encounters sets of numbers, such as $\mathbb{R}$, and sets of sets, such as $\{\{\}\}$, but never sets of numbers and sets, such as $\mathbb{R} \cup \{\{\}\}$. Similarly, the domains and co-domains of functions are homogenously typed relative to the aforementioned intuitive notion of type; thus functions like f are never encountered. (Homogeneity is an important concept, which we will return to in §5.3.5.)

Thus in practice, mathematicians do not need to decide arbitrarily hard problems in order to comprehend mathematics. Ideally, we would determine the precise strength of reasoning needed to determine types, and encode this into our theory. This is hard to do in practice. The strength of reasoning appears to tail off rather than hitting a sharp limit: one finds fewer and fewer examples that require harder and harder reasoning. This makes the strength of reasoning hard to formally characterise. As such, the best option might be to regard it as a psychological parameter not to be specified in the present theory.

We have outlined the approach we would take if we had encountered this first problem in isolation. Having said this, we will see that the second problem with the notion of types as properties completely changes the picture; the notion of reasoning itself will need to be adjusted. This will to some degree make the above discussion obsolete; but the essential point made therein, that an unbounded difficulty of determining types is not a major problem for a theory of linguistics (or even a computer using that theory), should not be forgotten.

---

[5] In fact, no compromise is required in this case. The fact that one needs 'infinite' computational power here is a red herring: the problem is fundamentally one of the lack of computational power to handle the worst-case. The key characteristics of this situation are that all *practical* cases require much less computational power than the worst-case, but one cannot find a hard bound on the amount of computational power needed in practice. There are strategies which can handle such situations. We intend to present one such strategy in a separate paper, as noted in §6.5.

Failure of Extensionality

We may now turn to the second problem, which is much more fundamental. It is characterised by the failure of extensional properties to capture the required types. More formally, we will (in §5.3) find a series of examples where:

1. Overloading requires a distinction to be drawn between types T_1 and T_2.
2. We can find expressions e_1, e_2 which have types T_1 and T_2 in their respective contexts.
3. It is possible to deduce that e_1 and e_2 refer to the same object, i.e. that $\ulcorner e_1 = e_2 \urcorner$.

These examples will force us to abandon the simple view that types are merely properties, and to shift to a non-extensional approach. Having separated the distinct strands are bound together in the usual notion of 'type', we are finally in a position to show that 'non-extensional type' is not a contradiction in terms, but a meaningful and precisely definable concept. We define a *non-extensional type* to be a type that is a formal tag in the sense of §5.1.1, but not a property in the sense of §5.1.2.

In §5.3, we will look at the different kinds of types that are needed to describe mathematics, and we will find that each one must be treated as being non-extensional. We will not find any overarching pattern to non-extensional types. Each kind of type will be non-extensional in a different way, due to a different kind of example. However, despite this variety in underlying causes, the different kinds of non-extensional type will raise similar issues. We will comment on these briefly now, and return to them in §5.3.4, after we have seen the actual types needed to describe mathematics.

The fundamental difficulty with non-extensional types is that it is a priori unclear how we should reason about them. When we are dealing with types which are also extensional properties, we have a connection to an independent notion of semantics, which induces technical standards of valid inference, soundness and completeness. These in turn give us one natural level of reasoning: we can allow 'infinite reasoning strength', allowing any valid inference. As discussed above, this gives a compact, clean, objective standard of reasoning which is well-suited to mathematical logic.

Once extensionality does not apply, we are forced to give explicit rules about how one should reason with non-extensional types. This is hard to do in a principled way. As we will see, most of our reasoning will be motivated by the idea that in practice, non-extensional types are 'close to' properties: the type describing integers is 'close to' the property of being an integer, and so on. Such similarities will be the only handle we have on non-extensional types, and we will exploit them to the full.

5.3   Type Distinctions in Mathematics

There are large number of ways of constructing incorrect type systems for mathematics, which we do not have space to present in detail. Instead, in this section, we will work through key examples that show that any adequate type system must make certain type distinctions and must not make certain other distinctions. All of the examples given below are novel.

5.3.1   Methodology

Type Checking and Type Overloading

As a general point of methodology, we will only introduce types where they are necessary for linguistic purposes; in other words, we will we will motivate types based only on the role they need to play as formal tags (§5.1.1), rather than their role as properties (§5.1.2). We noted in §5.1.1 that this comprises two overlapping functions, namely enabling type checking and enabling type overloading.

It is easy to see when a particular type distinction is needed to support type overloading: we only have to exhibit a sequence of symbols that can have multiple meanings. Motivating types in order to support type checking is much harder, for the reason that the failure of type checking in a given example is invariably difficult to separate from other phenomena, such as presupposition failure (cf. §3.3.5). For example, consider the finite fields denoted '$\mathbb{F}_p$'. p needs to be a prime number for '$\mathbb{F}_p$' to be a valid expression. A priori, this requirement could be encoded either by requiring an object of a type PRIME as a subscript or by requiring an object of type NATURAL NUMBER (or INTEGER or NUMBER or etc.) which carried a presupposition that it was a prime number. (As we noted in §5.2, incorrect typing cannot be clearly classified as either syntactic or semantic, so that both of these treatments are reasonable.)

Our response to this freedom of choice among mechanisms is based on a desire to keep the theory as simple as possible. The mechanism of type is complex and intertwines with both syntax and semantics, and so should only be used in cases where it is absolutely necessary. We will therefore introduce type distinctions *only* where they are necessary for type overloading rather than type checking. These distinctions will necessarily induce some type checking — but we will never introduce distinctions in order to support type checking, and will prefer to use simpler mechanisms, such as presuppositions (§3.3.5), instead. (Note that this leaves open the possibility of raising 'prime number' to the status of a type to handle some example(s) other than '$\mathbb{F}_p$'; we will rule this out in §5.3.3.)

Actual and Potential Distinctions

There is one point on which we should be particularly careful. Not all of the type distinctions that could arise in theory do arise in practice. For example, we will find below that a non-extensional type 'SET OF NUMBERS' will be directly necessary for disambiguation purposes; by contrast, we will not exhibit an actual example showing that, say, SET OF SET OF NUMBERS is (directly) necessary for disambiguation purposes. Nevertheless, we will posit a type SET OF SET OF NUMBERS based on the fact that one could plausibly define notation which is only defined on SETS OF SET OF NUMBERS.

Thus the key feature licensing type-hood is potential use to disambiguate rather than demonstrated use to disambiguate. This is partly a point of methodological cleanliness; attempting to specify the exact depth of nesting that can occur in real types is messy in the same way that attempting to specify the exact depth of syntactic nesting that can occur in sentences is. But there is also a point regarding monotonicity: new notations are introduced into mathematics over time, and if this could cause a new type distinction to arise among existing objects, then our interpretation of mathematics would be non-monotonic. We prefer to avoid this on both practical and philosophical grounds.

5.3.2 Examining the Foundations

Sets as Building Blocks

Under the conventional account of the foundations of mathematics, all mathematical objects *are* sets. So, for example, the natural number 0 is the empty set $\{\}$, the natural number 1 is the set $\{0\} = \{\{\}\}$, and the natural number 2 is the set $\{0, 1\} = \{\{\}, \{\{\}\}\}$.[6] Similarly, all other mathematical objects — functions, sequences, ordered pairs, equivalence classes, matrices, groups, and so on — are defined as particular sets.

Many of the most common mathematical notations are overloaded for sets. If A and B are sets, then we may refer to the sets $A + B$ ('symmetric difference'), $A - B$ (elements in A but not B) and A^B (functions from A to B).[7] Now, these operations are not the same as the corresponding operations on numbers. For example,

$$\underbrace{\{0\}}_{'=1'} + \underbrace{\{0, 1\}}_{'=2'} = \{1\}$$

and $1 + 2 = 3$, but $\{1\} \neq 3$.

---

[6] There are philosophical problems with this viewpoint, which we will discuss in detail in §7. Nevertheless, this remains the view of the foundations of mathematics which is most often presented to undergraduates, and it is therefore the one which we will take as our starting point.

[7] See, for example, pp. 17–18 and p. 30 of Halmos (1960).

Since '$x + y$' has different interpretations when x and y are interpreted as
sets and when they are interpreted as numbers, we require a type distinction
between sets and numbers. If we maintain that numbers are sets, then we
have no choice but to conclude that there exist distinct *non-extensional* types
corresponding to natural numbers and sets. In fact, because the standard
account claims that all objects are in fact sets, we find that superficially
similar mathematical notations clash regardless of what objects they are
defined on, and we need every type to be non-extensional.

Number Is a Single Type

Mathematics contains many kinds of numbers: natural numbers, integers,
rational numbers, real numbers and complex numbers (among others). According to the most common account of the foundations of mathematics,
each kind of number in this list is constructed out of the previous kind.
For example, rational numbers are often defined as equivalence classes of
ordered pairs of integers. Suppose that this is the case, and we also adopt
the aforementioned conventional view that the tools used in the construction
(ordered pairs and equivalence classes) are particular sets. Then, the Axiom
of Foundation from set theory tells us that the different kinds of number are
disjoint, i.e. that no object can be both a natural number and an integer, etc..
Thus the integer 3 must be a different object to the natural number 3, both
of these must be distinct from the rational number 3, and so on. (A fuller
discussion of this point may be found in §7.2.2.)

Suppose that we looking at the specific question of whether there should be
a type distinction between, say, integers and rational numbers. To motivate
this in accordance with the methodology presented above (§5.3.1), we would
need an expression involving some rational numbers whose interpretation
depended on whether those real numbers were necessarily integers. (The
qualifier 'necessarily' here is important: we want to distinguish between expressions which range over integers, and expressions which range over rational
numbers, including integers.) We know of no such examples. Nevertheless,
given the foundational concerns noted above, it is worth examining this issue
in greater detail. We will briefly illustrate the problems that would arise if
we were to *ignore* our methodology and posit a type distinction here.

The crudest type distinction that we could draw is to create separate
types, INTEGER and RATIONAL NUMBER, together with type coercion from
INTEGER to RATIONAL NUMBER (cf. §5.1.1). The problem with this simple
system is that it is far too liberal; it allows the possibility that the integer '3'
satisfies

$$coerce_{\text{RATIONAL}}(3 + 3) \neq coerce_{\text{RATIONAL}}(3) + coerce_{\text{RATIONAL}}(3)$$

To be rigorous, one would need to repeatedly rule out pathologies of this kind by proving that they cannot occur. This clearly does not correspond to actual practice in mathematics.

The next option is to have INTEGER as a *subtype* of RATIONAL NUMBER; under this option, integers *are* rational numbers.[8] Because this involves no casts, it avoids the problems associated with the last example. The issues here are subtler:

1. **Accommodation.** In practice, mathematicians are able to silently *accommodate* the fact that certain real numbers are integers. For example, one defines

$$^nC_r = \frac{n!}{r!(n-r)!}$$

   This quantity is clearly defined as a rational number, but it can be used as an integer without any explicit assertion of its integral status. In order to assign the type INTEGER to ^nC_r and similar quantities, we would need to use very high reasoning strength.

2. **Undiscovered Facts.** For many of the numbers that occur in actual mathematical texts, it will not be clear to the reader whether or not the number is an integer.[9] (Cf. the fact that the irrationality of $\sqrt{2}$ requires a nontrivial proof.) Some instances of rational numbers may turn out to be integers, using methods currently unavailable to mathematics. These would need to be assigned the type RATIONAL in order to model the behaviour of real mathematicians.

Together, these issues require us to specify the exact reasoning strength that mathematicians use to determine whether or not a particular rational numbers is an integer. This is a considerable burden, and as we noted above, it carries no associated benefit. Thus we will obey our methodology (§5.3.1), and avoid introducing INTEGER as a subtype.

We should emphasise that the existence of accommodations, etc., does not change the fact that in *some* cases, an attempt to use, say, a real number like an integer seems anomalous; for example, one cannot refer to the group SO_π. In accordance with our methodology, we will handle such cases using presuppositions (§3.3.5); the expression 'SO_x' will carry with it the presupposition that x is a positive integer.

The argument given above also applies to real numbers as compared to complex numbers, and so on. (For example, in '$zz^* < 1$', the fact that zz^*

---

[8] This is in accord with day-to-day mathematical practice; cf. De Bruijn's observation that in 'ordinary mathematical language', 5 is simultaneously a real number and an integer (De Bruijn, 1987, p. 869).

[9] This observation is much stronger than the assertion that there is no general method for determining whether a given real number is an integer, due to the halting problem. If difficult examples are rare in practice, we can contain that issue, as noted in §5.2 above.

is a real number is accommodated.) As a result, we end up having a single type, NUMBER, to represent numbers of all kinds.[10]

Mismatch with Conventional Foundations

The examples we have just considered show that the actual usage in mathematics depends on a picture about the relationships between basic mathematical objects, about the *ontology* of mathematics, that is very different from the picture obtained from the conventional account of foundations. (Cf. Figure 5.1.)

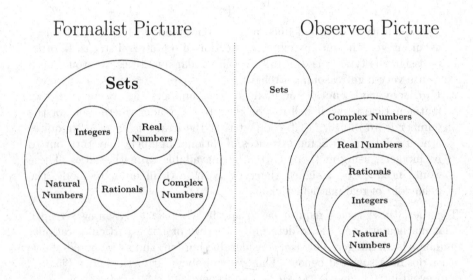

Fig. 5.1 The Ontology of Mathematics.

We could try to work around this issue by specifying that the genuine ontology is the formalist one of Figure 5.1, and that all types are non-extensional; under this view, '0' and '∅' refer to the same object, but via

---

[10] We have found that the argument given in this section has has sometimes lead to confusion in the following respect. We are not making any kind of normative claim; that is, we are not claiming that the real number 3 *ought* to be the same object as the integer 3. Rather we are making an empirical observation about mathematical language: mathematicians' actual use of language is simply not consistent with having more than one '3'. Correspondingly our remark that there is a single type NUMBER is a positive assertion about the type system needed to accurately model mathematical language; it should not be confused with normative assertions about the type systems used in computer science and elsewhere.

different non-extensional types. We will not take this approach, for a very simple reason. *No mathematician genuinely believes that numbers are sets, etc.*. The definitions of numbers *as* sets, etc. are convenient fables designed to support the position that mathematics can in fact be done inside ZF set theory. (The position is essentially correct, but the fable is problematic.) Mathematicians are told this fable as undergraduates, and assimilate it at a very superficial level. They will repeat it as a rote catechism, but do not restructure their internal picture of mathematical objects to reflect it.[11] This can be demonstrated — and we will demonstrate it, in §7.1.

Trying to force are a linguistic account to follow the formalist dogma is ultimately a losing game. One finds that mathematicians' actual beliefs about objects are repeatedly reflected in their use of language; as soon as one papers over one crack, another turns up. We will therefore need to build an account of the foundations of mathematics that is closer to what mathematicians actually believe, while still demonstrating that mathematics can be done inside ZF set theory. This is a major task, which we will take up in Chapter 7.[12]

5.3.3   Simple Distinctions

Objects Created *Out of Thin Air* Have Fresh Types

It is important to note that there is no single correct order in which all of mathematics may be encountered; for example, one could read a first text on group theory before reading about any real analysis, or vice versa. In order to be slightly more precise, we will say that two texts are unrelated if someone who knows nothing about the subject of text A could understand text B, and vice versa. When we have two texts of this kind, we require that the material in each must be independent of the material in the other, in the sense that the material in text A must be interpreted in the same way whether or not we have read text B.

A particularly strong form of independence occurs when two texts A and B share no dependencies, i.e. there is no third text which must be read before each of A and B. This is rare in practice, because so much of real mathematics depends on set theory; but there are examples of objects that one can learn

---

[11] The situation is very similar to that of an English speaker who believes that it is 'wrong' to end a sentence with a preposition, while frequently doing just that. Trying to build a theory of mathematical language that claims numbers are sets is as futile and unproductive as trying to build a theory of English that claims that sentences ending with prepositions are invariably ungrammatical.

[12] As we will note in §7.1, once a theory gives the correct predictions, the line between intension and extension is ultimately subjective; thus a determined reader can resolve to maintain that numbers are sets, by shifting the boundary between intension and extension. But, as we will show in Chapter 7, this is not necessary on epistemological grounds or for any other reason.

about without knowing about sets, such as natural numbers (in particularly careful presentations) and terms of the lambda calculus. In such treatments, all of these objects need to be defined axiomatically; they are introduced in terms of the way they behave rather than what they are. We will say that such objects are introduced *out of thin air*. When dealing with such objects, the above requirement of independence leads us to state:

> The types of classes of objects that are created *out of thin air* will necessarily be distinct from each other and from all other types.

Were this not the case, the texts introducing these objects might be interpreted differently depending on whether they were read consecutively or in isolation. Objects that are created *out of thin air* will be discussed more extensively in Chapter 7. In particular, in §7.5.1 we will argue that a number of classes of objects, including ordered pairs, relations, functions, sequences, vectors and matrices, need to be created in this way if we are to avoid both problems similar to those we discussed in §5.3.2 and related philosophical problems.

Structure Types are Always Fresh

Mathematicians often build up new kinds of object by combining old kinds of object. (We will refer to such objects as *structures*.) For example, the following definition sets up groups from sets and functions.

> **Definition.** A *group* is a set G together with a function $m : G \times G \to G$ satisfying ...

An individual group consists of a specific set and a specific function. In many ways, the group is like an ordered pair consisting of a set and a function. But there is an important difference: the syntactic behaviour of a group cannot be fully predicted from the syntactic behaviour of the aforementioned ordered pair. The notations which a group can participate in will be introduced by subsequent definitions. For example, the following definition sets up a 'direct product' notation on groups:

> **Definition.** If H and K are groups, then their *direct product*, denoted by $H \times K$, is ...

In order to overload the '$\bullet \times \bullet$' notation for groups, as opposed to e.g. rings, we need a type GROUP. We will refer to such types for structures as *structure types*.

One might consider that the overloading of notation on structures could be handled by treating structures as ordered pairs, and defining e.g. GROUP to be a synonym for ORDERED PAIR OF A SET AND A FUNCTION, a type which we will make sense of in §5.3.4 below. But there is a problem with this approach: the same kind of ordered pair could be used to represent different things in different areas of mathematics. One area might use ORDERED PAIR OF A SET

AND A FUNCTION to represent a group, and another might use it to represent, say, a metric space. If a mathematician had read the definitions from both areas, corresponding group and metric space notations would collide and every usage of such a notation would be ambiguous. This clearly does not correspond to the observed behaviour in mathematics.

As when we considered numbers and sets, we have two options; either we can insist that structures are ordered tuples and use non-extensional types, or we can take structures to be objects of some other kind. We will again choose the latter option. As before, this is primarily because we have never seen mathematicians *manipulate* structures as if they were ordered tuples, or conceive of a metric space 'happening' to be a group. But in this case, there is an additional reason. There is a linguistic convention whereby any structure can be treated like the object underlying the structure: a group can be considered as a set, so that one can write '$g \in G$' or '$|G|$'; a manifold can be considered as a topological space; etc.. This convention, which we will return to in §5.4.8, is much harder to account for if we treat structures as ordered tuples.

We will therefore specify that every time one creates a new kind of structure — for example, when one defines a group as a 'set together with a function' subject to certain properties — a new class of objects is created and has a new type, distinct from all existing types. Thus GROUP, METRIC SPACE, TOPOLOGICAL SPACE, etc. will all be distinct types.[13] We will still allow the 'ordered tuple'-like notation (as in '$G = (S, \circ)$'), but we will interpret it as an intrinsic notion applicable to structures rather than anything to do with ordered tuples as such.

The only issue with this approach is that it raises ontological questions; it opens the question of what groups are and whether they can be constructed using the ZF axioms. This question can be answered using the mechanisms we will construct in Chapter 7, but in this case, there is a more compactly stated alternative. We can eliminate structures at the level of the semantic representation: every time we see a reference to a structure, we replace that reference with references to the components of that structure, increasing the arity of semantic functions and predicates appropriately. For example, every time we find a group $G = (S, \circ)$ in the semantic representation, we replace that with references to the underlying set and the group operation; hence '$is\_Abelian(G)$' would become '$is\_Abelian(S, \circ)$', and so on. We will not actually carry out this operation — the fact that it is available in theory is enough to assuage foundational concerns.

---

[13] One consequence of the freshness of structure types is that our system of types does not fit well into the standard paradigms of type theory. See §5.5 for a full discussion.

Absence of Subtypes and Dependent Types

Our general methodology requires that we should only introduce type distinctions where they are needed to resolve overloading. In §5.3.2 we remarked that we know of no example where the distinction between, say, 'integers which are necessarily rational numbers' and 'other integers' was needed to resolve a concrete example of overloading. This reflects a much more general property; with one exception (noted below), we know of no instance where a proper subtype of a type is necessary to resolve overloading. Following our methodology, we will therefore stipulate that:

> Properties defined on types do not give rise to subtypes.

(Or equivalently: there are no subtypes.) We will draw a single exception to this rule in §5.3.4, when we come to discuss 'inferential types'.

This rule states, for example, that 'prime number' will not be raised to a type. As we noted in §5.3.1, if some notation needs to be defined on prime numbers (only), it will be defined on all numbers, and carry a presupposition that the number in question is prime. It is worth noting that this treatment is psychologically appealing in that it posits that mathematicians do not need to be able to tell whether large numbers like '30,031' are prime in order to simply understand mathematical notation.

In a similar vein, we do not know of a single instance where a type which contains a value as part of its name, which logicians call a dependent type, is needed to resolve overloading. That is, we do not know of any examples where a type like '3 × 3 MATRIX' is needed to resolve overloading; it always suffices to have a type MATRIX, and to encode information about the size of matrices into presuppositions. For example, the notation for the product of matrices of all sizes is captured by a single syntactic rule,

$$\text{Term}_{\text{MATRIX}} \rightarrow \text{Term}_{\text{MATRIX}} \; \text{Term}_{\text{MATRIX}}$$

Constraints on the sizes of matrices that may be multiplied together are encoded as presuppositions (§3.3.5) in the semantic representation attached to this rule.[14]

Summary

At this point, it will be useful to summarise the constraints we have discussed above. The three issues we have discussed so far have led us to conclude that:

1. Types created *out of thin air* are always distinct from each other and from all other types.
2. Every structure type is distinct from all other types, including 'isomorphic' structure types.
3. There are no subtypes.

---

[14] See also §8.3 for a discussion of related issues.

(Note that the first two criteria reflect our intuitive notions of type; that is, they ensure that SET is distinct from MATRIX, GROUP is distinct from METRIC SPACE, and so on.)

If we were to take these criteria, with no further changes, we would end up with a clean, minimal type system with a number of elegant properties; for example:

The type system is the weakest 'reasonable' type system.
The following non-formal diagnostic may be used to determine whether or not two objects should be of the same type:

> If (and only if) one can introduce an object of type T, and then show that it turns out to have type T', *and vice versa*, then $T = T'$.

So, for example, since one can introduce a ring $\mathbb{Z}[X]/(X^2 + 1)$ and then show that it happens to be a field, and also all fields are rings, rings and fields must have the same type. In other words, there is no type 'FIELD'; fields belong to the type 'RING'. But since it is impossible to introduce a ring and then show that it turns out to be a matrix, 'RING' and 'MATRIX' are distinct types.

As it happens, the system just discussed is not sufficient to describe mathematics; in fact, it seems to be insufficient in just two precisely delineable respects, which we shall return to below. But this system is elegant enough and useful enough that many useful parts of our theory are best stated with reference only to it, and not to the two exceptions. Accordingly, in our formalisation in §5.4 we will distinguish different kinds of types, turning the above system into a particular kind of type ('fundamental type'); and the exceptions discussed below into other kinds of type ('relational type' for types induced by relationship to an independent object, and 'inferential type' for containers and similar objects).

5.3.4 Non-extensionality

All of the types we have discussed so far seem to correspond to extensional, semantic properties; that is, they all seem to correspond to mathematical predicates that can be evaluated on objects. For example, NUMBER seems to correspond to 'being a number', and so on. This gives rise to a number of attractive properties; for example, whenever $X = Y$, it is the case that X and Y have exactly the same types.

Ideally, we would preserve this property of extensionality for the entire type system. In practice, extensionality breaks down for a variety of reasons. Both of the kinds of type which we have yet to introduce ('relational type' and 'inferential type') are non-extensional for distinct reasons, and even fundamental type is not extensional in the way which one would expect. We will now introduce the new kinds of type and explain the failure of extensionality for each kind.

Relationships to Independent Objects

There is an important class of mathematical objects which are not assigned any fundamental types. Consider the following fragment of a mathematical discourse:

Definition. If G is a group and a is an element of G, then the *order of a* is $|\langle a \rangle|$, the number of elements in $\langle a \rangle$.

a is neither of a class of objects created out of thin air (such as sets) nor a structure. As such it is not assigned any fundamental types. The ways in which a participates in mathematical notation are governed solely by the fact that it is related to some other object, namely the group G. In order to keep track of this information, we will need to create a new class of types, *relational types*. The particular relational type that we will assign to a is ELEMENT OF SOME GROUP (abbr. ELT OF GP). This type will licence a to participate in notation such as group multiplication, which is described by the following rule:

$$\text{Term}_{\text{ELT OF GP}} \to \text{Term}_{\text{ELT OF GP}} \ \text{Term}_{\text{ELT OF GP}}$$

Note that the type ELEMENT OF SOME GROUP will not track which group(s) an object is an element of: this information is never needed to resolve type overloading. (The determination of the appropriate group makes no reference to type information, and relies purely on the information in DRSs. This process is discussed in §8.3.)

The failure of extensionality for relational types is best illustrated by an example. Consider the two-element set $S = \{\pi, SO_3\}$. We can define a multiplication function $m : S \times S \to S$ as follows:

m	π	SO_3
π	π	SO_3
SO_3	SO_3	π

It is trivial to verify that there is a group $G = (S, m)$ on S with group operation m. It follows that π and SO_3 have the type ELEMENT OF SOME GROUP, and we are licensed to use group notation with them. We can write, for example

$$\pi SO_3$$

to denote SO_3, or

$$\pi^{-1}$$

to denote π.

Now we come to the crucial point: if relational types are extensional then π and SO_3 *always* the type ELEMENT OF SOME GROUP, even when we have never seen any reference to the group G on $\{\pi, SO_3\}$. Thus we are always able to write expressions like 'πSO_3', even when we have never seen any reference to a group.

The state of affairs is clearly absurd. To avoid it, we are forced to make relational types non-extensional. As noted above, this opens up a question as to the exact circumstances under which we are entitled to deduce that an object has a given relational type. We will return to this question later in this section.

It is also worth emphasising that relational types only apply to objects which *do not* have fundamental types. The key example motivating this involves a group of matrices in which the group inverse does not correspond to the matrix inverse, i.e. a group of matrices which is not a matrix group. If one attempts to apply the inverse notation 'M^{-1}' to a matrix M which happens to have been explicitly presented as a member of such a group, the 'inverse matrix' reading appears to hide the 'group inverse' reading. Consequently, matrices must not be assigned relational types, even if they are explicitly presented as being members of groups.

Inference

Mathematicians frequently use symbolic set notation as a shorthand for long textual assertions; so, for example, one often sees:

Let $x \in \mathbb{N}$.

acting as a shorthand for 'let x be a natural number'. When we see this kind of statement, we typically need to make inferences about type. In this particular instance, we need to infer that x has the type NUMBER.

In the system of types described so far, there is no type inference that can tell us that x has the type NUMBER. In order to deduce that fact, we need to resort to general semantic reasoning based on the following facts:

- x is an element of $\mathbb{N}$.
- Every element of $\mathbb{N}$ is a natural number.
- All natural numbers have type NUMBER.

So the system of types described so far is not inferentially complete, even on cases that occur frequently in mathematics (as opposed to pathological but mathematically legal 'worst cases'). This is not an issue. As noted in §5.2.2, we are first and foremost giving a theory of mathematical language; if we need to make concessions to computability we will do so elsewhere. And, in contrast to the example in §5.2.2, the reasoning that needs to be done is relatively simple, so our predictions do not risk becoming psychologically implausible. Let us emphasise the point: based on the evidence just presented, there is no need to add any additional types.

A problem strikes this picture, coming from an unexpected angle. Again, it is best illustrated by an example. If S is a finite set of natural numbers, then one sometimes can refer to the sum of the elements of S. So if, say, $S = \{1, 2, 3\}$, then the sum of the elements of S is 6. By convention, if S is empty, then one defines the sum of the elements of S to be 0.

This convention is both natural and important — it could not be dispensed with without damaging a nontrivial amount of mathematics.

Now, natural numbers are not the only objects that can be added together. Occasionally one refers to the sum of other kinds of objects. For example, we could refer to the sum of a finite set of functions, or a finite set of vectors, or a finite set of elements of an abelian group. Let us focus on, say, the sum of a finite set of functions from natural numbers to natural numbers. If, we define say,

$$f : \mathbb{N} \to \mathbb{N} \qquad n \mapsto n$$
$$g : \mathbb{N} \to \mathbb{N} \qquad n \mapsto n^2$$
$$S = \{f, g\}$$

then we can say that the sum of the elements of S is

$$h : \mathbb{N} \to \mathbb{N} \qquad n \mapsto n^2 + n.$$

And if a set S of functions from natural numbers to natural numbers is introduced and turns out to be empty, then convention requires that the sum of the elements of S is the function

$$k : \mathbb{N} \to \mathbb{N} \qquad n \mapsto 0.$$

This brings us to the crux of this example. Some foundational theories, such as polymorphic type theories, support the existence of an 'empty set of natural numbers' and a distinct 'empty set of functions (from natural numbers to natural numbers)'. But in Zermelo-Fraenkel set theory, there is *only one empty set*, $\phi = \{\}$. Suppose that we define

$$S_1 = \{n \in \mathbb{N} \mid n < 0\}$$
$$S_2 = \{f \in \mathbb{N}^{\mathbb{N}} \mid f(0) < 0\}.$$

Both S_1 and S_2 denote the *same* object, namely the unique empty set. Despite this, the phrases 'the sum of the elements of S_1' and 'the sum of the elements of S_2' denotes *distinct* entities.

This example forces us to introduce two non-extensional types which distinguish objects presented as finite sets of natural numbers from objects presented as finite sets of functions from natural numbers to natural numbers. For the reasons given in §5.3.3, the finiteness of the sets, etc., are irrelevant; the types that we need are SET OF NUMBERS and SET OF FUNCTIONS FROM NUMBERS TO NUMBERS.[15]

---

[15] Note that the issue here is not the parametricity of these types. One could introduce a type which was identical to 'SET OF NUMBERS', but which had a name that did not mention numbers and which was introduced in such a way as to refer *directly* to numbers rather than being an instance of a parametric 'SET OF α'.

The problem is not in fact restricted to sets; one finds the same issue with objects such as functions and relations. (The role played by the empty set in the above example is filled by functions and relations whose domain and co-domain turn out to be empty.) As a general principle, whenever one finds a property T on an object X and there exists a nondegenerate binary formula ψ such that whenever $\psi(X, Y)$ holds we may deduce that Y has a type T', examples of the above kind force us to make T (part of) a distinct non-extensional type. Or, speaking more loosely, any properties that license inferences about types of other objects need to be made (part of) a non-extensional type.

Following this principle, we will introduce a class of non-extensional *inferential types* such as SET OF NUMBERS, SET OF SETS, SET OF SETS OF NUMBERS, FUNCTION FROM NUMBERS TO NUMBERS and RELATION ON NUMBERS. (This class will also include types like ORDERED PAIR OF A SET AND A FUNCTION although, because we do not treat structures as ordered tuples (§5.3.3), these are not of any great use.) Once again, we have an open question as to how exactly we may infer that a given object has one of these types. We will turn to this question next.

Reasoning without Extensionality

In §5.1 and §5.2, we separated the aspect of types as tags which discriminated linguistic readings from their aspect as mathematical properties. By doing so, we made sense of the very concept of a non-extensional type; but at the same time, we left open the question of how non-extensional types, considered as tags, should be determined in concrete examples. As a result, we need to answer this question, both for relational types and for inferential types. We will do so when we present each of these types formally, in §5.4.

Our basic approach will rely on the fact that each of the types we have listed is 'close to' a property. For example, having the type SET OF NUMBERS cannot correspond to the property of being a set of numbers, as we saw earlier in this section, but there is certainly a connection between the two. We will list deduction rules for each kind of non-extensional type, constrained to resemble specific inference rules for the corresponding property. For example, because a subset of a set of numbers is itself a set of numbers, we will licence an inference from the assignment of the type SET OF NUMBERS to X and the fact that Y is a subset of X to assign the type SET OF NUMBERS to Y.

5.3.5 Homogeneity and Open Types

We will now motivate a desirable property of types by considering a specific example of ambiguity, relating to the inverse 'f^{-1}' of a function f. It is not generally realised that there are in fact three distinct notions (and corresponding notations) in use here. Consider the following three excerpts, all taken from the same textbook:[16]

1. Let $g = f^{-1}$.
2. $f^{-1}(0) = A$
3. $f^{-1}(D) = T$

The notation from the first excerpt, allowing the use of 'f^{-1}' to denote the inverse function, may be used to map objects to objects in notations like '$y = f^{-1}(x)$'. In the second excerpt, an object 0 is mapped to a set A; and in the third, a set D is mapped to another set T. So, in general, if we see an expression of the form:

$$f^{-1}(\bullet)$$

there are three distinct notations that could be in use. (Object to object, object to set and set to set.) In theory, the first and second usages are distinguished depending on whether f is bijective or not — but authors tend to distinguish them based on whether f is *obviously* bijective or not, and this criterion is too subjective to be linguistically useful. A theory of mathematical language ought to be able to resolve ambiguity by predicting which notation is used in individual instances of '$f^{-1}(\bullet)$' in texts. We will now highlight a property of the type system described above which enables such disambiguation.

With respect to our intuitive notion of type, we think of most of the sets we encounter in mathematics as being *homogenous*, i.e. as containing objects of the same type. Thus we generally find sets of numbers, and sets of matrices, but *inhomogenous* sets that contain both numbers and matrices are both rare and disconcerting. As the domains and co-domains of functions are themselves sets,[17] we tend to encounter, say, functions from matrices to numbers rather than functions mapping both matrices and sets to both numbers and groups. To a considerable extent, this has already been reflected in our formal type system; when we set up inferential types like SET OF NUMBERS or FUNCTION FROM MATRICES TO MATRICES, we were relying on homogeneity.

Let us illustrate the importance of homogeneity using the context surrounding the second and third examples above:

Let D denote $\{0,1\}$ with the discrete topology. Suppose that $A|B$ partitions [a topological space] T. Define $f : T \to D$ by

$$f(x) = \begin{cases} 0, & x \in A, \\ 1, & x \in B. \end{cases}$$

[...] Now $f^{-1}(\phi) = \phi$, $f^{-1}(0) = A$, $f^{-1}(1) = B$, $f^{-1}(D) = T$.

(Sutherland, 1975, p. 95)

---

[16] The excerpts are taken from p. 66, p. 95 and p. 95 of Sutherland (1975) respectively.

[17] See §7.1 concerning a subtlety regarding the co-domains of functions.

In this example, we have that:

- 0 and 1 are NUMBERS,
- T is a TOPOLOGICAL SPACE,
- D is a homogenous TOPOLOGICAL SPACE OF NUMBERS,
- A and B are homogenous SETS OF ELEMENTS OF A TOPOLOGICAL SPACE and
- f is a FUNCTION FROM ELEMENTS OF A TOPOLOGICAL SPACE TO NUMBERS, homogenous with respect to both domain and co-domain.

Bearing this in mind, consider a particular usage of $f^{-1}(\bullet)$, such as:

$$f^{-1}(0) = A$$

Because f is a homogenous function to NUMBERS, and 0 is a NUMBER (rather than a SET OF NUMBERS), we know that either the 'object to object' or 'object to set' sense of $f^{-1}(\bullet)$ must be intended. Because A is a homogenous SET OF ELEMENTS OF A TOPOLOGICAL SPACE (and not an ELEMENT OF A TOPOLOGICAL SPACE), we know that the 'object to set' sense of $f^{-1}(\bullet)$ must be intended. In this way, the homogeneity of type enables us to disambiguate expressions of the form '$f^{-1}(\bullet)$'.

We should note four points before moving onwards. First, the standard foundations of mathematics (the ZF(C) axioms) allow the construction of sets which are *not* intuitively homogenous. Stronger, such sets actually occur in textbooks; we will discuss concrete examples in §7.2.7.

Second, even if all sets are homogenous, notation may be ambiguous; for example, in, '$f^{-1}(0) = f^{-1}(1)$' (interpreted with respect to the above example) it is impossible to tell whether equality of objects or equality of sets is intended.

Third, in general disambiguation requires harder reasoning than was the case above: we will not always be so lucky as to begin with a situation stating that '$f^{-1}(\bullet)$' is equal to an object of known type. In most real cases, the available type information is sufficient to disambiguate expressions, but the actual operation of 'chasing around type information' to do so is a non-trivial task. In particular, we should emphasise that types are not always deduced compositionally, i.e. 'bottom-up'; for example, when we encounter '$f(X) = Y$', we may find that the only way to deduce the type of X is to deduce it from the types of f and Y. The general process of inferring types for mathematical language is the primary focus of Chapter 6.

Finally, there are a few cases where, although a kind of homogeneity obtains, the distinction between 'objects' and 'sets' that we have used above breaks down. Just encountering, say, SETS OF SETS OF NUMBERS is not problematic; we distinguish readings based on whether we see SETS OF NUMBERS (corresponding to 'objects' above) or SETS OF SETS OF NUMBERS (corresponding to 'sets' above). However, when one is dealing with Von Neumann ordinals, which are effectively SETS OF SETS OF SETS OF ..., the distinction cannot be applied; but in fact, in such cases, even real mathematicians need to be extremely careful about what 'f^{-1}' actually denotes.

Thus homogeneity is not a silver bullet, disambiguating everything that we might encounter; but it is extremely effective in practice. It is a property that we would like all of our inferential types to have, when applied to examples that actually crop up in mathematics. This brings us to the next section.

Closures and Open Types

Often in mathematics one wants to take an existing set of objects and *close* that set under some operation to form a larger collection. For example, one might take a metric space M and close it under the operation of sequence convergence to construct another metric space, called the *completion of M*. Alternatively, one might take a field k and close it under the operation of finding a root for every polynomial to form the *algebraic closure of k*. But the most important example relates to *numbers*. First one takes the natural numbers and closes them under subtraction to form the integers; then one closes the integers under division to form the rational numbers; and so on.

For the reasons given immediately above, we want the sets which are constructed as the result of closure to be homogenous. This presents a particular problem with regard to concrete constructions. For example, suppose that we have the set of natural numbers, which have the type NUMBER, and we wish to close this set with respect to subtraction to form the integers. The usual concrete construction of the integers constructs them as equivalence classes of ordered pairs of natural numbers, i.e. objects which have the type SET OF ORDERED PAIRS OF NUMBERS. A priori it is unclear how the natural numbers relate to integers. If natural numbers *are* integers then the set $\mathbb{Z}$ of integers is necessarily inhomogenous as it contains both NUMBERS and SETS OF ORDERED PAIRS OF NUMBERS. As noted above, this is very unattractive; we would like $\mathbb{Z}$ to be a homogenous set, so that our disambiguation mechanisms are as effective as possible.

The relationship between natural numbers and integers is a major topic; it is one of the primary examples motivating our analysis of the foundations of mathematics in Chapter 7, and we will discuss it extensively there. For the moment we will merely assume that we have a way of constructing integers so that they also have type NUMBER, natural numbers are integers and $\mathbb{Z}$ is a homogenous set containing only NUMBERS. For present purposes, the key point is as follows: in whatever way we constructed the integers, we have introduced *more* objects of the type NUMBER. Because of our desire to keep the set $\mathbb{Z}$ homogenous, we have been forced to allow the type NUMBER to expand. Originally, it contained only natural numbers; when we introduced integers, it had to contain those as well; later it expand again to contain rational numbers; and so on. (Note that in talking about expansion, we are depending on the notion of time introduced in §1.2.2.)

This kind of expansion is found most often with numbers; on repeatedly introduces objects of new kinds. However, it is not exclusive to numbers. For example, the δ-function is something that can be used in many notations involving functions, and it is therefore useful to be able to expand the type FUNCTION to encompass δ-functions.

More generally, we have no way of knowing which fundamental types will need to expand; if one encounters enough mathematics, it is plausible that any given fundamental type will need to stretch to accommodate new object. As a result, we are forced to specify that *all* fundamental types are able to expand to encompass additional objects. We will describe this property by saying that all fundamental types are *open*.

We are now in a position to state the key observation of this section. If types are open, they cannot be the extensions of the properties we would expect them to be. For example, we cannot make the type FUNCTION the extension of the property of being a function; if we were to do so, FUNCTION would not be able to stretch to accommodate δ-functions. Thus even fundamental types are not extensional in the way that we would expect them to be.

Finally, we should note that the existing names for fundamental types are something of a misnomer; if we were being strict we should refer not to FUNCTION but to FUNCTION-LIKE, the type of objects which are like functions. And, indeed, the type NUMBER should really be called NATURAL NUMBER-LIKE; it starts by containing only natural numbers and repeatedly expands to encompass objects which are like the numbers it already contains. (An extensive discussion of this expansion is given in §7.5.) However, as most fundamental types do not expand substantially, we have chosen to use compact but technically incorrect labels like 'FUNCTION'. We draw a specific exception in the case of the type of numbers, which expands repeatedly. Because having the type 'NATURAL NUMBER' contain integers is confusing (and the label 'NATURAL NUMBER-LIKE' is unwieldy), we label the relevant type NUMBER. This is the one case where the name we use for a type is one that cannot be mechanically derived from mathematical texts.[18] (Cf. also the discussion of this point in §7.5.4.)

5.4 Types in Mathematics

We will now present the system of types needed to model mathematics faithfully, i.e. to support the resolution of ambiguity in mathematical statements.

In the same way as one typically separates the discussion of types in programming languages into descriptions of atomic types, polymorphic types, record types, etc., we have constructed several different kinds of type. The three kinds that will concern us here can be described briefly as follows:

---

[18] Naturally, this also extends to derived types; if we were being rigorous, SET OF NUMBERS should be called SET OF NATURAL NUMBER-LIKES, etc..

Fundamental Type. This is the intrinsic type that is intuitively associated with a mathematical object; examples include 'NUMBER', 'SET',
'GROUP', 'METRIC SPACE', 'FUNCTION' and 'MATRIX'. Any mathematical
object will have at most one fundamental type.

Relational Type. This is a kind of type which is not an extensional
property of an object but derives from membership of some structure;
examples include 'ELEMENT OF A GROUP', 'ELEMENT OF A METRIC
SPACE' and 'ELEMENT OF A RING'.

Inferential Type. This is a kind of type supporting inference about the
types of other objects, applying primarily to containers; examples include
'SET OF NUMBERS', 'GROUP OF MATRICES', 'MATRIX-VALUED FUNC-
TION', 'SET OF ELEMENTS OF A RING' and 'SET OF SET OF NUMBERS'.

In addition to these, we have a 'top type' 'OBJECT' which falls into none of
these categories; every mathematical object has this type, and every type is
a subtype of 'OBJECT'. Because 'OBJECT' conveys no information, we will
sometimes refer to it as the *trivial* type, and all other types as *non-trivial*
types.

5.4.1 Presenting Type: Syntax and Semantics

In the rest of this chapter, we will be specifying particular configurations that
trigger the creation of new types or type inferences. Often these will be given
in specific syntactic forms; so, for example, we might say that a statement
like

If x_1 is a T_1, then P.

triggers the creation of a new type. Such remarks are generally not intended to
require a specific syntactic configuration, that is the use of formulaic language.
So we would draw no distinction between the above example and

P if x_1 is a T_1.

or

P for every x_1 which is a T_1.

with regard to whether these behave as triggers for the creation of new types.
The creation of a type is actually triggered by the *shape of the semantic
representation* rather than the shape of the sentence. Throughout the rest
of this document, we will emphasise this indifference to syntactic form by
saying that type creation or type inference is triggered by a configuration
that *essentially* has a particular form.

5.4.2 Fundamental Type

Fundamental type is the intrinsic type that is intuitively associated with a mathematical object; examples include 'Number', 'Set', 'Group', 'Metric Space', 'Function' and 'Matrix'. Any mathematical object will have at most one fundamental type.[19]

Properties

1. Most mathematical objects will have a fundamental type. In practice, all exceptions occur when one sees something of the form 'Let $x \in S$', and one does not have enough information about S to deduce a type for x.

2. Fundamental type names are atomic; that is, no proper part of the name of a fundamental type bears any significance. So e.g. 'METRIC SPACE' is an indivisible description.

   Equally, one cannot construct a fundamental type like 'Function from A to B'; the fundamental type is 'FUNCTION', and the 'from A to B' part is captured by an inferential type.

   We will encounter a single class of exceptions to this principle when we consider a particular kind of structure type later in this section.

3. The following diagnostic may be used to determine whether or not two objects should be of the same fundamental type:

   > If (and only if) one can introduce some object of fundamental type T, and then show that it happens to have fundamental type T', *and vice versa*, then $T = T'$.

So, for example, since one can introduce the ring $\mathbb{R}[X]/(X^2 + 1)$ and then show that it happens to be a field, and all fields are rings, rings and fields must have the same fundamental type. In other words, there is no fundamental type 'Field'; fields belong to the fundamental type 'RING'. But since it is impossible to introduce a ring and then show that it turns out to be a matrix, 'RING' and 'MATRIX' are distinct fundamental types. The significance of the 'and vice versa' caveat becomes apparent when we consider objects with two separate kinds of structure, such as topological groups. It is not possible to introduce a topological space and show that it happens to also be a group. (One can show that a topological space is a group *under some concrete operation*, but that is another matter; cf. the fact that one can show that a topological space is metrizable, but not that it is a metric space.) As a result, TOPOLOGICAL GROUP is a separate fundamental type to both TOPOLOGICAL SPACE and GROUP. On the

---

[19] In some respects, fundamental types resemble *ground types* in the type systems studied in type theory. However, the similarity should not be overemphasised; in particular, as we will see in §5.4.3, fundamental types can have proper subtypes. More generally, we should emphasise that the type system as a whole is not suited to analysis in type theoretic terms; see §5.5 for a full discussion.

other hand, a TOPOLOGICAL GROUP *can be considered as* a TOPOLOGICAL SPACE or as a GROUP; cf. §5.4.8 below. Assignment of distinct types to e.g. topological groups and topological spaces is the key to making the next property hold.

4. Fundamental types are strictly disjoint. In other words, any mathematical object has at most one fundamental type.

   In §6.5 we will outline an efficient algorithm for determining types. The disjointness of fundamental types will be the single most important fact underpinning that algorithm.

For reasons presented in §5.3 and elaborated on in Chapter 7, all the familiar kind of numbers must share a single fundamental type; we will call this type 'NUMBER'.

Creation

There are only two ways in which fundamental types can be created:

1. *Ex nihilo*. This involves the introduction of a kind of mathematical object that is not constructed out of other mathematical objects. This is extremely rare in mathematical texts; the only instances we know of are the introduction of sets and the introduction of categories. When a new kind of object is created *ex nihilo*, a corresponding fundamental type is created. For example, the introduction of sets results in the creation of a fundamental type SET.

2. **Structures.** The use of the constructors 'consists of' and/or 'together with' can create a new *structure type* out of old types. There are several variants, but the basic pattern is:

   A T consists of a T_0 [together with a T_1, a T_2, ..., and a T_n] such that ... .

For example, topological spaces are introduced by the following fragment:

Definition 3.1.1
A topological space $T = (A, \mathscr{T})$ <u>consists of</u> a non-empty set A <u>together with</u> a fixed collection $\mathscr{T}$ of subsets of A satisfying:
(T1) $A, \phi \in \mathscr{T}$,
(T2) the intersection of any two sets in $\mathscr{T}$ is [again] in $\mathscr{T}$,
(T3) the union of any collection of sets in $\mathscr{T}$ is [again] in $\mathscr{T}$.
The collection $\mathscr{T}$ is called a topology for A, and the members of $\mathscr{T}$ are called the open sets of T. Elements of A all called points in the space T.
(Sutherland, 1975, p. 45; underlining ours)

Every instance of such notation introduces a new structure type, and two structure types are distinct even if they consist of the same components.

Apart from this restriction, structure types behave just like tuples, and one can use tuple-like notation for them, as in:[20]

Let $(A, \mathscr{T})$ be a topological space.

There is one isolated anomalous case which needs to be discussed individually. In real mathematics, an ideal of a ring is defined to *be* a particular kind of subset of the ring. Additionally, one can define concatenative multiplication both on ideals of a ring and on subsets of a ring — and these two operations are defined *differently*. (The product of ideals is necessarily closed under addition, and the product of subsets is not.) As a result, we need a type IDEAL OF A RING which is distinct from the type SUBSET OF A RING. Whether or not we analyse this type as a non-extensional type, there is no way to motivate its existence based only on the text of the underlying mathematics; there are plenty of subsets of structures which are genuinely subsets, rather than behaving like ideals. In this isolated case, the idealisation of language required to meet full adaptivity (1.2.3) is, unusually, of a kind which would not be immediately obvious to a mathematician, at least until the point concerning multiplication of ideals was made. An appropriate idealised variant might look like this:

An ideal of a ring R **consists of** a set I of elements of R which are ... .

The key point is that this introduces IDEAL OF A RING as a (one-component) structure type. Types of this kind are the only exception to the above principle stating that the names of structure types are atomic. Note that no further emendation is required; the definitions of the product of ideals and all other operations on ideals may be left unchanged.

We should finally note that it is possible that it is possible that there are other isolated cases which behave like 'ideal'; at least, it would be rash to rule out the possibility. We are however certain that they are extremely rare.

Note that both methods for creating a fundamental type name the type created; hence there are no 'anonymous' fundamental types. All of the types presented in this book have names that can actually be derived from definitions, excepting only NUMBER (and types referring to NUMBER). As we noted in §5.3.5, we use the label NUMBER as the actual label for this type is potentially confusing. We will comment further on this issue in §7.5.4.

Finally, a phenomenon called *identification* can cause two fundamental types to be collapsed into a single type. We will describe this phenomenon in Chapter 7. (Narrow technical details of identification are given in §7.4.2, but the earlier parts of the chapter introduce the necessary context.)

---

[20] Despite the similarity, this use of $(\bullet, \bullet, \dots, \bullet)$ is *not* tuple notation. This notation for structures is inherent in the language of mathematics whereas tuples and tuple notation are defined in mathematical texts. See §5.3.3 for details.

5.4.3 Relational Type

Relational type is a kind of type which is not an extensional property of an object but derives from membership of some structure; examples include 'Element of some Group', 'Element of some Metric Space', 'Element of some Ring'.

Properties

1. Only objects that do not have a fundamental type have a relational type.
2. Nearly all of the objects with a relational type that one encounters are elements of structures which have underlying sets. However, because the linguistic theory given here is not tied to any mathematical framework, including ZF(C) set theory, relational types cannot be characterised in this way.

   As promised in §1.1, this cautious separation of linguistic theory from mathematical content is rewarded when one reaches category theory; both OBJECT OF A CATEGORY and MORPHISM OF A CATEGORY can be modelled as relational types.
3. Although relational types are non-extensional (§5.3.4), we do not need to give dedicated rules governing their behaviour here. In §6.1 and §6.2 we will give general rules governing the behaviour of types during parsing, and these will completely determine the behaviour of relational types.

Creation

Relational types are created in two ways:

1. **Definitions involving 'of'.** If x is an object which has no fundamental type and y is another object which has a fundamental type T, then a definition which has the essential form

   x is a *[phrase]* of y [if ...].

   will create a relational type [PHRASE] OF A T.

   For example, the following definitions triggers the creation of the relational type ELEMENT OF A SET:

   - Let S be a set, and let $x \in S$; we say that x is an element of S.

2. **Structure Type Closure.** Whenever '<*phrase*> OF A T_0' is a relational type, and T_1 is a structure type which has T_0 as its first element, then '<*phrase*> OF A T_1' is a (distinct) relational type.

   For example, if ELEMENT OF SOME SET is a relational type, as in the example above, then ELEMENT OF SOME GROUP, ELEMENT OF SOME RING, ELEMENT OF SOME METRIC SPACE, etc. must all be distinct relational types.

5.4.4 Inferential Type

Inferential type is a kind of type supporting inference about the types of other objects, applying primarily to containers; examples include 'Set of Numbers', 'Group of Matrices', 'Matrix-valued Function', 'Set of Elements of a Ring' and 'Set of Set of Numbers'.

Properties

1. Inferential types exist in order to support inference; the actual operation of inference will be described in the next section.
2. Every inferential type is based on another type: SET OF NUMBERS is based on SET, GROUP OF NUMBERS is based on GROUP, SET OF SET OF NUMBERS is based on SET OF NUMBERS, and so on. The remainder of the name only bears a meaning when combined with the base type; for example, OF NUMBERS means nothing in itself, and also an X OF NUMBERS and a Y OF NUMBERS are *a priori* unrelated.
3. In practice, all useful inferential types are based on objects like sets (including categories) and objects like functions (including sequences, vectors, matrices and functors). Inferential types based on structures are induced from the appropriate inferential type on the object underlying the structure; for example, a GROUP OF NUMBERS is really a GROUP which is a SET OF NUMBERS.
4. Inferential types are not the same as 'parametric' types, i.e. families of types which are indexed by types (such as SET OF T for T a type). One may introduce a type which is identical to 'SET OF NUMBERS', but which has an *atomic* name that did not mention numbers. Nevertheless, in practice, all of the (handful of) inferential types are introduced as parametric types. (Parametric types are described in §5.4.6 below.)

Creation

All inferential types are created in one of two ways. First, inferential types may be created by statements that essentially have the form

> Let x be a D. x is a D'' if whenever a_1 is a D_1, a_2 is a D_2, ... a_n is a D_n and $\alpha(a_1, \ldots, a_k, x, a_{k+1}, \ldots, a_l, y, a_{l+1}, \ldots, a_n)$, then y is a D'.

where the a_i, x and y are variables, D (resp. D') is a N' corresponding to the type T (resp. T'), each D_i is a N' corresponding to the type T_i, $\alpha(...)$ translates into an atomic semantic predicate $\hat{\alpha}(...)$ and D'' is a N' (which will correspond to the type being created). Note that some of the types T_i may be 'OBJECT', making the restrictions on the corresponding a_i vacuous.

So, for example, the inferential type SET OF MATRICES could be set up in the following way:

> Let A be a set; A is a set of matrices if for all y,
> $y \in A$ implies that y is a matrix.

Here $T = \text{SET}$, $T_1 = \text{OBJECT}$, $T' = \text{MATRIX}$, and '$y \in A$' is translated into the atomic semantic predicate '$in(\mathbf{y}, \mathbf{A})$'.

Remembering that it is the underlying semantic form of a definition that counts, we could express the above statement more fluidly as

Let A be a set; A is a set of matrices if all of its elements are matrices.

or as

A set of matrices is a set whose elements are matrices.

As we shall see in the next section, a statement of this form creates an initial inference rule which is associated with the inferential type.

The second method of creating inferential types relates to structures, and results in the creation of types like GROUP OF NUMBERS based on SET OF NUMBERS. This method will be discussed in §5.4.8.

5.4.5 Type Inference

Deriving Inference Rules

In order to fully describe the behaviour of inferential types, like SET OF NUMBERS, we need to describe exactly which type inferences they take part in. Since our methodology requires that *all* mathematical content be derived from texts, rather than being built into the language, all inference rules must be derived from texts. Unfortunately, actual mathematical texts do not state this information explicitly; indeed, actual mathematical text do not define what it means to be a 'set *of numbers*' at all.

One option that is *a priori* attractive is to look at the behaviour of the mathematical objects that correspond to a type, and extrapolate rules about the corresponding type. For example, a subset of a set of numbers is a set of numbers; correspondingly, we should infer that a subset of a SET OF NUMBERS is a SET OF NUMBERS. Of course, for the reasons discussed in §5.3.4, there are certain facts which we must not convert into inference rules; in particular, we do not want to deduce that the empty set ϕ is a SET OF NUMBERS.

In general, one can actually characterise the inferences that must not be derived from facts, subject to a caveat (to be given below). For the moment we will assume a intuitive version of parametric types, i.e. types of the form SET OF T where T is another type; such types are discussed fully in §5.4.6 below. Given this, we can characterise the unwanted inference rules as being those in which a given type parameter T appears in the conclusion of the inference, but not in the premises. Thus, for example,

S is a SET OF T, x is an element of $S \vdash x$ is a T.

is a valid type inference because T, which is the only type parameter that appears in the conclusion, also appears in the premises. But by contrast,

$\vdash \phi$ is a SET OF T.

is an illegitimate inference because the type parameter T appears in the conclusion but nowhere in the premises.

Morally speaking, this criterion tells us exactly which inferences about objects should be raised to inferences about types. Its effect is precisely to ensure that no entity is ever assigned more than one fundamental type, even in e.g. arguments by contradiction where we take the hypothesis that x is an element of the empty set ϕ. (As we noted in §5.4.2, the efficient algorithm for typed parsing which we will refer to in §6.5 would not work were this not true; it relies on the fact that once one shows that an object is a NUMBER, one knows that is not also a SET.)

Unfortunately, as we noted, there is a caveat concerning this diagnostic. This caveat in fact comes in the form of two separate problems. First, one can introduce spurious parameters to the premises of the inference; for example, one can form the inference

S is a SET OF $T \vdash \phi$ is a SET OF T.

in which S serves no function but nevertheless licenses the inference according to the above diagnostic. If this were the only problem, we might attempt to reformulate the diagnostic using some variant of relevance logic. Unfortunately, the second problem is more serious. As we noted in §5.4.4, inferential types need not be parametric. A type like SET OF MATRICES is typically assumed to be an instantiation of a parametric type SET OF T, but this need not be the case; as in the example in §5.4.4, we can introduce it directly. Indeed, one can even write, say:

An alpha is a set whose elements are functions.

and

A beta is a set whose elements are matrices.

This sets up the types ALPHA and BETA, whose names makes no reference to sets, functions or matrices. Subsequently, both of the inference rules

$\vdash \phi$ is a ALPHA.

and

$\vdash \phi$ is a BETA.

are licensed by the diagnostic, as no type parameters are used at all. If we then suppose (during an argument by contradiction) that x is an element of ϕ, then type inference will allow us to deduce that x has both of the fundamental types FUNCTION and MATRIX — and this is precisely what we need to avoid at all costs.

Now, one might try to prevent this second problem from arising by banning types like ALPHA and BETA, which are morally instances of a parametric type but constructed as if they were not. Unfortunately, however, a SEQUENCE OF Ts is in the same way morally a special case of something like a FUNCTION FROM NUMBERS TO Ts.[21] Thus, if we ban ALPHA and BETA, we also ban SEQUENCE OF Ts, which is not an option.

We know of no way around this second problem. This is therefore a case where we have an informational gap (§1.2.3). The reason why this is not as serious as one might expect is that there are very few inferential types in mathematics; the main examples are sets, families, functions, sequences, vectors, matrices and (later) categories and functors.[22] Further, these divide into only two classes, namely objects that behave like sets (sets and categories) and objects that behave like functions (families, functions, sequences, vectors, matrices and functors).[23] The inference rules for objects in each class are almost identical; for example, to list the inference rules for vectors one takes the inference rules of functions and specialises them appropriately.

Specifying Inference Rules

We noted in §1.2.3 that wherever we encountered an informational gap, it would be possible to fill in the relevant information by adding a small amount of material to the text. It is therefore incumbent upon us to show that type inference rules can be explicitly stated in this way. We will outline one possible scheme in this section. The gist of the scheme is that we will explicitly insert some mathematical statements in the appropriate texts, phrased in ordinary mathematical language, and describe a method for extracting inference rules from those statements.

---

[21] The qualification 'something like' here is important; a sequence and a function *cannot* be of the same type because they each support notations that the other does not. The mechanisms introduced in Chapter 7 will allow us to define sequences to be things that *behave like* functions without defining them *as* functions, and will therefore preserve the necessary type distinction; cf. §7.5.1 for details.

[22] Structures (like groups and metric spaces) need not be considered separately as they inherit they inferential behaviour from their nature of sets.

[23] If we had considered structures (like groups) to be ordered tuples, then we would also need to deal with a third class of inferential types like ORDERED PAIR OF A SET AND A FUNCTION; but as (in §5.3.3) we adopted an alternative analysis, such types turn out not to be necessary to describe real mathematics. *Homogenous* ordered tuples do occur, but these are just vectors.

Under the scheme, all inference rules fall into one of two classes. Rules of the first class are created by statements that essentially have the form

Let a_1 be a D_1, a_2 a D_2, ... and a_n a D_n.
If $\alpha(a_1, \ldots, a_k, x, a_{k+1}, \ldots, a_n)$, then x is a D'.

where the a_i and x are variables, each D_i is a N$'$ corresponding to the type T_i, D' is a N$'$ corresponding to the type T' and $\alpha(...)$ translates into an atomic semantic predicate $\hat{\alpha}(...)$. The rule created by such a statement is written as:

$e_1 : T_1, e_2 : T_2, e_n : T_n, \hat{\alpha}(e_1, \ldots, e_k, x, e_{k+1}, \ldots, e_n) \vdash x : T'$.

(Note that some of the types T_i may be 'OBJECT', making the restrictions on the corresponding e_i vacuous.) An example of a statement of this kind is given by:

Let A be a set of groups. If x is an element of A, then A is a group.

Here 'set of groups' corresponds to the type SET OF GROUPS, 'group' corresponds to the type GROUP, and 'x is an element of A' translates into the atomic semantic predicate '$in(\mathbf{x}, \mathbf{A})$'. Thus this statement creates the rule:

$e : $ SET OF GROUPS, $in(x, e) \vdash x : $ GROUP.

We should underline the fact that it is only the essential form of the statement that counts; this rule could equally well have been created by the statement

Every element of a set of groups is a group.

Further, whenever an inferential type is created, an inference rule of this first kind is automatically created. For example, consider the statement

A set of groups is a set whose elements are groups.

This statement creates both the type SET OF GROUPS and the inference rule just given in our example. It is worth emphasising that not all inference rules are created when types are created; a counterexample is given by the statement

Let A be a set of groups. If B is an subset of A, then A is a set of groups.

Rules of the second class are created by statements of the form:

Let a_1 be a D_1, a_2 a D_2, ... and a_n a D_n.
Then $f(a_1, \ldots, a_n)$ is a D'.

where the a_i are variables, each D_i is a N$'$ corresponding to the type T_i, D' is a N$'$ corresponding to the type T' and $f(...)$ translates into an semantic term $\hat{f}(...)$. The rule created by such a statement is written as:

$e_1 : T_1, e_2 : T_2, e_n : T_n \vdash \hat{f}(e_1, \ldots, e_n) : T'$

An example of a statement of this kind is given by

If a and b are sets of matrices, then $a \cap b$ is a set of matrices.

Here 'sets of matrices' corresponds to the type SET OF MATRICES, and '$a \cap b$' corresponds to the semantic term $intersect(a, b)$. Thus this statement creates the rule:

$$e : \text{SET OF MATRICES}, e' : \text{SET OF MATRICES}$$
$$\vdash intersect(e, e') : \text{SET OF MATRICES}.$$

It is worth noting that like some of the statements described in §4.1.5, statements which create inference rules have a dual role. On the one hand, they are actual mathematical statements with truth-conditional mathematical content, and should be verified by a reader; on the other hand, they alter the way in which the linguistic theory treats mathematical material.

The actual usage of inference rules during the parsing process will be described in §6.1.

5.4.6   Type Parametrism

If T is a type, then SET OF T and FUNCTION BETWEEN Ts are also types. Types like these, which depend on other types, are standardly described as *parametric* types. Parametric types are barely productive in mathematics; nearly all such types are set up in the foundations.[24]

Perhaps because parametric types primarily occur in foundational material, they are never explicitly introduced; that is, textbooks do not say what it means for something to be a 'set of Ds' (where D denotes 'integer', 'matrix', 'set of sets', etc.). Thus our assumption about mathematical language being idealised (§1.2.3), in the sense of providing definitions for every term used, is violated. In keeping with our general policy, we will describe one possible mechanism for introducing parametric types, chosen so that it fits closely with mathematical language. An example would be as follows:

Definition
Let D be a description. A set of D is a set S s.t. every element of S is a D.

Here 'description' is a synonym for the grammatical category N', chosen to be more natural to mathematicians.

Statements of this kind can introduce many types at once ('SET OF NUMBERS', 'SET OF MATRICES', 'SET OF ELEMENTS OF A RING', 'SET OF SETS', 'SET OF SETS OF SETS', etc.) but the individual types behave just like other

---

[24] Note that GROUP OF T and the like are not independently introduced types; as soon as one has defined SET OF T and GROUP, GROUP OF T automatically comes into being. The details of this process are given in §5.4.8.

types. There is no distinguished behaviour which is caused by parametrism in and of itself.

Similarly, one may have higher-order inference rules being explicitly introduced by assertions like:

Theorem
Let D be a description. Then:
i) If S is a set of D and T is a subset of S, then T is a set of D.
ii) Let S be a set of D and let $P(x)$ be a predicate. Then if $\{x \in S \,|P(x)\}$ exists, it is a set of D.

Again, we treat this as a collection of individual inference rules about specific types.

5.4.7   Subtyping

Every proper type is an *child type* of some other type, called the *parent type*. In the case of fundamental types and relational types, the parent type is always 'OBJECT'; so 'SET', 'NUMBER', 'GROUP', 'ELEMENT OF SOME GROUP', etc. are all child types of 'OBJECT'. In the case of inferential type, the parent type will be the type on which the inferential type is based; so we have e.g.:

- 'SET OF NUMBERS' is a child type of 'SET',
- 'GROUP OF MATRICES' is a child type of 'GROUP',
- 'MATRIX-VALUED FUNCTION' is a child type of 'FUNCTION',
- 'SET OF ELEMENTS OF A RING' is a child type of 'SET' and
- 'SET OF SETS OF NUMBERS' is a child type of 'SET OF SETS'.

We will define the *subtype* relation to be the reflexive transitive closure of the *child type* relation; so, for example, 'SET OF SETS OF NUMBERS' is a subtype of 'SET', and every type is a subtype of 'OBJECT'. Note that every type is considered to be a subtype of itself — when we want to exclude this possibility, we will refer to *proper* subtypes.

5.4.8   Type Coercion

The subtype relation captures many of the relations between types, but there are cases where we need to introduce additional structure. In particular, we may want to treat instances of a type T as if they were instances of a distinct type T' without stating that the former *are* instances of T'. We will refer to this as *type coercion* from T to T'.

The canonical example of type coercion comes from point-set topology; we define the notions of topological space and metric space, each a structure type, as follows:

Definition 3.1.1
A topological space $T = (A, \mathcal{T})$ consists of a non-empty set A together
with a fixed collection $\mathcal{T}$ of subsets of A satisfying:
(T1) $A, \phi \in \mathcal{T}$,
(T2) the intersection of any two sets in $\mathcal{T}$ is [again] in $\mathcal{T}$,
(T3) the union of any collection of sets in $\mathcal{T}$ is [again] in $\mathcal{T}$.
The collection $\mathcal{T}$ is called a topology for A, and the members of $\mathcal{T}$ are
called the open sets of T. Elements of A all called points in the space
T.

Definition A metric on a set A is a nonnegative map $d : A \times A \to \mathbb{R}$
satisfying:
i) For any x, y in A, $d(x, y) = 0 \Leftrightarrow x = y$.
ii) $d(x, y) = d(y, x)$ for all x, y in A.
iii) $d(x, y) + d(y, z) \leq d(x, z)$ for all x, y, z in A.
Definition 2.1.2 A metric space $M = (A, d)$ consists of a nonempty set
A together with a metric d on A.
(Condensed from Sutherland (1975).)

Having set up these concepts, we want to be able to treat metric spaces
as if they are topological spaces. We cannot say that a metric space *is* a
topological space; superficially, this was because they are distinct structure
types so that equality is impossible, but the deeper point is that it is not
possible to introduce a topological space and show that it happens to be a
metric space — the conversion from metric space to topological space loses
information. So a 'type coercion' is required.

In order to set up the desired conversion, one makes an assertion with the
following essential form:

A metric space can be considered as a topological space.

This bare formulation merely asserts that a conversion will be specified;
it needs to be fleshed out with an effective description of the conversion.
Textbooks are typically somewhat informal here, and the idealised version
treated by our theory (§1.2.3) needs to be more precise, as for example in:

Theorem
A metric space (M, d) can be considered as the topological space $(M, \mathcal{T})$,
where $\mathcal{T}$ is the set of open sets of M.
Proof
M and ϕ are trivially open sets of M, and are therefore elements of $\mathcal{T}$.
*[Verify that intersections of pairs of open sets of M are open sets of M, and
likewise for arbitrary unions — typically this is done by referring back to existing theorems. Deduce that the remaining topological space axioms
follow.]* □

Like some of the statements discussed in §4.1.5 and §5.4.5, the assertion of the
theorem above has a dual role. On the one hand, it is an actual mathematical

statement with truth-conditional mathematical content; on the other hand, it alters the way in which the linguistic theory treats mathematical material.

We say that a type T may be coerced to a type T' if there is a finite sequence of types $T, T_0, T_1, \ldots T_n, T'$ such that there is a cast from each type in the sequence to the next. (We need to think in terms of a sequence of individual coercions rather than just making coercion transitive because we will 'minimise' coercion during parsing.)

Structure Types

A structure type T which is constructed out of types T_0, T_1, T_2, ..., and T_n, may always be coerced to the type T_0; this coercion picks out the first element of the structure type 'tuple', discarding the remaining information. (Cf. forgetful functors in category theory.) Returning to our topological space example above:

> **Definition 3.1.1**
> A topological space $T = (A, \mathscr{T})$ consists of a non-empty set A together with a fixed collection $\mathscr{T}$ of subsets of A satisfying...

Following this definition, a topological space can be considered as a set, and the topological space $T = (A, \mathscr{T})$ can be considered as the set A.[25] As a result, topological spaces support set notation — for example, one can write '$x \in T$'.

We will also specify that whenever a structure type T which is constructed out of types T_0, T_1, T_2, ..., and T_n, any inferential types associated with the underlying T_0 are automatically extended to T; thus a GROUP OF MATRICES is simply a GROUP which can be considered as a SET OF MATRICES.

5.5   Types and Type Theory

The system of types that we have set out in this chapter bears a number of surface resemblances to the systems studied formally in *type theory*. For example, notions such as type parametrism (§5.4.6) and type coercion (§5.4.8) are studied extensively in type theory. Despite this, the system we have outlined does not actually fit within the standard formalisms of type theory. In order to substantiate this point, we will need to give a quick overview of certain parts of type theory.

The systems studied in type theory are of two kinds, *structural* and *nominal* (Pierce, 2002, pp. 251–4). Structural type systems contain a collection of

---

[25] Note also that, as in this example, the standard syntax

> A T consists of a T_0 together with a T_1, a T_2, ..., and a T_n.

distinguishes T_0 from the other T_i; this deliberate asymmetry conceptually meshes with the automatic cast to T_0.

atomic *ground types* and various operators which act on types to form new types, such as 'sum' and 'product'. In such systems, whenever one introduces a named complex type, that type is simply an alias for an appropriate combination of ground types using operations; for example, one could define 'Group' to be an alias for the product of ground types 'Set × Function'.

Although structural type systems have historically been the main focus of attention, they turned out to be ill-suited to describing programming languages. This is because most programming languages allow the creation of 'record types', which are like product types except for the fact that two record types are necessarily distinct, even if they consist of the same components. In this respect, the record types of programming languages are similar to the structure types of §5.4.2. Structural type systems are not equipped to treat either of these in a natural way.

Nominal type systems were developed in order to handle record types and similar constructs. The core principle of such systems is that types with distinct names are necessarily distinct. In such a system, one could define 'Group $\simeq$ Set × Function' and also 'Metric Space $\simeq$ Set × Function', and the types 'Group' and 'Metric Space' would necessarily be distinct by virtue of having different names.

For present purposes, the key problem with the nominal approach is it implies that the names of types are unique, i.e. that one never encounters two types with the same name. While this is rare, it does occur. For example, in addition to the familiar rings of algebra, one sometimes encounters a distinct kind of 'ring' in functional analysis or measure theory. More generally, given that maths texts are written by many authors, it is inevitable that collisions of type names will eventually occur. Any descriptive theory of the language of mathematics must cope with this eventuality, just as it must accommodate the existence of many senses of 'prime' (§4.2.2). Stronger, it must resolve ambiguous type names where there is information to do so; for example, it must be able to deduce that a 'Noetherian ring' is necessarily a ring in the algebraic sense. The theory presented in Chapter 6 is fully capable of doing this, so long as we do not preclude the very existence of types with the same name.

Thus neither of the standard approaches from type theory are appropriate for our purposes. The central issue seems to be that type theoretic approaches attempt to present type systems in a timeless way, so that they are more amenable to mathematical analysis. By contrast, our approach involves an irreducible notion of time: when the declaration of a structure type is encountered, a new type is created. We will return to this notion of creation over time in Chapter 7.

6

Typed Parsing

This chapter builds on Chapter 4 and Chapter 5 to describe the combined type inference and parsing procedure needed to interpret and disambiguate mathematics. Although some type-related concepts are used in this chapter, few of the actual technical details from Chapter 5 are needed. In particular, readers need not assimilate the details of the technical presentation of types from §5.4.

In this chapter, we will face some of the hardest problems considered in this book. The first of these relates to the fact that type inference is a notion which is applied to artificial languages, and specifically to computer languages.[1] It is not clear how to extend such notions to natural languages, or even what it would mean to do so. To take one simple example, consider noun phrases. These do not in general denote single entities. It is plausible that a noun phrase like 'the smallest natural number' has the type NUMBER, but what is the type of 'every natural number' or 'some natural number'? Or, worse, what is the type of 'some natural number or set'? Does this have both of the types NUMBER and SET, or neither, or some complicated hybrid type?

The second problem relates to the rich syntax of mathematics. Classical type inference methods, such as the one in Milner (1978), operate on artificial languages with extremely simple syntax. As a result, the interaction of each syntactic rule with the type inference procedure can be manually described. But to describe mathematics, we need a wide range of syntactic rules, both textual and symbolic; and, even more problematically, new syntactic rules will be introduced over time due to adaptivity. Thus manually specifying the interaction of type and syntax is not an option. We will need some novel methods to describe the interaction of type and syntax.

The third problem relates to the interaction between text and symbol. Even if we can say what it means for pieces of textual mathematics to have

---

[1] One of many notions of *type* has been applied to natural languages, and even to mathematics, as we noted in §1.5.1. But this notion of type is unrelated to the one we use to describe mathematics in the previous chapter, or to the kind of type inference we now need to handle; cf. §5.1 and §5.2.

types, how do we give a unified analysis for textual and symbolic material?
How does type information cross the boundary between text and symbol? We
may illustrate these points with respect to the sentence:

> An ideal I in a commutative ring R is prime if and only if the factor ring R/I
> is an integral domain.

In this sentence, type information needs to somehow flow from the word
'ideal' into the symbolic variable I, and then be carried across the textual
structure of the sentence until it reaches the constituent 'R/I', where (in
conjunction with similarly carried information about R) it must predict that
we are dealing with the quotient of a ring by an ideal rather than, say, division
of numbers.[2] There is nothing in the literature that even remotely resembles
this kind of reasoning about information flow inside mixed mathematical
sentences. We will need an entirely new method.

Chapter Structure

We will give a declarative, inefficient, characteristically linguistic formulation
of the typed parsing procedure by describing it as a filter on parses. (A parse
is the pair of a parse tree and the DRS compositionally constructed from
that parse tree.) The essential idea behind this approach is that we start
with the collection of all possible parses for a given sentence, and apply this
filter to sieve out most of them; if just one parse is left, then the sentence is
grammatical.

The better part of the description of the filter will be taken up by a check
that the types have been assigned to the given parses in a valid manner.
§6.1 will describe how to compute the types assigned to a parse, and §6.2 will
describe how to compute the types required to be present within a parse. §6.3
will combine these type assignments and type requirements to form a 'type
filter' on parses, and specify some other simple filters, such as a filter ensuring
that variables are bound; these small filters are then chained together to give
the filter which characterises the typed parsing process. §6.4 will illustrate the
mechanisms presented here using a real sentence that contains both symbolic
and textual ambiguity. §6.5 is a brief note concerning a separate paper we
intend to produce on the algorithms needed to implement the typed parsing
process efficiently.

---

[2] Note that in a more complex example, information about I could even have
determined the syntactic structure of the symbolic constituent. Thus, as noted
in §3.6, we can effectively assign a syntactic category to an object like I in one
part of a sentence and use it in another; there is no parallel to this in any natural
language.

6.1 Type Assignment

In the semantic representation of a sentence, every instance of an element of the category e or E (i.e. discourse referents, variables and terms) is *assigned* a collection of types. It is important to note that this happens on a per-instance basis; that is, we assign types not to a referent x but each place where 'x' occurs inside our DRS.[3]

In some cases types are *intrinsically assigned* to an instance of an element; informally, this means that the element has the said type by virtue of its nature. For example, a DRS term of the form '$sqrt(\bullet)$' (corresponding to the notation '$\sqrt{\bullet}$') always has the type 'NUMBER'. Other types are *externally assigned* by a DRS-condition. For example, a DRS-condition '$ring(\bullet)$' (corresponding to the N' 'ring') externally assigns the type 'RING' to certain objects, as specified later in this section. And, in a few cases, types are *compositionally assigned* to elements with complex internal structure. For example, '$0() \oplus 1()$' (corresponding to '0 and 1') is compositionally assigned the type 'NUMBER'.

In order to introduce some restrictions on external assignment, we will need to recall the notion of command which we introduced in §3.3.5. As command will be one of our central tools in this chapter, we will repeat the relevant definition and example.

We define the relation of *command* between two DRS-conditions to be the smallest relation such that:

- In a DRS of the form $[x_1 \ \ldots \ x_n | \gamma_1; \gamma_2; \ldots; \gamma_n]$, each γ_k commands each of $\gamma_{k+1}, \ldots, \gamma_n$.
- In a DRS-condition of the form $[\ldots | \gamma_1; \gamma_2; \ldots; \gamma_n] \Rightarrow [\ldots | \gamma_1'; \gamma_2'; \ldots; \gamma_m']$, each γ_i commands every γ_j'.
- If γ commands γ', then γ commands any DRS-condition contained within γ' (at any depth).

Note that the command relation is both transitive and irreflexive — it is therefore a (strict) partial ordering on DRS-conditions.

We may illustrate this notion using the sentence:

We can write $\sqrt{2} = a/b$, where $a, b \in \mathbb{N}$ and a and b are relatively prime.

The compositionally constructed DRS for this sentence is:

---

[3] We will follow the standard convention of taking the assignment to be minimal, i.e. we will assume that types are not assigned unless they can be proven to be assigned by some finite application of the rules below.

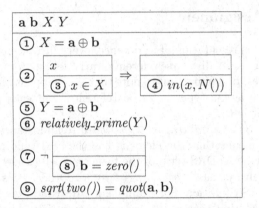

① commands ② – ⑨; ② commands ⑤ – ⑨; ③ commands ④; ④ commands nothing; ⑤ commands ⑥ – ⑨; ⑥ commands ⑦ – ⑨; ⑦ commands ⑨; ⑧ commands nothing; ⑨ commands nothing.

We will always regard the sentence being processed as being merged at the insertion point (§3.5) in the context DRS; one consequence of this is that each of the DRS-conditions belonging (directly) to the context DRS will command all the DRS-conditions of the sentence. So if we have:

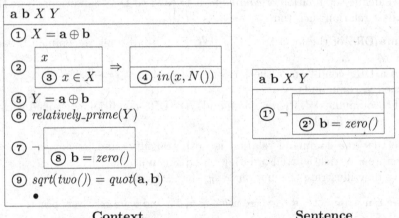

Context   Sentence

then ①, ②, ⑤, ⑥, ⑦ and ⑨ all command ①' and ②'. As promised in §3.5, this allows a unified treatment of intra-sentence and discourse phenomena.

If a DRS-condition γ commands an atomic DRS-condition γ', then we will say that γ *commands* all instances of elements of the categories e or E which are contained within γ' (at any depth). So, the last example, we have that ⑤ commands the instances of **b** in the atomic conditions ⑧, ⑨ and ②', but not the instances of **b** in ① or ⑤ itself.

DRS-conditions can (externally) assign types *for* several reasons, but they always assign types *to* all instances of a particular element which they command (and nothing else). We should emphasise that conceptually, type is applied to instances of an element rather than elements themselves; so above, ⑤ assigns type to certain instances of **b** but not to others. Nevertheless, because it is extremely awkward to repeatedly state that a condition "assigns a type T to all the instances of x which it commands", we will abbreviate this to "assigns T to x". This is emphatically a secondary notion; in order to understand the type system we will always need to look at individual instances of elements.

Occasionally it will be useful to speak of the types assigned to an element without reference to specific instances. To this end, we say that the *final type* assigned to an element in a given DRS is the type which would be assigned to an instance of that element if it were merged to the end of the DRS (as part of a dummy atomic condition). So, for example, the final type assigned to c in

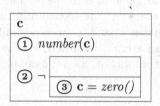

is the type that would be assigned to the instance of **c** in ④ in the modified DRS

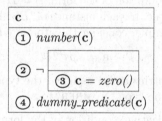

6.1.1 Mechanisms

The complete list of type assignment mechanisms is as follows:

1. **Definitions.** When a Term or NBar is defined (cf. §3.4), it *inherits* all the types assigned to its definiens (i.e. the RHS of the definition) in the circumstances under which the definition applies. For example, consider:

   Definition 2.3.1
   Given a metric space $M = \{A, d\}$, a point a in A and a positive real number ϵ, the open ball about a with radius ϵ, $B_\epsilon(a)$, is the set $\{x \in A \mid d(x, a) < \epsilon\}$.
   Excerpt from (Sutherland, 1975).

   The definiens,

   $$\text{the set } \{x \in A \mid d(x, a) < \epsilon\},$$

has the fundamental type 'SET' and the inferential type 'SET OF POINTS OF METRIC SPACE' (and no further types). So the two phrases being defined, namely the NBar 'open ball [about •] [with radius •]' and the Term '$B_\bullet(\bullet)$', each inherit these two types.

When a new Term is defined, it will be associated with a new DRS function. Any instance of that DRS function will be intrinsically assigned the types inherited by the Term. So, given the definition above, the defined term '$B_\bullet(\bullet)$' would be associated with a DRS function $B\_(\bullet, \bullet)$; and then instances of this function, such as $B\_(\epsilon, one())$, will be intrinsically assigned both of the types 'SET' and 'SET OF POINTS OF METRIC SPACE'.

When new NBar is defined, it will be associated with a new DRS relation — for example, the NBar 'open ball' in the definition above would be associated with '$open\_ball(\bullet, \bullet, \bullet)$'. (The second and third argument positions correspond to the variables 'a' and 'ϵ' in the definition.[4]) Any instance of that DRS relation in an atomic condition will assign the types inherited by the NBar to its first argument. So, for example, the atomic condition

$$open\_ball(\mathbf{b}, \mathbf{x}, \delta)$$

will assign the types 'SET' and 'SET OF POINTS OF METRIC SPACE' to '$\mathbf{b}$' (i.e. to all instances of '$\mathbf{b}$' which it commands).

2. **Equality.** Any DRS-condition of the form '$A = B$' will assign all the types assigned to 'A' to 'B' (i.e. to each instance of 'B' which it commands), and vice versa. So, for example, consider the atomic DRS-condition

$$\mathbf{a} = sqrt(2)$$

Because '$sqrt(2)$' is (intrinsically) assigned the type 'NUMBER', this DRS-condition will assign the type 'NUMBER' to $\mathbf{a}$.

3. **Plurals. i.** Any 'implicative' condition of the form:

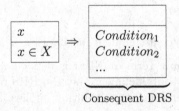

Consequent DRS

will assign the final type of x in the consequent DRS to X. Further, if the entire implicative condition is *commanded by* any condition of the form

---

[4] Note that in many uses of the phrase 'open ball', the centre and radius will not be specified. The semantic representation of such phrases will still use the ternary DRS relation $open\_ball(\bullet, \bullet, \bullet)$, but the second and third slots will be marked as 'gaps'. These gaps are filled in by a separate mechanism described in Chapter 8.3, which discusses the treatment of ellipsis in both textual and symbolic mathematics.

$X = a_1 \oplus a_2 \oplus \cdots \oplus a_n$, then the implicative condition assigns the final type of X to each a_i.[5]

ii. An expression

$$a_1 \oplus a_2 \oplus \cdots \oplus a_n$$

is compositionally assigned any types which are assigned to *all* the a_i. (More precisely: any common supertypes of the types of the a_i are assigned to $a_1 \oplus a_2 \oplus \cdots \oplus a_n$. Thus if we are considering the expression $a_1 \oplus a_2$, a_1 is assigned the type SET and a_2 is assigned the type SET OF NUMBERS, then $a_1 \oplus a_2$ is compositionally assigned the type SET.)

Note in particular that this rule interacts with the above rule governing equality to predict that a condition of the form

$$X = a_1 \oplus a_2 \oplus \cdots \oplus a_n$$

will externally assign any types assigned to *all* the a_i to X.

For example, if we are considering the condition $X = a_1 \oplus a_2$, a_1 is assigned the type SET and a_2 is assigned the type SET OF NUMBERS, then the condition assigns the type SET to X.

4. **Inference.** In §5.4.5, we noted that type inference rules were of two kinds. Rules of the first kind took the form:

$$e_1 : T_1, \; e_2 : T_2, \; e_n : T_n, \; \hat{a}(e_1, \ldots, e_k, x, e_{k+1}, \ldots, e_n) \vdash x : T'.$$

where $\hat{a}$ is an atomic predicate. (Note that some of the types T_i may be 'OBJECT', i.e. may be trivially held by all elements.)

Rules of this kind should be read as formally stating that if in a condition of the form

$$\alpha(e_1, \ldots, e_k, x, e_{k+1}, \ldots, e_n)$$

e_i is assigned the type T_i for each i, then the condition externally assigns the type T' to x. Note that e_i may be arbitrary expressions, but x must be a discourse referent.[6]

---

[5] This last condition requires some justification. It is unique in looking back into the history of previously processed material, and extracting certain relationships from there. Its special status arises from the fact that in a real mathematical text, one knows the type of any 'normal' term as soon as that term is encountered, so that lookback is unnecessary; plural discourse referents are an exception because they can be *aliases* for other objects, and the 'alias' relationship is much stronger than mere equality.

[6] Note we could have formulated this in a stronger way, to say that if any instance of x was *jointly* commanded both by $\hat{\alpha}(e_1, \ldots, e_k, x, e_{k+1}, \ldots, e_n)$ and by conditions assigning the type T_i to e_i for each i, then that instance should be assigned the type T'. In effect, this allows one to e.g. state that x is an element of a set A, later state that A is a set of numbers, and then later still have x treated as a number. We choose not to adopt this stronger formulation as this kind of reasoning does not happen in actual mathematical texts; if a set is a set of numbers, it is invariably known to be a set of numbers as soon as it is introduced.

Rules of the second kind took the form:

$$e_1 : T_1, e_2 : T_2, e_n : T_n \vdash \hat{f}(e_1, \ldots, e_n) : T'$$

where $\hat{f}$ is an atomic function. (Again, some of the types T_i may be 'OBJECT'.)

Rules of this kind should be read as formally stating that if in an expression

$$f(e_1, \ldots, e_n)$$

each sub-expression e_i is assigned the type T_i, then the entire expression is compositionally assigned the type T'.

Note that because command is a (strict) partial ordering, there can never be a cycle of DRS conditions in which each DRS-condition commands the next. As a result, the above mechanisms can only assign a finite amount of type information within any given DRS.

6.1.2   Example

We will illustrate the type assignment mechanisms with reference to our example:

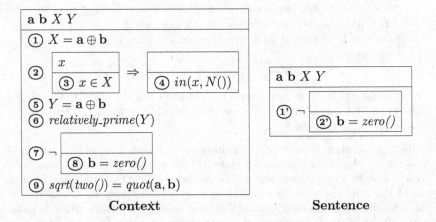

Context   Sentence

The first step is to mark the type assignments which can be obtained from definitions:

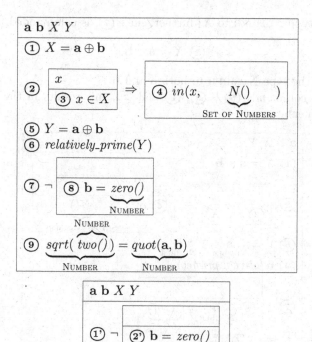

We may now note that the constant $N()$ is the semantic representation of the set $\mathbb{N}$ of natural numbers, and is intrinsically assigned the inferential type 'SET OF NUMBERS'. As we saw in §5.4.5, the statement creating this inferential type also created a type inference rule,

$e :$ SET OF NUMBERS, $in(x, e) \vdash x :$ NUMBER.

This inference rule applies in

$$\text{④}\ in(x, N())$$

so that ④ assigns the type NUMBER to x.

Now, since ④ does not command any conditions, this assignment has no direct effect; but it does ensure that the final type of x in

is NUMBER. This in turn triggers the rule on plurals with the effect that assigns the type NUMBER to X; further, since ② is commanded by

$$① \; X = \mathbf{a} \oplus \mathbf{b},$$

② assigns the type NUMBER to both **a** and **b**.

Since ② commands ⑤ – ⑨, ①' and ②', this results in the following type assignments:

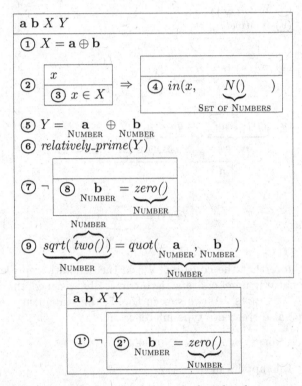

Finally, we apply the second part of the rule for plurals to

$$⑤ \; Y = \underset{\text{NUMBER}}{\mathbf{a}} \oplus \underset{\text{NUMBER}}{\mathbf{b}}$$

to see that ⑤ assigns the type NUMBER to Y; since ⑤ commands ⑥, the final type assignment picture is like the one above but with

$$⑥ \; relatively\_prime(\underset{\text{NUMBER}}{Y})$$

in place of ⑥ $relatively\_prime(Y)$.

6.2 Type Requirements

Whenever a new DRS relation or function is created by definition, any slot arising from a variable in the definition is annotated with the type of that variable. If the variable has more than one type, we require that one of the types is a subtype of all the other types, and this maximally specific type is used to annotate the definition. We can illustrate this by returning to our example from 6.1:

Definition 2.3.1
Given a metric space $M = \{A, d\}$, a point a in A and a positive real number ϵ, the open ball about a with radius ϵ, $B_\epsilon(a)$, is the set $\{x \in A \mid d(x, a) < \epsilon\}$.
(Sutherland, 1975)

'a' has the type POINT OF METRIC SPACE and 'ϵ' has the type NUMBER. The new DRS relation, $open\_ball(\bullet, \bullet, \bullet)$, is therefore annotated as:

$$open\_ball(\bullet, \underset{\text{REQ:PointOfMetricSpace}}{\bullet}, \underset{\text{REQ:Number}}{\bullet})$$

If the types of a variable have no common subtype, the definition is illegitimate.

It is worth noting that the only slots which do not arise from variables are the first arguments of DRS relations arising from NBars; thus all other slots are marked with type requirements. These requirements may be vacuous for the few positions accepting any mathematical object, such as the first argument of the set membership notation '$\bullet \in \bullet$'. We still annotate the corresponding DRS function or relation with a null requirement by writing 'REQ:OBJECT'; this serves to distinguish DRSs that are annotated with requirements from those that are not.

6.3 Parsing

The parsing process works as follows: we start with the collection of all context-free parses which have the correct terminal string, and we successively pare down this collection by a series of operations. If there are no parses at the end of this process the sentence is ungrammatical; if there is just one parse the sentence is grammatical and unambiguous; and if there are two or more parses the sentence is ambiguous.

The operations used in parsing are as follows:

1. **Type.**
2. **Variables.**
 2.1. No free variables.
 2.2. No multiple binding.
 2.3. No spurious binders.
3. **Structural Disambiguation.**
4. **Type Cast Minimisation.**
5. **Symmetry Breaking.**

We will express many of these operations as constraints; it should be taken as read that those parses which do not satisfy the constraint are discarded.

6.3.1   Type

Given a parse, we compute type assignments (§6.1) and type requirements (§6.2) on that parse. If any type requirement is not fulfilled by a corresponding type assignment, we discard the original parse.

Note that an assigned type need not exactly match the type requirements to fulfil it; its suffices that the assigned type is a subtype of the required type. Thus an assignment of the type SET OF NUMBERS can fulfil a requirement for the type SET. Similarly, types may be assigned where they are not required; such superfluous assignment is ignored.

6.3.2   Variables

1. **No free variables.**

   Every occurrence of a variable must be bound.

   Note that variables may be introduced in 'let'-statements or syntactic variants thereof (§2.5, §3.5). Such variables are introduced into the context DRS and so will be bound whenever they occur in a sentence.

2. **No multiple binding.**

   If a variable is bound twice within a given sentence, the binding domains must be disjoint.

   This rules out examples like

   Then for all $a > 0$, for all $a > 0$, $f(a) \leq 0$.

   (Cf. also §4.3.2.)

3. **No spurious binders.**

   Whenever a variable is bound, that variable must occur at least once inside the binding domain of the binder.

   This rules out examples like

   Then for all $a < 0$, $\mathbb{N} \subset \mathbb{R}$.

   in which the variable binding serves no purpose.

6.3.3 Structural Disambiguation

As we noted in §4.2.3, there are disambiguation conventions specific to textual mathematics. For example, 'P and Q or R' means '(P and Q) or R'.

Such rules are implemented during parsing process by means of filters that discard parses with the incorrect form, in this case those with the structure 'P and (Q or R)'. One crucial point is that this filter must discard such trees even if the corresponding 'correct' tree with the form '(P and Q) or R' does not exist. In other words, the filter considers each tree in isolation; we say that it acts *pointwise* rather than being *comparative*. The reason is that the 'correct' tree might have been ungrammatical for some unrelated reason, and have been ruled out by another filter. Whether or not this is the case, our original tree remains ungrammatical. If our filter had acted comparatively, then changing the order in which filters acted might have changed the end result, which would be a clear error.[7]

Additionally, all of the disambiguation conventions for symbolic mathematics (§4.1.5) are assimilated as filters which behave just as the textual filter just described. In particular, they operate pointwise, removing incorrect parses even if the 'correct' parse has been removed for some other reason.

6.3.4 Type Cast Minimisation

If α and β are parses, and the type casts in α are a strict subset of the type casts in β, then we discard α in favour of β. Note that the individual type casts must exactly match – they must be casts of the same instances of the same terms. (Equivalently, they are must be type casts of the same group of terminal symbols interpreted in the same way.)

6.3.5 Symmetry Breaking

In some cases one will find that even after application of all of the operations listed above, a sentence remains ambiguous but that the ambiguity is *spurious* — i.e. it is a syntactic ambiguity which happens not to affect the meaning of the sentence. An example of this phenomenon is:

Then $f(0) = 0$ and $f(x) \neq 0$ for $x \neq 0$.

which can be read either as

Then $f(0) = 0$ and $(f(x) \neq 0$ for $x \neq 0)$.

or

Then $(f(0) = 0$ and $f(x) \neq 0)$ for $x \neq 0$.

---

[7] More pithily: pointwise filters commute.

In this case the ambiguity relating to the scope of the binder 'for' has no effect on the meaning of the sentence. When such situations are detected, we may break symmetry and choose a reading at random.

6.4 Example

We will illustrate the preceding theory with respect to the sentence,

> An ideal I in a commutative ring R is prime if and only if the factor ring R/I is an integral domain.

For simplicity's sake, we will focus on the ambiguity due to the existence of different mathematical senses for the word 'prime', ignoring other ambiguities. We will also consider only two senses of that word, corresponding to 'prime number' and 'prime ideal'.

As discussed in §3.6, the lexical ambiguity of the word 'prime' is represented by having two separate rules in the grammar, containing distinct semantic predicates:

$$
\mathrm{AP}_{dist} \rightarrow \mathbf{prime} \quad \left\{ \lambda x. \begin{array}{|c|} \hline \\ :e \quad \fbox{$prime\_ofnumber(x)$} \\ \hline \end{array} \right\}
$$

$$
\mathrm{AP}_{dist} \rightarrow \mathbf{prime} \quad \left\{ \lambda x. \begin{array}{|c|} \hline \\ :e \quad \fbox{$prime\_ofideal(x)$} \\ \hline \end{array} \right\}
$$

When we compositionally construct the semantic representation of our sentence, the word sense ambiguity results in the creation of two distinct DRSs. The one corresponding to the 'ideal' reading is:

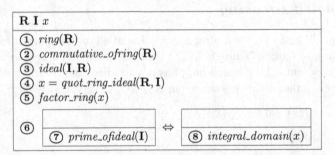

The relations '$ring(\bullet)$' and '$ideal(\bullet, \bullet)$' arise from NBars, and therefore assign types ('RING' and 'IDEAL', respectively) to their first arguments. Thus ① assigns the type RING to $\mathbf{R}$, and ③ assigns the type IDEAL to $\mathbf{I}$. Since ① commands ② – ⑧ and ③ commands ④ – ⑧, we have the following type assignments:

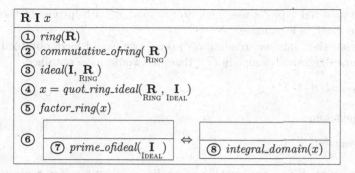

Further, $quot\_ring\_ideal(\bullet, \bullet)$ corresponds to a Term and is intrinsically assigned the type RING. Statement ④ is an equality and therefore assigns this type to x, yielding:

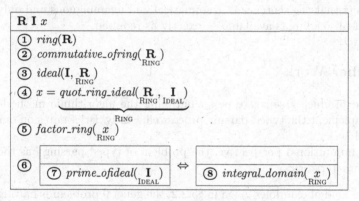

(Statements ⑤ and ⑧ also assign the type RING to x, but this assignment is redundant.)

These are all the types assigned in this DRS. Following the rules from §6.2 tells us that the type requirements are as follows:

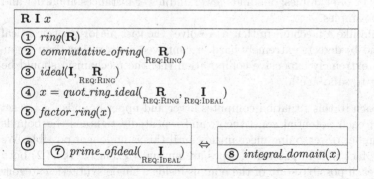

Each of the required types is assigned. So the reading with 'prime' in the sense of 'prime ideal' is legitimate.

If we had used the 'number' reading of 'prime', we would have obtained exactly the same diagrams, except in ⑦; there we would have obtained

⑦ $prime\_ofnumber(\underset{\text{IDEAL}}{\mathbf{I}}$)

in the assignments and

⑦ $prime\_ofnumber(\underset{\text{REQ:NUMBER}}{\mathbf{I}}$)

in the requirements. Since an IDEAL cannot be a NUMBER (for reasons discussed in §5.4.2), this reading is illegitimate.

Thus the theory given here rules out the 'prime number' reading and accepts the 'prime ideal' reading. Since exactly one reading remains, the theory predicts that the sentence is grammatical and unambiguous and only the 'prime ideal' reading is available — exactly as required.

6.5 Further Work

We intend to produce a separate paper outlining the algorithmic methods needed to implement the typed parsing process efficiently. Brief notes on our approach follow.

From a computational perspective, the problem of typed parsing has the following characteristics:

1. Due to the kind of examples given in §5.2.2, the general problem is halting equivalent.
2. There is no hard, uniform upper bound on the amount of computation that is required to resolve examples that occur *in practice*.
3. However, amount of computation required tails off rapidly relative to the complexity of examples; one finds fewer and fewer instances of harder and harder examples.
4. We would like a mechanism that a) resolves the vast majority of practical cases and b) detects extremely hard or contrived cases rather than beginning an extremely expensive computation (i.e. the mechanism should be 'resilient to sabotage').

Our approach to this situation computes lower and upper bounds for the set of types of each potential constituent, and repeatedly tightens the bounds using a number of reasoning mechanisms until this is no longer possible. We exploit the fact that fundamental types are mutually exclusive (§5.4.2) both to encode each possible state of the bounds inside a single syntactic category and to make strong inferences about bounds, making the entire process

extremely rapid. In all the difficult but realistic examples we have studied, all
pairs of bounds converge and types are completely determined; in artificially
hard examples like that given in §5.2.2, some upper and lower bounds will
diverge in reasonable time. The mechanisms used to make inferences about
bounds are specified orthogonally to the tracking of the bounds, and can
therefore be adjusted easily if harder examples are found in some particular
area of mathematics, although our preliminary analysis suggests that this
will not be necessary.

7

Foundations

In §5.3, we noted that type distinctions among various elementary objects were needed in order to avoid two linguistic problems. The first of these was *notational collision*; we saw that if we took, say, natural numbers and sets to be of the same type, then our theory incorrectly predicted that expressions like '1 + 1' had multiple readings. Constructing this type distinction was hard because the standard foundational account defines natural numbers *as* sets. The second problem was that of *unwarranted distinctions*; we saw, for example, that the actual use of mathematical language required real numbers and complex numbers to be of the same type in order to assign a reading to an expression such as '$zz^* < 1$'. Preventing a type distinction here was difficult because the standard foundational account defines complex numbers as particular structures containing real numbers.

In order to resolve these problems, we promised to reconstruct the foundations of mathematics so that natural numbers were not sets and real numbers were complex numbers. This chapter presents that promised reconstruction. We will approach this as an interesting problem in its own right, rather than as merely as an obstacle to our linguistic theory. Thus the question we will ask and answer is not, 'how should numbers be constructed?', but rather, 'what are the legitimate mathematical operations needed to give a satisfactory account of the foundations of mathematics?'. Similarly, our approach will widen to cover far more than the two concerns that led us here; these form only the tip of an iceberg of issues in the foundations of mathematics. Some of these issues, including notational collision and unwarranted distinctions, are directly linguistic; some are philosophical, including particularly a famous criticism of the foundations raised in Benacerraf (1965); yet others relate to how a theory should be constructed in order to have the best chance of characterising mathematics that we are not ourselves aware of, or even mathematics that does not yet exist.

This chapter is structured as follows. In §7.1, we will explain why our approach to mathematics in the foundations is slightly different to our approach to the rest of mathematics; in doing so, we will explain why we did not simply make NUMBER and SET into non-extensional types in accordance with our strategy for handling the other problems encountered in Chapter 5.

Subsequently, in §7.2, we will discuss and criticise all of the standard approaches to the foundations of mathematics, noting the particular problems encountered by each one. While doing this, we will introduce a novel notion of *ontogeny* in mathematics, relating to the way in which an individual mathematician's representation of mathematics changes as more mathematics is learnt. The ontogenetic perspective will be our most important tool in the remainder of the chapter. It will give us novel insights in many situations, and we consider it to be the most important contribution of the chapter; indeed, it is not too much of a stretch to say that the entire chapter should be considered as an illustrative application of ontogeny.

§7.3 will then extract from the discussion of inadequate approaches a concise account of the particular difficulties that any account of the foundations of mathematics must overcome. In particular, it will note that stating that mathematical objects such as numbers *are* sets causes one fatal problem, and stating that such objects *are not* sets causes another fatal problem. It will also underline the role that some notion of identification must play in any account of the foundations, and will recapitulate the difficulties involved in giving a successful account of identification. Finally, it will emphasise the importance of ontogeny and note the numerous ways in which this constrains any theory of the foundations.

§7.4 will then introduce the three formal mechanisms which we will use to give an adequate account of the foundations. Subsequently §7.5 will present the development of a large part of the foundations of mathematics using these mechanisms. In the course of these two sections we will highlight and illustrate the way in which our theory overcomes the problems outlined in §7.3

Finally, §7.6 outlines projected further work based on the philosophical implications of the material given in this chapter.

7.1 Approach

The status of the foundations is different from the status of the remainder of mathematics. The easiest way to see this is to look at the formal definition of a function:

DEFINITION. Let A and B be sets. A *function* $f : A \to B$ is a subset f of $A \times B$ such that
(F1) If $x \in A$ there exists $y \in B$ such that $(x,y) \in f$.
(F2) Such an element y is unique: in other words, if $x \in A$ and $y, z \in B$ are such that $(x,y) \in f$ and $(x,z) \in f$, it follows that $y = z$.

(Stewart and Tall, 1977, p. 86)

Essentially the same definition is given in every textbook.[1] One consequence of this definition is that the co-domain is not an (extensional) property of a function; the definition predicts, for example, that

$$f : \mathbb{Z} \to \mathbb{Z} \qquad x \mapsto x^2$$

and

$$f' : \mathbb{Z} \to \mathbb{N} \qquad x \mapsto x^2$$

are one and the same function.[2] Yet no mathematician actually believes that these two functions are the same, or manipulates them as if they were.

The key fact here is the status of the mismatch between formal predictions and belief. If our beliefs about, say, sheaves do not match with the definition of a sheaf, then our beliefs are wrong. But when our beliefs about functions do not match with the definition of a function, it is the definition that is wrong. More generally, sufficiently advanced mathematics proceeds inductively from definitions, so that the definitions are the final arbiter of truth. But definitions in the foundations are post hoc rationalisations, formal constructs created to mimic the objects that we study in pre-formal 'high school' mathematics, such as numbers and functions. Despite this conceit about formality, we often continue to manipulate our pre-formal objects; that is, we continue to treat functions as if they had co-domains, and so on.[3] As a result, formal definitions in the foundations can genuinely fail to match with the actual mathematics.

This mismatch between concepts in foundational mathematics and their formalisations causes us to adopt a stance towards the foundations of mathematics which differs from our stance towards the remainder of mathematics. Elsewhere, we took it as read that mathematics was precisely that which was found in mathematical texts, and our purpose was to model this as faithfully as possible. In the foundations, we consider our task to be the construction of a formal theory that matches mathematicians' actual intuitions as closely as possible. To give a very specific example, working in the foundations, we consider ourselves licensed to *replace* the above definition of the function with one which does state that functions have co-domains. The key fact underpinning this is our belief that few mathematicians would object to this emendation if the deficiency in the definition above was pointed out to them.

This difference in approach does not license us to completely discard existing material; we will still exert considerable effort to stay as close to standard formal accounts as possible. (One might say that our concern is to

---

[1] See, for example, (Enderton, 1977, p. 42), (Halmos, 1960, p. 30), (Hamilton, 1982, p. 83), (Henle, 1986, p. 12), (Schumacher, 1996, p. 104) or (van Dalen et al., 1978, p. 58).

[2] As far as we are aware, this observation is novel.

[3] Often our pre-formal concepts are adjusted or refined during formalisation. For example, the pre-formal concept of a function might not encompass functions that cannot be written down. For present purposes, the key point is that there is a sharp difference between cases where pre-formal notions influence the way in which we manipulate objects, and other cases.

repair the foundations rather than to completely reconstruct them.) Nevertheless, this difference in emphasis can tip the scale regarding certain problems. For example, in Chapter 5, we encountered a number of problems which were similar to notational collision and the existence of unwarranted distinctions in the foundations, in that they arose from mismatches between our type system and the properties of the underlying mathematics. Our general approach to this was to make our types non-extensional; for example, we took the type 'SET OF NATURAL NUMBERS' to mean something different from the property 'is a set of natural numbers'. We could have resolved our foundational problems by taking a comparably non-extensional approach, taking e.g. the type 'NATURAL NUMBER' to mean something different from the property 'is a natural number'. The fundamental reason why we did not choose to do this, and chose to adjust the foundations instead, is because no mathematician genuinely *believes* that natural numbers are sets.[4]

Finally, we should note that we do not claim to be doing mathematics, or consider any of the material presented here to have *mathematical* significance: mathematicians' existing intuitions about the foundations are adequate for doing mathematics, and in that respect nothing more is required. Our purpose is rather to develop a foundational account which is precise enough to satisfy linguists and philosophers of mathematics. In this regard, we should also note that when we criticise foundational textbooks, we are doing so from a linguistic or philosophical perspective; we are not attempting to assert that these textbooks should be rewritten. The primary function of these textbooks is to convey certain mathematical ideas to their readers; as long as they succeed in doing so, the means which they use to do so are not a concern, at least to mathematicians.

7.2   False Starts

This section considers a number of standard approaches to the foundations of mathematics, and outlines the ways in which each such approach is inadequate or incorrect.

7.2.1   All Objects as Sets

The classical viewpoint has it that all mathematical objects, including numbers of every kind, are sets.[5] Under this view, the natural number 0 is just

---

[4] We should however note that once one has a theory that makes the correct linguistic predictions, the distinction between intension and extension is largely a matter of choice; a determined reader could take the material in this chapter and reinterpret it so that co-domains, and all other loci of mismatch between formal and intuitive, were handled intensionally.

[5] Cf. 'Since the Second World War, the dominant position on the foundations of mathematics has been the view that mathematics should be thought of as formalised in some extension of Zermelo-Fraenkel axiomatic set theory ZFC (including the axiom of choice).' (Grattan-Guinness, 2003, p. 680).

the empty set ϕ; the natural number 1 is the set $\{0\} = \{\phi\}$; the natural number 2 is the set $\{0, 1\} = \{\phi, \{\phi\}\}$; and so on.[6]

This viewpoint is problematic. We have already noted that it is difficult to reconcile it with the actual use of mathematical language (§5.3.1). More specifically, we saw that it caused *notational collision*. For example, although 0 is ϕ and 1 is $\{\phi\}$, '$0 + 1$' means something different from '$\phi + \{\phi\}$'. (Similar clashes occur with many intuitive kinds of objects.) It has also come under considerable criticism from philosophers of mathematics. In a famous paper (Benacerraf, 1965), Benacerraf argued that the existence of distinct methods for constructing natural numbers from sets, together with the fact that mathematicians using different methods could communicate about natural numbers without difficulty, meant that natural numbers could not be sets.

Most modern mathematics textbooks pay lip service to this observation, in that natural numbers are defined with appropriate hedging. But the underlying point of Benacerraf's objection has not been assimilated; a vast majority of the objects that Benacerraf's argument applies to are still constructed in an entirely concrete way. For example, as we noted above, a function is invariably defined in the following way:

DEFINITION. Let A and B be sets. A *function* $f : A \to B$ is a subset f of $A \times B$ such that
(F1) If $x \in A$ there exists $y \in B$ such that $(x, y) \in f$.
(F2) Such an element y is unique: in other words, if $x \in A$ and $y, z \in B$ are such that $(x, y) \in f$ and $(x, z) \in f$, it follows that $y = z$.

(Stewart and Tall, 1977, p. 86)

Yet alternative definitions are certainly possible; for example, one could reverse the order of elements in the ordered pairs, writing '$(y, x) \in f$' in place of '$(x, y) \in f$' (and so on). Because working mathematicians never treat functions as sets, mathematicians using different definitions remain able to communicate, and Benacerraf's objection applies. Thus the standard definitions of many mathematical objects remain problematic from a philosophical perspective.

We will encounter these linguistic and philosophical criticisms again. Notational collisions occur wherever there is a gap between the way we think of objects and the way in which they are formally defined. Benacerraf's criticism applies wherever objects are explicitly constructed out of simpler objects, and some details of the exact construction are irrelevant. Most instances of both of these phenomena apply to cases where simple objects that we intuitively think of as being *sui generis* (i.e. as being of their own kind rather than being instances of other kinds of object), such as numbers, are formally defined via explicit construction. (Note that in such cases, many details of the construction are necessarily irrelevant.) As a result, the two criticisms tend to occur hand-in-hand.

---

[6] Cf. Halmos (1960), pp. 43–44.

We may also add a final, simple criticism of viewpoint under discussion. It implies that it is not possible to learn formally about, say, natural numbers without knowing about sets. This implication is slightly unsettling. We will shortly come to introduce a concept called 'ontogeny', and to present this criticism as an example of the use of that concept (§7.2.5).

7.2.2   Hierarchy of Numbers

There are two standard ways of defining the larger classes of numbers (i.e. integers, rationals, real numbers and complex numbers). We will present the simpler and more widespread approach here, and leave the more sophisticated approach to §7.2.7.

Under this simpler approach, each kind of number is directly constructed out of the previous kind using tools such as ordered pairs, relations and equivalence classes, themselves constructed as specific sets via the approach of §7.2.1. This is easiest to illustrate with an example:

> Let $a, b, c, d \in \mathbb{N}$. We say that (a, b) is related to (c, d), written $(a, b) \Diamond (c, d)$, if $a + d = b + c$.
>
> *[Proof that $\Diamond$ is an equivalence relation.]*
>
> We define the integers to be equivalence classes under the relation $\Diamond$. As an example, the set $\{(a, b) : a + 1 = b\}$ is an equivalence class (it is the class determined by $(0, 1)$), and we are defining the integer -1 to be this set.
>
> (Hamilton, 1982, p. 12–13)

Even if we assume that the problems of §7.2.1 have been solved, so that ordered pairs, etc. are not sets, a number of problems occur. One can give alternative constructions for each kind of number; for example, we could just reverse the order of elements in the ordered pairs. As mathematicians using different constructions remain able to communicate, Benacerraf's criticism still applies. Also, as many different kinds of object are constructed using equivalence classes and ordered pairs,[7] objects of different intuitive types may 'turn out' to be equal, again causing notational collision. But in this case, there is also a second linguistic issue, distinct from notational collision.

Under the very explicit kinds of construction that we are using, natural numbers are not integers, integers are not rational numbers, and so on. For example, under the standard construction, the integer 3 (or '$3_{\mathbb{Z}}$') is equal to the equivalence class $[(3_{\mathbb{N}}, 0_{\mathbb{N}})]$, which is distinct from $3_{\mathbb{N}}$. Yet, as we saw in §5.3.2, mathematical usage consistently treats the two as the same object. Thus our linguistic theories posit *unwarranted distinctions*.

---

[7] For example, quotients of many kinds are constructed using equivalence classes and, under the standard account, structures such as groups and metric spaces are constructed as ordered tuples. We use a different analysis of structures precisely to avoid notational collision; essentially, we eliminate the 'tuples' during interpretation by having each structure take up multiple slots in the functions and predicates of the semantic representation. (Cf. §5.3.3.)

Note that in a loose sense, this is the 'dual' problem to notational collision. Notational collision covers cases where the formalism treats objects that should be distinct as equal; here the formalism treats objects that should be equal as distinct. In both cases, a disparity between the way we think about mathematical objects and the way they are formally defined causes our linguistic theories to make incorrect predictions. In order to obtain the correct predictions about language, we need to make sure that the formal situation matches actual usage.

Mathematicians are more aware of the issues here than when handling, for example, notational collision. Cf.:

> The above is only a temporary warning, however. Once the properties of integers have been derived from the properties of natural numbers, we can forget about the apparatus of construction, and treat integers in the intuitive way that we are accustomed to. Part of this intuition is the idea that $\mathbb{N}$ is a subset of $\mathbb{Z}$, i.e. that natural numbers are just non-negative integers. Our construction of $\mathbb{Z}$ renders this convenient idea false. However, we may recover the situation by the following process. [...]
>
> (Hamilton, 1982, p. 16)

(The 'process' detailed by Hamilton will be discussed in §7.2.6.)

Hamilton's explicitness is unusual. Most authors signal their awareness in more implicit way, by making statements like:[8]

> [...] each such special complex number $(x, 0)$ is simply to be identified with the corresponding real number x.
>
> (Birkhoff and Mac Lane, 1941, p. 109)

The key notion in this excerpt is that of *identification*. Identification is not confined to the number systems, but is found throughout mathematics. For example, one sometimes identifies an integral domain with part of its field of fractions, a metric space with part of its completion or a field with part of its algebraic closure. In general, when one wants to 'close' a set under some operation (such as subtraction, division, convergence of sequences, or taking the root of a polynomial), it is conventional to first construct the closure under that operation and then identify the original set with the appropriate part of the closure.

The actual term 'identify' is not always used in mathematical texts. For example, Enderton states that 'we will streamline our notation by omitting the subscript "Z" on $+_Z$, [...], etc.' (Enderton, 1977, p. 101) and Stoll remarks that 'we agree to adopt names of representatives (that is, members) of rational numbers as names of rational numbers' (Stoll, 1979, p. 141). But the effect of these circumlocutions is the same: one removes an unwarranted distinction

---

[8] Often such remarks are preceded by the formulaic phrase, 'by abuse of language', signalling an underlying linguistic convention which is not spelt out.

by in some fashion obliterating the difference between two kinds of object. Henceforth, we will refer to this operation as identification, regardless of the exact locution used.

The explicitly declared operation of identification is an important source for us. If we could pin down its formal effect, we might be able to 'neutralise' the unwarranted distinctions. Thus we will aim to determine the exact effect of identification on the language of mathematics, and to separate legal and illegal usages. (For example, what is it that makes the above legitimate but 'we will now identify 0 with 1' illegitimate?)

The simplest and most natural approach would be to take identification as the addition of an axiom asserting that the relevant objects are the same. This is troubling from an epistemological perspective,[9] as one does not want to expand the collection of axioms which underpins mathematics — but for the moment, we will leave that worry aside and concentrate on seeing whether the approach might work. A concrete example of the effect of this approach would be to add the assertion that

$$3_{\mathbb{N}} = 3_{\mathbb{Z}}$$

to the language. That is, we need to assert that

$$3_{\mathbb{N}} = [(3_{\mathbb{N}}, 0_{\mathbb{N}})].$$

If we take equivalence classes and ordered pairs to be sets, this assertion violates the Axiom of Foundation. Even if we do not, it remains extremely problematic; for example, it entails the fact that there are certain mathematical objects which cannot be constructed as sets.

Thus this notion of 'identification as equality' is not viable, and the problem of unwarranted distinctions persists. Another simplistic approach to identification will be ruled out in §7.2.4. Subsequently, in §7.2.5, §7.2.6 and §7.2.7, we will consider two methods mathematicians sometimes use to try and eliminate unwarranted distinctions without relying on identification, and illustrate the ways in which these are inadequate. In the course of these sections we will build up more sophisticated conceptual tools which we will use to consider and rule out a subtler analysis of identification than the one given here (§7.2.9); and eventually, we will come to hone and utilise a specific formal

---

[9] Epistemology is the study of knowledge and especially of the bases on which we can have knowledge. In a mathematical setting, epistemology focuses particularly on the axioms from which all other mathematical facts are deduced. It encompasses questions of two kinds. First there are questions internal to mathematics, such as the question of which axioms are necessary to build up mathematics. Second there are external questions, such as the question of how we can have knowledge of those axioms. In this book we are only concerned with the former. More specifically, given our conservative approach (§7.1), we will need to ensure that any foundational approach we develop rests on the standard ZF(C) axioms. This issue is discussed further in §7.3.1.

notion of identification as part of a general solution to the problems faced in this chapter (§7.4.2).

7.2.3 Summary of Standard Picture

The standard ontological picture of mathematics is taken by combining the approaches given in the last two sections,[10] i.e., taking all mathematical objects to be sets, and taking each class of numbers to be constructed using ordered pairs, etc.. It gives an ontology that is markedly different from the actual ontology which mathematicians believe in and which their use of language reflects, as Figure 7.1 indicates:

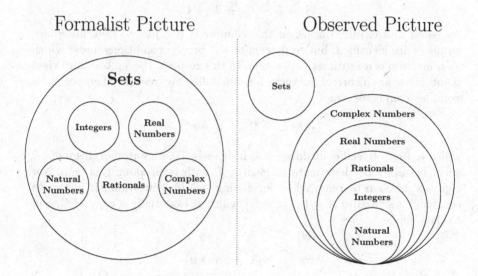

Fig. 7.1 The Ontology of Mathematics

---

[10] Ontology is the study of what objects exist. In mathematical setting, it reduces to the study of what mathematical objects exist. As with epistemology (cf. footnote 9), it encompasses questions of two kinds. First there are questions internal to mathematics, such as the question of what kinds of mathematical objects (numbers, sets, etc.) we need to posit in order to develop mathematics. Second, there are external questions, such as the question of whether any of these mathematical objects 'really' exists. In this book we are only concerned with the internal questions. More specifically, we will ask what kinds of mathematical objects exist, and how they relate to each other. This includes particularly questions asking whether one kind of mathematical object is a special case of another kind; for example, the question of whether numbers are sets. We will return to these issues in §7.3.1.

7.2.4 *Invisible Embeddings*

Another approach that is sometimes taken is to state that (sets of) objects which are 'identified' remain distinct, and that identification actually consists of the provision of an embedding connecting them.[11],[12] These embeddings are *invisible*, i.e. are never realised in actual mathematical notation.

Under this view, natural numbers are entirely distinct from integers, and 'identification' of natural numbers and integers consists of the provision of an isomorphic embedding from the set of natural numbers into the set of integers. Thus one has not

$$\mathbb{N} \subset \mathbb{Z} \subset \mathbb{Q} \subset \mathbb{R} \subset \mathbb{C}$$

but rather

$$\mathbb{N} \overset{i_0}{\hookrightarrow} \mathbb{Z} \overset{i_1}{\hookrightarrow} \mathbb{Q} \overset{i_2}{\hookrightarrow} \mathbb{R} \overset{i_3}{\hookrightarrow} \mathbb{C}.$$

As noted above, our concern in this chapter is not just to determine how numbers are identified, but to determine the precise conditions under which identification is a legitimate operation. In this respect, the 'embedding' viewpoint gives an incorrect account for the following reason: there exists a 'complex conjugate' map

$$\Theta : \mathbb{C} \to \mathbb{C} \qquad z \mapsto z^*$$

which is a non-trivial embedding of $\mathbb{C}$ into itself (i.e. an automorphism of $\mathbb{C}$); yet it certainly not legitimate to identify $\mathbb{C}$ with itself along this map. Nor can this problem be removed by forbidding 'self-identification'. It is easy to construct a structure $A = \{a_z \mid z \in \mathbb{C}\}$ which is essentially a copy of $\mathbb{C}$, and to then define

$$\Theta_1 : \mathbb{C} \to \mathbb{A} \qquad z \mapsto a_z$$

$$\Theta_2 : \mathbb{C} \to \mathbb{A} \qquad z \mapsto a_{z^*}$$

If we do this, one may either identify A with $\mathbb{C}$ along Θ_1, or make that identification along Θ_2, but not both — so we have two locally legitimate identifications which cannot be combined in a global way. Excluding examples of the kind we have just given will be an ongoing concern in the remainder of this chapter.

Digressing briefly, we may note that our counterexample using a non-trivial automorphism of $\mathbb{C}$ is indebted to an observation in Burgess (1999), noting

---

[11] For example, Schumacher (1996) advocates precisely this approach. Stewart and Tall (1977) discusses both this approach and the one given in §7.2.7. Category theorists often favour this approach, although surprisingly, in Birkhoff and Mac Lane (1941) Saunders Mac Lane prefers the approach given in §7.2.7.

[12] An embedding is an injective map which preserves some structure; the exact structure to be preserved is determined by the context.

that the existence of this automorphism presents a problem for the version of *ante rem* structuralism presented in Shapiro (1997).[13] This is not coincidental: the notion of identification which we develop in this chapter is connected to structuralist positions in the philosophy of mathematics. We intend to discuss this connection in further work, described briefly in §7.6. We should also emphasise that this approach does nothing to solve either Benacerraf's criticism or our problem of notational collisions; it is narrowly focused on removing unwarranted distinctions by making sense of identification. In fact, in the presence of the concrete constructions that cause both Benacerraf's phenomenon and notational collisions, this approach exhibits an additional problem. If, say, $\mathbb{R}$ and $\mathbb{C}$ are defined as sets in the usual concrete manner, then they have structure as sets of equivalence classes above and beyond their arithmetical structure. Yet when checking that a given map is an embedding, we need to ignore this kind of structure. Although any mathematician can intuitively see which kinds of structure need to be checked and which do not, finding a general principle that predicts this is difficult. (The essential reason for this is the considerable gap between the intuitive conceptions of $\mathbb{R}$, etc. and their realisation as concrete constructions.)

Even if we leave aside the problems noted above, the 'invisible embeddings' viewpoint remains unsatisfactory from a linguistic viewpoint because it does not predict where the invisible embeddings need to be inserted. Specifying this in a general way is difficult because there are many instances where numbers from a larger class turn out to lie in some smaller class due to idiosyncratic properties. (In such cases, the inverse of the embedding needs to be inserted.) For example,

Therefore $zz^* < 1$

needs to be emended to

Therefore $i_3^{-1}(zz^*) < 1$

---

[13] Regarding the definition of *ante rem* structuralism, cf.

Now we may contrast three ways of interpreting a subject like number theory or real analysis. On the one hand, an *eliminative* structuralist interpretation would take the former to be the study of all infinite discrete well-ordered sets, it being known that all such ordered sets are isomorphic; and it would take the latter to be the study of all complete orderable fields, it again being known that all such fields are isomorphic. On the other hand, an *ante rem* structuralist interpretation would take each to be the study of a single specific system, *the* natural numbers in the case of the former, and *the* real numbers in the case of the latter, but would insist that the systems in question are *ante rem* structures, and that natural and real numbers have no *nonstructural* properties, but only structural relations to other natural or real numbers.

(Burgess, 1999, p. 5)

It turns out that there is no easier way to flesh out the details of this approach than to formulate a theory in which natural numbers *are* integers (and so on), such as the one we will give in §7.4, and use that to infer where the assorted injections are present. Given that most mathematicians do genuinely think of natural numbers as being integers (and so on), and that the approach just described 'involves littering the landscape with unsightly isomorphisms which confuse what is really a simple situation' (Stewart and Tall, 1977, p. 179), there seems little reason to pursue it.[14]

7.2.5 *Introducing Ontogeny*

When they are confronted with the problems outlined in §7.2.2, some mathematicians suggest a very direct workaround.[15] They construct the set $\mathbb{C}$ of complex numbers, and then define $\mathbb{N}$, $\mathbb{Z}$, $\mathbb{Q}$ and $\mathbb{R}$ as specific subsets of $\mathbb{C}$. Then

$$\mathbb{N} \subset \mathbb{Z} \subset \mathbb{Q} \subset \mathbb{R} \subset \mathbb{C}$$

holds by direct construction.

This approach is simple; it removes the unwarranted distinctions that plagued §5.3.2 without relying on identification; and it is no more susceptible to Benacerraf's criticism or to notational collision than any other method we have considered. Unfortunately, it is not without its own problems. To understand these, we will need to introduce a new concept, which will play a central role in the remainder of this chapter.

Ontogeny in Mathematics

Since the publication of *Proofs and Refutations* (Lakatos, 1976), philosophers have paid considerable attention to the notion of mathematical change over time. Apparent informal proofs of a result come into being; time passes

---

[14] A exception rests in computer science; if one is required to treat, say, natural numbers and integers as distinct types, then explicitly predicting the injections has some use.

[15] For example, Stewart and Tall (1977) tends towards advocating this view, albeit starting with $\mathbb{R}$ rather than with $\mathbb{C}$:

[...] we assume no more and no less if we postulate that $\mathbb{R}$, rather than $\mathbb{N}_0$, exists. But $\mathbb{R}$ is much more convenient, for it is relatively easy to locate within it a chain of subsets

$$\mathbb{R} \supseteq \mathbb{Q} \supseteq \mathbb{Z} \supseteq \mathbb{N}_0$$

giving the rationals, integers, and natural numbers.

(Stewart and Tall, 1977, pp. 174)

Having said this, this text also stresses the importance of the constructability of the real numbers from the natural numbers, and touches on the positions discussed in §7.2.4 and §7.2.7.

and counterexamples are discovered, refuting the proofs; time passes again, definitions are adjusted to accommodate the counterexamples, and new informal proofs are provided; and the cycle repeats. Thus informal mathematics changes over the centuries.

Central to Lakatos's view is the idea that mathematics *develops as time passes*. But Lakatos' notion of time is not the only such notion that may be productively applied to mathematics. We have already used another such notion extensively throughout this book (cf. §1.2.2). When we spoke of adaptivity, and said that definitions *changed* an individual mathematician's representations of mathematics, we were implicitly relying on a notion of time. Similarly, when a mathematician observes that a binary operator is associative, and uses this to licence the omission of brackets (cf. §4.1.5), this operation irreducibly depends on some notion of time; the bracket-free notation that is syntactically ambiguous *beforehand* is unambiguous *afterwards*. And the most refined use of this notion of time occurs with reanalysis (§2.6): as we saw, a single piece of notation, such as 'A^B' when applied to numbers, may refer to many different things depending on the *time* in a mathematician's development at which it is encountered.

This notion of time is indispensable for any linguistic or philosophical theory of mathematics. It is meaningless to make assertions about, for example, what 'A^B' is defined to be unless we qualify such assertions using this notion of time. Mathematics does not suddenly appear, magically forming in the mind of a mathematician as a monolithic whole. Mathematics is incrementally learnt. Any individual mathematician encounters particular definitions, instances of reanalysis, identifications and similar phenomena in some concrete chronological sequence. And, further, if we want to assert that a particular mathematical fact holds, we cannot do so in a vacuum; we can only make assertions of this kind if an individual mathematician could have deduced the fact after seeing a plausible chronological sequence of the kind discussed.

The notion of time which we are discussing needs to be sharply distinguished from the notion of time stemming from Lakatos (1976). Lakatos deals with the development of mathematics over decades and centuries; roughly speaking, he deals with the evolution of mathematicians as a species. Our remarks concerning the development of an individual mathematician's representation of mathematics over months and years. We will distinguish and contrast these two notions of development, relating to the 'species of mathematicians' and the individual mathematician respectively, by referring to them as *phylogeny* and *ontogeny*. Lakatos deals primarily with *phylogenetic time*, although he uses an ontogenetic metaphor (in the form of individual mathematicians holding a dialogue). We deal exclusively with *ontogenetic time*, which we will sometimes call *ontochrony*.

This terminology allows us to rephrase our earlier remarks in a more precise way; for example, we might say that an individual mathematician encounters definitions, reanalyses and similar phenomena in some concrete *ontochronic* sequence. Equally, we can only assert that a mathematical fact holds if an individual mathematician could have deduced the fact after seeing a plausible ontochronic sequence of this kind, i.e. at the end of some reasonable *path of ontogenetic development.*

In this chapter, we have already encountered a concrete case where the concept of ontogeny was in play. Identification, as discussed in §7.2.2, is an irreducibly ontogenetic notion. When an individual mathematician encounters an identification, their internal model of mathematics *changes*. Before the identification, two specific objects, say the natural number 0 and the integer 0, were not formally considered to be the same; after the identification these objects were known to be the same. Thus the mathematician's picture of the ontology of mathematics has changed. In this example, all of the notions of 'change', 'before' and 'after' are irreducibly ontogenetic; they relate to the passage of ontogenetic time, and cannot be construed in any other way.

In regard to this example, we should add one caveat. Mathematical statements are never qualified using explicit ontochronic markers; that is, we do not make statements like 'the principle of induction holds until you learn about the complex numbers'. Thus the ontochronic evolution of our picture of mathematics must be *monotonic*. ('True facts remain forever true.') In this regard, it would be illegitimate to say that the natural number 0 and the integer 0 were distinct objects before identification, and became the same object afterwards. When we analyse this phenomenon, we will have to find a subtler, ontochronically monotonic, analysis of identification. We will return to this point in §7.2.6.

Even within the notion of ontogeny, we can distinguish two variants. When we refer to the ontochronic order in which mathematical concepts are learnt, we may either be referring to the order in which such concepts are genuinely learnt, or the order in which they are formally presented to us. That is, we might be referring to *psychological ontogeny* or *formal ontogeny*. For sufficiently advanced mathematics, these notions always agree, because advanced mathematical concepts are learnt directly from formal treatments; but when we come to consider elementary material, this is not the case. For example, formally one learns about sets before learning about numbers or any other mathematical objects; but psychologically one could well learn about numbers, functions, vectors and matrices before encountering the concept of a set.

In this chapter, whenever we speak of 'ontogeny' without explicit qualification, our aim should be taken to be the development of a formal ontogeny that is as close as possible to the psychological ontogeny. On one level, this is part of our programme to construct a theory of the foundations of mathematics that agrees with the way mathematics is actually done (cf. §7.1). But there is also a more practical aim. As we shall see later in this section, if we posit overly large differences between formal and psychological ontochrony, we may be led to the conclusion that large swathes of mathematics, including entire textbooks, are incorrect. This is untenable.

Looking back, we can find a concrete example of these two variant notions. When in §7.2.1 we criticised the requirement that one learn about sets before learning about numbers, we were really criticising the disparity between the formal and informal accounts of mathematical ontogeny. The formal account seems unsatisfactory precisely because it is at odds with the genuine psychological progression.

The ontogenetic perspective that we have introduced above will be our single most important tool in the remainder of this chapter by a considerable margin. Stronger, we would say that the main contribution of this chapter is not the collection of precise, formally satisfactory foundational mechanisms which we give in §7.4; rather, it is this notion of mathematical ontogeny. Our discussion of the foundations, and particularly our criticism of existing approaches in the remainder of §7.2, are an end to illustrating the effectiveness of ontogeny as a critical tool, rather than vice versa.

Applying Ontogeny

Ontogeny draws out two problems with the 'subsets of $\mathbb{C}$' method discussed above. First, the picture created by this method is not compatible with the psychologically correct ontochronic development of numbers. Intuitively, we expect there to be a time when an individual mathematician knows about, say, $\mathbb{N}$, $\mathbb{Z}$ and $\mathbb{Q}$, but not $\mathbb{R}$ or $\mathbb{C}$. This stage of knowledge cannot be accommodated as a precursor to the picture created by the 'subsets of $\mathbb{C}$' method under discussion. To put it another way, as ontogenetic time progresses, we expect the individual mathematician's model of numbers to evolve as shown in Figure 7.2.[16] This is clearly not possible if, say, $\mathbb{N}$ is *defined as* a subset of $\mathbb{C}$.

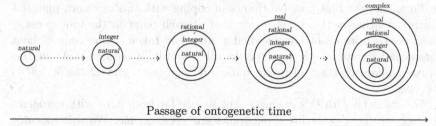

Passage of ontogenetic time

Fig. 7.2 Ontogenetic evolution of numbers

One could try and escape from this difficulty by appealing to a disparity between psychological ontochrony and formal ontochrony, as occurs with numbers and sets in §7.2.1. That is, one could argue that informally one learns about real numbers before complex numbers, but that formally the opposite occurs. But this would entail that a formal textbook which introduced real numbers but not complex numbers was not genuinely formal, or not genuinely correct. That position seems untenable.

---

[16] There is a subtlety here, regarding the question of whether people encounter fractions before negative numbers; we will return to this issue in §7.5.6.

The second problem occurs because, briefly put, mathematics continues forever. Ontogenetic time is semi-infinite: it has a beginning but no end. As a consequence, there is no final vantage point from which we can look back and say, 'this is all the mathematics that there is'. In particular, in this example, there is no way to know that $\mathbb{C}$ is the 'end of the line'; as ontogenetic time progresses, there is an ever-present possibility of finding a new, 'larger', class of numbers of which $\mathbb{C}$ is a proper subset.[17] At that point, the method described in this section would break down completely: because we chose to evade the problems of identifying $\mathbb{R}$ with a subset of $\mathbb{C}$, etc., we would have no way of identifying $\mathbb{C}$ with a subset of our new class. So we have only evaded the problem of identification in a very superficial, temporary manner.

Stepping back, we can draw a useful generalisation from this discussion. The two problems we encountered occurred because we attempted to privilege one stage of ontogenetic development, namely knowledge of $\mathbb{C}$ and precursors, above both earlier stages (such as knowledge of $\mathbb{Q}$ and precursors) and later stages (such as knowledge of some 'larger' class of numbers). Methodologically, this move was ill-chosen. To avoid similar problems elsewhere, we will adopt a principle that no stage of ontogenetic development should be privileged above any other. By analogy with the notion of isotropy in physics, we will refer to this principle as that of *isochrony*.

One important corollary of isochrony is as follows. We do not know what mathematics a human mathematician will encounter in the (ontogenetic) future, both because mathematics is continually being created (in a phylogenetic sense) and because we have not seen more than a tiny fraction of the mathematics that exists. Yet we need a way to give our theories, philosophical or linguistic, the best possible chance of coping with this unknown material. Isochrony achieves this by ensuring that at each point in the (ontogenetic) past, the theories *could have* handled a 'snapshot' taken at that time without reference to material yet to come. In other words, it ensures that our theories handle each stage of mathematical development *without the benefit of hindsight*.

We are done with this example, but we are far from done with ontogeny; in fact, its most powerful applications are yet to come. We will continue to expand on its aspects and applications throughout the remainder of this chapter.

7.2.6 Redefinition

Certain authors attempt to avoid the problems of identification by changing the definition of one of the (collections of) objects that needs to be identified.

---

[17] In fact, we know of several possible candidates; one example is the algebraic closure of Conway's surreal numbers (Conway, 2001). But the key point is not the identification of concrete examples of this type, but the idea that the intuitively natural occurrences of 'closure' to more general kinds of number can continue endlessly.

It is easy to do injustice to this particular strategy because the exact choice of wording can affect the content of the approach in subtle ways. To avoid this, we will concentrate on the concrete presentation of the approach in Hamilton (1982), which gives a particularly clear exposition.

Hamilton begins by defining the natural numbers using Peano's axioms, rather than via Von Neumann's construction. He then defines the notion of a model of Peano's axioms, describes the everyday model as $(\mathbb{N},',0)$, and proceeds to demonstrate the existence of other models, such as $(2\mathbb{N},^*,0)$ (where * is defined by $x^* = x'')$. Because the version of the induction axiom that is adopted refers to a background universe of sets, rather than being a first order axiom schema, Hamilton is able to prove that distinct models of Peano's axioms are isomorphic. He concludes:[18]

> Models of Peano's axioms exist which are different from, but isomorphic to, $(\mathbb{N},',0)$. Mathematically, such models are essentially the same, and for mathematical purposes it really does not matter whether natural numbers are taken to be the elements of $\mathbb{N}$ or the elements of a different but isomorphic model. This will form the basis of our construction of natural numbers within set theory in section 4.3. In a sense it is only a matter of labelling. If two models are isomorphic then their mathematical characteristics are the same but the elements may be objects of different sorts.
>
> (Hamilton, 1982, pp. 9–10)

Having introduced natural numbers, Hamilton proceeds directly to integers and other number kinds. Integers are constructed as equivalence classes of ordered pairs of natural numbers in the usual way. Hamilton then remarks:

> Care must be taken in such proofs to distinguish between elements of $\mathbb{Z}$ and elements of $\mathbb{N}$. [...]
>
> The above is only a temporary warning, however. Once the properties of integers have been derived from the properties of natural numbers, we can forget about the apparatus of construction, and treat integers in the intuitive way that we are accustomed to. Part of this intuition is the idea that $\mathbb{N}$ is a subset of $\mathbb{Z}$, i.e. that natural numbers are just non-negative integers. Our construction of $\mathbb{Z}$ renders this convenient idea false. However, we may recover the situation by the following process.
>
> Consider the set S of integers of the form $(n, 0)$ $(n \in \mathbb{N})$.
>
> *[Shows that $(S, f, (n, 0))$ is a model of Peano's axioms.]*
>
> Consequently, we can take the elements of S to represent the natural numbers. This satisfies the formal mathematical requirements. In practice, there is no need to do other than just imagine that $\mathbb{N}$ is a subset of $\mathbb{Z}$, in

---

[18] In passing, we should note that the notion of 'sort' that appears at the end of this excerpt corresponds to an intuitive notion of type. Hamilton's actual choice of wording, 'the elements may be objects of different sorts', carries with it the assumption that models are homogenous, consisting of objects of a single sort. This tends to support the view that mathematicians intuitively think of sets as homogenous collections (§5.3.5).

effect regarding and n and $(n, 0)$ as different labels for the same object. From now on we actually do so. It should not lead to confusion.

(Hamilton, 1982, pp. 16–17)

There are a number of technical problems with this approach, but before we turn to those, we should address a much more significant philosophical problem. The key to the entire approach is the sentence:

Consequently, we can take the elements of S to represent the natural numbers.

This statement is (ontogenetically) non-monotonic. It *changes* the denotation of natural number for a reader who encounters it. From a philosophical perspective, this is deeply troubling. In particular, because ontogenetic time is semi-infinite (i.e. has no end), the operation may be repeated an indefinite number of times in the mathematics yet to be encountered by any (fixed) reader. The corollary to this is that one can never be certain of knowing the final denotation of 'natural number' — and, because natural numbers are in no way privileged, one can never be certain of having the final denotation of any mathematical concept. Again, this is extremely troubling from a philosophical viewpoint.

Leaving this aside, we may move to technical issues. Benacerraf's criticism and notational collision continue to be concerns; as in previous cases, we will pass over these and focus on the problems that are unique to this attempt to avoid unwarranted distinctions without using identification.

First, we may observe that $\mathbb{Z}$ is defined *in terms of* $\mathbb{N}$. So if we redefine the meaning of $\mathbb{N}$, the denotation of $\mathbb{Z}$ will also shift. So the 'new' $\mathbb{N}$ may be a subset of the old $\mathbb{Z}$, but the old $\mathbb{Z}$ is defunct; and, the new $\mathbb{Z}$ does not contain the new $\mathbb{N}$ as a subset. Avoiding this requires us to choose very careful wording; we need to make it clear that we are constructing a new $\mathbb{N}$, but that the old $\mathbb{N}$ remains in existence, and is still used to define the one and only version of $\mathbb{Z}$. At the same time, most other terms and objects which are defined in terms of the old $\mathbb{N}$ (such as 'prime number') need to be redefined to use the new $\mathbb{N}$. There is no principled basis on which to distinguish the objects which need to shift to use the new denotation, and the objects that do not.

Second, isomorphism or no isomorphism, there are concrete mathematical statements whose truth value is changed by this operation. For example, immediately before the operation the statement '$0_{\mathbb{Z}} = 0_{\mathbb{N}}$' is false; after the identification it is true. If this is left unchecked, it constitutes a definite *mathematical* error. So one needs to formulate some principle arguing that statements of this kind are not genuine mathematical statements — and it is hard to see how such a principle could be grounded in the actual formal content of mathematics as it is developed under this approach.

Third, we will on occasion want to identify natural numbers with objects other than integers. For example, it is standard to identify natural numbers with finite cardinals. How are we to do this? If we redefine natural numbers to be certain finite cardinals, they will cease to be integers, and vice versa. (The relationship between the natural numbers and cardinals is an important example; we will return to it in §7.5.4 when we have formulated our actual solution.)

Finally, as in §7.2.4, there is no general principle that specifies the respects in which two sets need to be isomorphic before one can be replaced with the other. A concrete example arises during the construction of the rational numbers. There is a stage where one needs to redefine $\mathbb{Z}$ to be a subset of $\mathbb{Q}$. Immediately before this point, both $\mathbb{Z}$ and $\mathbb{Q}$ are sets — so as well as arithmetic operations, they admit the set membership operator $\in$. It is intuitively clear that $\in$ is irrelevant as regards isomorphism, i.e. that we do not need to check statements of the form '$x \in \mathbb{Z}_{old} \Leftrightarrow x \in \mathbb{Z}_{new}$' to license the replacement. However, we know of no general principle rooted in the mathematics of the approach that predicts this. (Note that in one sense, this is a problem with concrete construction rather than with replacement *per se*.) In fact, the problems related to isomorphism run much deeper than this example indicates; we will return to them in §7.2.9.

We should emphasise that the real problems with this issue are not technical, but philosophical: ontogenetic monotonicity should be an absolute constraint.

7.2.7 *Manual Replacement*

We now turn to another approach which attempts to avoid the unwarranted distinctions of §7.2.2 without utilising explicit identification.[19] This approach works by constructing each class of numbers as in §7.2.2, but manually substituting elements of the previous class to achieve the required identifications. We may illustrate this approach using the integers, which were defined in §7.2.2 essentially as

$$\mathbb{Z} \stackrel{\mathrm{df}}{=} \mathbb{N}^2 / \sim$$

where $\sim$ is the equivalence relation defined on $\mathbb{N}^2$ by

$$(a,b) \sim (c,d) \quad \text{if} \quad a+d = c+b.$$

Under the new approach, one forms this set '$\mathbb{N}^2 / \sim$', but then cuts out the equivalence classes corresponding to natural numbers, and substitutes the original natural numbers. Thus $\mathbb{Z}$ is defined to be

$$(\mathbb{N}^2 / \sim) \underbrace{- \{[(n,0)]_\sim \mid n \in \mathbb{N}\}}_{\text{Remove equivalence classes}} \cup \, \mathbb{N}.$$

---

[19] The clearest description of this approach is given in (Birkhoff and Mac Lane, 1941, pp. 54–57). (Stewart and Tall, 1977, p. 180) also suggests it as an explicit, formal way of avoiding the invisible embeddings of §7.2.4.

This alternative definition of $\mathbb{Z}$ ensures that $\mathbb{N}$ is a subset of $\mathbb{Z}$ by explicit construction. Arithmetic operations are then defined on $\mathbb{Z}$ using the natural bijection from $(\mathbb{N}^2/\sim)$.

This approach remains vulnerable to Benacerraf's criticism as, for example, one could construct integers in an analogous way but with the order of elements in the ordered pairs reversed. It also suffers from notational collision because, for example, negative numbers *are* equivalence classes. And, unlike the approaches discussed previously, this approach abounds with inhomogenous sets; for example, $\mathbb{Z}$ is a set containing both natural numbers and sets of ordered pairs of natural numbers. As well as reducing the effectiveness of the type system in disambiguation (cf. §5.3.5), such sets are simply *ugly*. But we will leave these issues aside, and consider this approach only as an alternative to identification, i.e. as a way of avoiding unwarranted distinctions.

Unlike the approach given in §7.2.5, 'manual replacement' reflects the incremental nature of the real, psychological, ontogenetic development of numbers. Layers of numbers are built up one by one, and at any given stage in construction no knowledge of future layers is used. Thus isochrony is satisfied, and the two ontogenetic problems discussed in the previous section do not arise. Yet there is still a problem which we can discern by considering ontochrony, as we shall now do.

The idea behind manual replacement is to fuse the operations of definition and identification. Rather than defining, say, $\mathbb{Z}$ and then identifying part of it with $\mathbb{N}$, we fuse these into a single operation, namely the definition of '$\mathbb{Z}$-including-$\mathbb{N}$'. The key property that allows us to do this is the fact that *no ontogenetic time* passes between the definition and the identification. In other words, this approach requires that as soon as we define an object, we immediately know all required identity-relationships between that object and all existing objects, and encode those relationships within the definition.

With regard to the examples we have considered, this is a plausible requirement: as we define the integers, we do intend nonnegative integers to be natural numbers; as we define rational numbers, we do intend certain rational numbers to be integers; and so on. More generally, all the examples we have considered to date are examples of closure of a set under some operation — and in such cases we are constructing the closure itself with a view to identifying part of it with the original set. This suggests that we look for an example of identification which does not arise from closure, and more specifically one in which ontogenetic time passes between the creation of some objects and their identification. In such an instance of *late identification*, the fusion of definition and identification, and manual replacement itself, would become problematic.

One example of late identification is surprisingly close to hand. When they are first encountered, the complex numbers are always introduced as ordered pairs of real numbers, some of which are immediately identified with real numbers. Yet eventually, after one has introduced the notion of algebraic closures, $\mathbb{C}$ is identified with the algebraic closure of $\mathbb{R}$.

In all accounts, a substantial span of ontogenetic time will pass between the introduction of $\mathbb{C}$ and of algebraic closures and the identification in question. For example, Hamilton (1982) defines $\mathbb{C}$ and notes that the Fundamental Theorem of Algebra, which is needed to licence the identification under discussion, 'requires methods which are not the concern of this book, so we shall omit it'. Lang (1993), which presupposes knowledge of $\mathbb{C}$, introduces algebraic closures and proves the Fundamental Theorem of Algebra in separate chapters.

As promised, this example creates an immediate problem for manual replacement. Manual replacement defines both $\mathbb{C}$ and the algebraic closure of $\mathbb{R}$ as specific concrete sets; it very carefully ensures that both of these sets contain $\mathbb{R}$, but does not ensure that they coincide. Thus we are left with the need to identify unequal *concrete* sets, which is precisely the situation that manual replacement was designed to avoid.

The only way to avoid this problem would be to change the definitions with the benefit of hindsight, i.e. to violate isochrony. This then causes the problems discussed in §7.2.5 to recur. It is worth spelling out the form that these two problems take. First, we are forced to normatively conclude that the standard definition of either $\mathbb{C}$ or of algebraic closures is incorrect. Neither option seems viable. Second, we have no way of coping with the broad class of problem if it recurs: if we happen to set up two new objects and later prove a result (like the Fundamental Theorem of Algebra) showing that we should think of these objects as one and the same, we have no way of identifying them. In fact, it is not hard to see that both of these problems apply to the attempt to evade identification via any kind of concrete construction, whether by manual replacement or otherwise; identification is an abstract phenomenon and we need abstract machinery to handle it.

Notes

There are two related observations about this 'identifying $\mathbb{C}$ with $\bar{\mathbb{R}}$' example which we should make before closing this section. First, this is the first example where we do not have a linear 'chain' of identifications. Pictorially, we have:

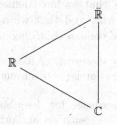

We may consider this as a graph, in which $\mathbb{R}$, $\bar{\mathbb{R}}$, $\mathbb{C}$, etc. are nodes and each operation of identification corresponds to an edge. We should regard it as an undirected graph because, in general, there is no reason why one of the objects in question should become a subset of the other. (To give a concrete example, one can certainly define cardinal numbers and complex numbers, and then identify the two versions of the natural numbers that lie inside these.)

The key point about the example we have just given is not that it is not a chain, but that it contains a cycle. Cycles gives us the ability to approach or construct objects in (at least) two different ways; in this case, we may either approach $\mathbb{C}$ directly from $\mathbb{R}$, or approach it via $\bar{\mathbb{R}}$.[20] The need to make sure that the different approaches are·compatible is precisely what causes the problems that derailed manual replacement, as discussed earlier in this section. A corollary is that we should be particularly careful to evaluate any proposed approach against a cyclic identification graph; we shall do precisely this in §7.5.6.

Second, this is the first example which admits more than one legitimate path of ontogenetic development. To wit: one could reasonably either learn about real numbers, then algebraic closures, and then complex numbers, or about real numbers, then complex numbers, and then algebraic closures. The latter is certainly more likely, but the former remains a reasonable path of development. Whatever theory of the foundations we develop, we will need to take care to ensure that in any domain admitting *ontogenetic variations*, i.e. admitting more than one reasonable path of development, the theory is compatible with all such paths. This reflects the fact that there is no central coordinating authority stipulating the order in which mathematics should be learnt.[21] Mathematics is described locally, not globally, and theories of the language and philosophy of mathematics need to accommodate this.

7.2.8 Identification and Conservativity

In this section, we will suppose that we had some formal mechanism of identification, and look at a way in which that mechanism could behave in an undesirable manner if it had not been constructed in exactly the right way.

We will concentrate on a concrete example. Suppose that we have defined natural numbers using Peano's axioms in the usual way, and that we are using the first order version of Peano's axioms, i.e. the version that encodes

---

[20] In fact, the direct construction of $\mathbb{C}$ from the algebraic closure $\bar{\mathbb{R}}$ of $\mathbb{R}$ is not straightforward, and raises interesting issues; but these are unrelated to our main concerns.

[21] Note that one could say that the inadequacy of precedence for describing mathematical language also stemmed from the absence of such an authority (§4.1.3).

induction via an axiom schema rather than as a second-order axiom or by reference to sets.[22] This version of Peano's axioms is famously incomplete (Gödel, 1930); that is, there are arithmetical properties which cannot be proved to be either true or false by deduction from the said axioms. The standard example is the Gödel sentence G.

Now consider the situation where we are identifying natural numbers with some other class of objects. We need to be very careful to ensure that in the course of this operation, G (and other undecidable properties) do not become either true or false. This is not only because 'adding properties' to the natural numbers is unsatisfactory; it is because one mathematical text could cause G to become true, and another could cause $\neg G$ to become true. Each text functions monotonically and is individually coherent; but taken together, the two texts become inconsistent.

The particular point that this underlines is that in order to identify the natural numbers, defined as above, with some other objects, it is not enough merely to know that those objects satisfy the axioms which were used to define the natural numbers (i.e., Peano's axioms). We need to ensure that those objects have no properties that could not be deduced from Peano's axioms. So in *some* respect, identification must be *conservative*, must not introduce new mathematical facts. But this notion is not as straightforward as it might seem. Consider the case where we identify natural numbers with integers. Before identification, we cannot prove that $0_N = 0_Z$; after identification, we can. Nor is the problem limited to statements involving equality; for example, before identification, we cannot prove whether the set $\{0_N, 0_Z\}$ has size 1 or 2; after identification, we can prove that it has size 1.

Thus giving a precise criterion that specifies what kind of new facts may not be introduced is difficult. One possible approach would be to say that systems must be isomorphic before they can be identified; this brings us to the next section.

7.2.9 Isomorphisms Are Inadequate

The approaches discussed in both §7.2.4 (on invisible embeddings) and §7.2.6 (on redefinition) assumed that the existence of an isomorphism was enough to licence some substitute for identification. This reflects an implicit notion that an isomorphism is precisely what would be needed to licence identification, if the formal details of identification could be worked out. In §7.2.4, we saw one respect in which this view was incorrect: we cannot identify $\mathbb{C}$ with itself along a nontrivial automorphism, or make a sequence of identifications which combine to have the same effect. We will now discuss two further deficiencies of this view on identification, which did not apply in the exact

---

[22] In practice, the 'second-order' axiom is invariably implemented by reference to a background universe of sets which specify the available properties.

circumstances of §7.2.4. The first of these makes the view that isomorphism licenses identification difficult to hold; the second makes it entirely untenable.

First, observe that the kind of isomorphism we wish exhibit is not an actual set-theoretic function; this would cause our mechanism of identification to depend on set theory. Instead, we want to use a circumlocution involving higher-order properties, of the kind that is used to state the Axiom of Replacement. This is most easily illustrated using a concrete example; let us suppose that we wish to identify the natural numbers with finite cardinals. Intuitively, we would want to show that these two collections of objects have the same structure with respect to $+$ and $\times$. Formally, we would wish to exhibit a two-place property $P(x, y)$ such that:

- For every natural number n there is a unique finite cardinal κ such that $P(n, \kappa)$;
- for every finite cardinal κ there is a unique natural number n such that $P(n, \kappa)$;
- Suppose that we have natural numbers n, m and finite cardinals κ, λ such that both $P(n, \kappa)$ and $P(m, \lambda)$ hold. Then $P(n + m, \kappa + \lambda)$ and $P(n \times m, \kappa \times \lambda)$ also hold.

Exhibiting such a property is essentially equivalent to exhibiting an isomorphism between the natural numbers and finite cardinals, but without using any set-theoretic machinery. The surprising fact is that this property is *not* sufficient to licence an identification. The reason is as follows: there are salient properties of natural numbers or of finite cardinals which cannot be stated in terms of $+$ and $\times$. One example of such a property is,

The set of natural numbers exists.

A priori, we can envisage a situation in which we knew that this was true, but where we did not know that the corresponding property,

The set of finite cardinal numbers exists.

was true. In this kind of situation licensing an identification would be tantamount to introducing a new fact about finite cardinal numbers.

In practice, this example is slightly absurd because we are so used to the fact that if some Xs and Ys are in one-to-one correspondence, then the set of Xs exists if and only if the set of Ys exists. It is easy to forget that this fact depends on the ZF Axiom of Replacement. As stated in Chapter 1, none of the material we develop in this book is tied to any mathematical theory; *all* mathematical content, including the ZF axioms, is extracted from mathematical text. Our account of the foundations must handle all the phenomena encountered when using ZF set theory, but may not be tied to it. In particular, we cannot depend on the Axiom of Replacement having been stated.

Thus, even if we ignore the issues surrounding automorphisms of $\mathbb{C}$, isomorphism still allows the possibility of 'new facts' being introduced to one of the systems being identified.

The second deficiency is much more serious. It is most easily introduced by an example. Let us take a concrete example of a legitimate identification, such as, say, the identification of the natural numbers and the nonnegative integers. Let us ignore the issues discussed above, and suppose that identification is licensed by the presentation of an isomorphism i between, perhaps, $(\mathbb{N}, +_\mathbb{N}, \times_\mathbb{N})$ and $(\mathbb{Z}_{\geqslant 0}, +_\mathbb{Z}, \times_\mathbb{Z})$ — the exact details will not matter for our purposes.

Now, let us define some objects called 'pseudo-integers', which are introduced using exactly the same text as integers *except* that we add as part of their definition the following statement:

($*$) Pseudo-integers are not natural numbers.

This remark is necessarily imprecise, because we have not yet described how one can introduce integers so that they are not specific, concrete sets; but we will in any case need to do so before we can make sense of the notion of identification. Once we have defined our formal mechanisms for introducing objects more abstractly than as concrete sets (in §7.4.1), we will return to this question (in §7.4.2) and show that the above remarks about the introduction of 'pseudo-integers', and the argument that will now follow, can be made completely precise.

If we know how to construct integers, it is not difficult to mimic the construction for pseudo-integers, but modify it so that pseudo-integers are provably not natural numbers. (For example, we can take each pseudo-integer to be the ordered pair of an integer and $\mathbb{N}$.) Once we have constructed pseudo-integers, we construct the set $\mathbb{Z}'$ of pseudo-integers, by mimicking the process we used to construct $\mathbb{Z}$. Because mathematics is *monotonic*, the availability of an extra fact ($*$) cannot interfere with this construction in any way. And once we have constructed $\mathbb{Z}'$, we can mimic the construction we used to create the isomorphism i in order to create an isomorphism i' between $(\mathbb{N}, +_\mathbb{N}, \times_\mathbb{N})$ and $(\mathbb{Z}'_{\geqslant 0}, +_{\mathbb{Z}'}, \times_{\mathbb{Z}'})$. Again, monotonicity means that ($*$) cannot interfere with the construction in any way.

Finally, once we have i', we are licenced to identify natural numbers and nonnegative pseudo-integers. But to do so would allow us to deduce a contradiction. Thus isomorphism *cannot* be what licenses identification.

A final note: one might try to salvage the situation by disallowing ($*$) and similar statements. The simplest approach would be to disbar references to $\mathbb{N}$ in the introductions of integers and similar kinds of objects. This in itself is too crude. It turns out that however we set up the integers, the text introducing them must refer to $\mathbb{N}$ in some way, or else must provide some analogue of the Axiom of Induction for integers — and this last option changes the mathematical content too much to be acceptable.

A subtler approach would be to declare that assertions of equality or inequality between objects of different types (such as natural numbers and matrices, or natural numbers and pseudo-integers) are simply meaningless and may not be asserted. But if the ZF axioms have been introduced, then it is impossible to separate meaningless statements of this kind from statements that actually occur in mathematics. The reason for this is that a statement about (in)equality can be rephrased as an assertion about inhomogenous sets (cf. §5.3.5) — for example, the assertion that $0_{\mathbb{Z}'} \neq 0_{\mathbb{N}}$ is equivalent to the assertion that $|\{0_{\mathbb{Z}'}, 0_{\mathbb{N}}\}| = 2$. And while inhomogenous sets may be ugly, they are entirely unobjectionable from a technical viewpoint, and do genuinely crop up in mathematics. For example, Birkhoff and Mac Lane (1941) and other texts utilising manual replacement (§7.2.7) construct sets which include as members both natural numbers and sets of ordered pairs of natural numbers.

As in Chapter 5, we have to construct all of our mechanisms to allow for the possibility of inhomogenous sets; this is the price one pays for the expressivity of ZF. (It is substantially harder to build up mathematics in theories which disallow inhomogeneity, such as type theory.) And as we found in Chapter 5, this means that our types must imperfectly supervene on the underlying mathematics, rather than being extensional properties we can use to restrict the kind of mathematical statements that can be made. Thus there is no way to distinguish (∗) from statements that might actually occur in textbooks; and as a consequence, if we allowed isomorphism to license identification, then we would necessarily leave open the possibility of deriving both a statement (e.g. '$0_{\mathbb{Z}'} = 0_{\mathbb{N}}$') and its negation (e.g. '$0_{\mathbb{Z}'} \neq 0_{\mathbb{N}}$'). As a result, isomorphism cannot be taken to license identification.

7.3   Central Problems

The discussion in the previous section cast light on three major difficulties that any theory of the foundations must overcome. We will discuss these in order of increasing severity.

7.3.1   Ontology and Epistemology

The first problem relates to the ontological status of mathematical objects. Suppose that we take the orthodox position, and state that all mathematical objects are sets. In this case, whatever exact definitions we adopt, we will encounter notational collision. To take a concrete example, if, say, natural numbers are defined as sets, then whatever the actual definitions are, we will find that phrases like '1 + 1' have two readings, relating to addition as numbers and symmetric difference as sets respectively. Equally, if we take all mathematical objects to be sets, then Benacerraf's criticisms will apply in full as we will be forced to make arbitrary choices about construction, for example by settling on von Neumann's construction of the natural numbers rather than any other construction.

Both of these difficulties arise because mathematicians do not think of numbers as being sets. The idea that numbers are sets is a dogma that is repeated as a sop to epistemological concerns (discussed below), not an intuitive belief. As we noted in §7.1, our main concern in this chapter is to construct a theory of the foundations that reflects the way mathematics really is by, for example, not defining natural numbers as sets. Thus we need our ontological picture of mathematics, specifying what mathematical objects *are*, to match the picture that mathematicians actually have (cf. Figure 7.1, given in §7.2.3).

The real difficulty here arises because if we specify that natural numbers are *not* sets, then we have violated *epistemological* constraints. To wit: the ZF(C) axioms are the arbiters of truth for modern mathematics. Mathematical objects may only exist if they can be constructed using those axioms; mathematical statements are only true if they can be deduced from those axioms. From an epistemological perspective, the ZF(C) axioms form the *epistemic basis* for mathematics. These facts are non-negotiable. We cannot change them without changing modern mathematics itself.

Thus we face a central conflict between ontology and epistemology. If we take natural numbers to be sets, then epistemology is satisfied but we obtain an ontology that bears little relation to actual mathematics. If we take natural numbers not to be sets, then we have at least the possibility of obtaining the correct ontology, but we encounter fatal epistemological problems.

(The solution to this problem is discussed in §7.4.1, under the heading of 'Ontology and Epistemology'.)

7.3.2 Identification

As we saw in the previous section, identification forms an indispensable part of any theory of the foundations; any attempt to evade or replace it runs into serious technical problems (cf. §7.2.5, §7.2.6 and §7.2.7). But giving a technically adequate account of identification is a substantive and multifaceted problem. There are four difficulties that any theory of identification must tackle. First, it must stipulate what it actually means to identify two objects; that is, it must specify the formal effect the identification has. As we saw in §7.2.2 and §7.2.4, the straightforward approaches to this problem did not work. Second, an adequate theory must set out criteria licensing identification that exclude examples like the identification of the complex numbers with themselves in a non-trivial way. Third, it must not add properties to either of the objects being identified, even in certain cases where those properties refer to objects which are only indirectly related to the objects being identified. (Cf. especially the example involving the set of finite cardinals in §7.2.9.) Fourth, it must also exclude the identification of structures that are directly presented as being distinct, as in the example with 'pseudo-integers' from §7.2.9.

(The solution to this problem is discussed in §7.4.2, primarily under the heading of 'The Local Condition and Isomorphism'.)

7.3.3 Ontogeny

Finally, and most importantly, any account of the foundations must conform to the constraints we discovered by adopting an ontogenetic perspective. In particular, it must describe our picture of mathematics not as eternally fixed but as something that develops, and can continue to develop, as more mathematics is encountered. Reducing ontogeny to a list of sub-principles is dangerous; it is a perspective, a *way* of looking at mathematics, and conveys insights that will not be captured in any list of principles we might make. Nevertheless, there is some value in highlighting the most important points we have drawn out above; but we must emphasise that this narrow list is not the same as the wider perspective.

Firstly we saw that many mathematical operations, such as definition, reanalysis and identification, must be situated in an ontogenetic chronology. We also saw that all of these operations need to be ontogenetically monotonic: although our picture of maths changes as ontogenetic time passes, true facts cannot become false (as, for example, would happen during redefinition). Nor can we leap to 'the end of ontogenetic time' and look back to see all of mathematics laid out in perfection: ontogenetic time is semi-infinite, having a beginning but no end. (In other words, there will always be *more* mathematics.) Our theories must cope with the fact that we can describe only snapshots in the ontogenetic progression of mathematics, and must allow us to move from snapshot to snapshot as mathematics progresses. This leads us to a principle of *isochrony*: no stage of mathematical development may be privileged above another. As well as preventing us from assuming that mathematics is 'finished', this precludes us from operating with the benefit of hindsight: we force ourselves to treat each stage of mathematical development as if we had no insight into what might come next. This applies not only to objects that might be introduced in future, but connections that might be discovered; thus ontogenetic concerns force us to handle *late identification*. Equally, our theory must handle the existence of ontogenetic variations, that is of different paths that one might take when learning mathematical material.

We will keep ideas like these constantly in mind throughout the remainder of this chapter. This does involve remembering the ways in which ontogenetic considerations invalidated many of the approaches presented in §7.2, and ensuring that our own approach does not fall into the same traps. But, more significantly, it involves constantly maintaining the ontogenetic perspective; looking at our theories and ensuring that they can describe mathematics incrementally, as ontogenetic time passes and a given mathematician's representation of mathematics evolves.

(As we have noted, ontogenetic concerns cannot be solved in a localised way, but need continuous attention throughout both the development of our novel formalisms and their application to actual mathematics. We will highlight them where they arise.)

7.3.4 Further Issues

In highlighting these three particular problems which will constrain any eventual solution, we should not forget the general constraints on the work described in this book. In particular, we aim to be faithful to actual mathematics as far as is possible. Although we may now have to emend mathematical text more than in previous chapters (cf. §7.1), we should aim to do so no more than is necessary. In particular, foundational texts contain a great deal of important mathematical material, such as Von Neumann's concrete construction of the natural numbers from sets or the construction of the integers as equivalence classes of ordered pairs of natural numbers. It is clear that this material must have an important foundational role, even if we are not yet certain what that role is. We will aim to reuse this material in a way that keeps it as close to its original form as is possible.

Additionally, there are some constraints that are so obvious that they are easily missed. As elsewhere in the book, we aim for generality; we wish to construct foundational mechanisms that handle not just, say, numbers but as wide a range of mathematical phenomena as possible. Equally, we need our theory to be completely precise; we allow no 'abuse of language' or other hand-waving.

7.4 Formalism

We will now set out the novel formal mechanisms needed to give an account of the foundations that overcomes all of the problems listed above. This section is primarily concerned with formally characterising the mechanisms; their application to the foundations will be exemplified at length in §7.5. In keeping with the character of the remainder of the book, we will clothe the mechanisms in the kind of language that a real mathematician might use, rather than in, say, the apparatus of logic. As in the few other cases where we have had to invent language (cf. §5.4.2), the exact linguistic formulae chosen are irrelevant; it is their underlying effect that matters.

We will divide our mechanisms into two kinds: those concerned with abstraction (§7.4.1) and those concerned with identification (§7.4.2).

7.4.1 Abstraction

Systems

We introduce a new kind of block,[23] which we call a *system*. Systems are intended to contain direct axiomatisations of objects which we regard as being *sui generis* (§7.2.1), such as numbers. However, formally speaking, systems

---

[23] I.e., something that is typeset like a theorem or definition; cf. §2.5.

may contain any material whatsoever, including other blocks. All of the material in the system is regarded as collectively axiomatic; that is, any facts which are stated inside a system are assumed to be true rather than requiring proof.

A simple example of a system is as follows:

System 1.3 'Ordered Pairs'

Given arbitrary objects a and b, there is an object called the ordered pair of a and b and denoted (a, b). Two ordered pairs (a, b) and (x, y) are equal if and only if $a = x$ and $b = y$.   □

Note that in this example ordered pairs have effectively been constructed *out of thin air* in the same way that sets were in §5.4.2, as opposed to being defined in terms of existing objects. Construction of objects in this way is a frequent feature in systems.

Since it is unusual in mathematics to have anything other than sets explicitly constructed out of thin air, it is worth clarifying our formal stance concerning such objects. Although distinct classes of objects that are constructed in this way are stipulated to have different types (§5.4.2), we make no ontological commitment as to whether objects of different classes may or may not coincide. Thus, if we construct of sets and ordered pairs 'out of thin air', we make no commitment as to whether sets are ordered pairs or not. These are general remarks about objects introduced in this way; the fact that in this example ordered pairs happen to be introduced inside a system is neither here nor there.

Models

The second kind of block which we introduce is called a *model*. A model is a formal presentation of what the objects in some system could be, in a sense which we will shortly make precise. When considered as blocks, models are to systems as corollaries are to results: just as every corollary must be the corollary to some result, every model must be a model of some specific system.

A model may contain any mathematical material, with the sole exception that it may not construct new classes of objects out of thin air. A model must contain the following material:

1. Whenever a class of objects is constructed out of thin air in a system, the same class of objects must be defined in terms of existing objects in any model of that system.
2. Whenever a system contains a concrete definition, any model of that system must define the same entities in the same way; the surface form of the definition may differ, but its content must not.
3. Whenever a system introduces a variable or assumption, any model of that system must introduce the same variable or assumption; the surface form of the relevant statement may differ, but its content must not.
4. Whenever a system asserts a fact, any model of that system must deduce those facts from the definitions it has presented.

Additionally, a model must make sense as a concrete set of definitions and results even if read before the system to which it corresponds. (Equivalently, a model may not define objects of a system in terms of objects or concepts introduced in the same system, unless those objects or concepts have previously been defined in the model.) However, a model may freely utilise objects and concepts from any other system.[24]

The presentation of a model effects no formal changes on the reader's model of mathematics. (The primary purpose of models is not to effect such changes, but to ensure that the overall foundational system has the correct epistemological properties. We will discuss this topic later in this section.) In particular, ontological relationships between objects are not changed; the type system is unchanged; and objects that were defined in the corresponding system gain no new properties. Thus models could be removed from a mathematical text without affecting any other part of the text.[25] We will return to these remarks once we have a concrete example of a model which we may use to illustrate them.

If we look back at the example of a system presented earlier in this section, we see that it consists of one class of objects constructed 'out of thin air' (namely ordered pairs) and one assertion about such objects. Thus any model of this system must first define ordered pairs in some concrete way, and then prove that the ordered pairs defined in this way satisfy the assertion. One example of such a model is as follows:

Model 1.4 of System 1.3 'Kuratowski's Ordered Pairs'

Let a and b be arbitrary objects. The set $\{\{a\}, \{a, b\}\}$ is called the ordered pair of a and b, and denoted (a, b).

Theorem 1.4.1
Two ordered pairs (a, b) and (x, y) are equal if and only if $a = x$ and $b = y$.

---

[24] There is a technical subtlety here, involving the situation where one has systems S_1 and S_2, S_2 is stated in terms of material introduced in S_1, and one is trying to provide a model $\mathcal{M}_1$ for S_1 which uses material from S_2. In this situation, $\mathcal{M}_1$ may not depend on material given in S_1, but it may use material from S_2 despite the dependence of S_2 on S_1.

This stipulation does not introduce circularity; the real reason for preventing $\mathcal{M}_1$ from using terms and notation introduced in S_1 is that this causes every usage of such a term to become ambiguous. In other words, the condition is intended to simplify our use of language to the point where a human reader can following it without extensive effort, not to avoid circularity. Indeed, if one takes S_1 to be the system of complex numbers, one can give a nontrivial model $\mathcal{M}_1$ of S_1 which is built in terms of the very complex numbers introduced in S_1. (Cf. the possibility of identifying $\mathbb{C}$ with itself along the conjugation automorphism, as discussed in §7.2.4.)

We will discuss an example of this situation in detail in §7.5.3.

[25] An exception is drawn in the case where the text specifically refers to a particular model; examples of this kind will occur in §7.4.2.

Proof

Suppose that $(a, b) = (x, y)$, i.e.

$$\{\{a\}, \{a, b\}\} = \{\{x\}, \{x, y\}\}.$$

Hence,

$$\{a\} = \{x\} \quad \text{or} \quad \{a\} = \{x, y\},$$

and

$$\{a, b\} = \{x\} \quad \text{or} \quad \{a, b\} = \{x, y\}.$$

[...]   □

The use of a theorem in this model is a purely stylistic matter; it would have been perfectly legitimate to substitute an argument in the main text. It is important to note that the body of the above proof is taken essentially unchanged from (Hamilton, 1982, p. 130), satisfying our aim of reusing mathematical material in a way that keeps it as close to its original form as possible (§7.3.4).

As noted above, the presentation of this model effects no formal changes. In particular, ordered pairs do not become sets. We remain ontologically uncommitted as to whether ordered pairs are sets or are not sets. Similarly, the definition of an ordered pair is still just the definition given in the system. From the perspective of the text that follows the model, there is no relationship between (a, b) and $\{\{a\}, \{a, b\}\}$; ORDERED PAIR and SET continue to be distinct types, and it makes no sense to ask, for example, if an object x is an element of (a, b).

Ontology and Epistemology

As we noted in §7.3, one of the central problems we faced was that objects which we intuitively consider to be *sui generis* (such as numbers or functions; cf. §7.2.1) cannot be defined to be sets without creating a formal ontology that does not match the ontology that mathematicians intuitively hold. This in turn causes notational collision and opens us to Benacerraf's criticism. But conversely, if we specify that objects which are intuitively *sui generis* are not sets, we encounter fatal epistemological problems.

Systems and models provide a solution to this dilemma. When we need to introduce objects which are intuitively *sui generis*, we will define them out of thin air in a system, as we did for ordered pairs in the example above. By doing so, we are effectively axiomatising the objects directly. Because we carefully state neither that such objects are sets nor that they are not sets, these objects *might* not be sets. And, if we are careful, we can rely on this fact to ensure that there is a type distinction between sets and objects introduced in systems; this type distinction prevents notational collision. Additionally, Benacerraf's criticism does not apply to objects that are directly axiomatised.

Thus our method of systems solves the ontological issues we encountered when dealing with these objects. However, it has come with a price; we have expanded the epistemic basis of mathematics, i.e. the set of axioms which are necessary to derive all of mathematics. This is untenable. As we noted above, it is a fact that modern mathematics takes the ZF(C) axioms as its epistemic basis, and we are not free to adopt a different position. Fortunately, we can recover from this fumble. Epistemological considerations do not actually require that all objects are sets; they only require that all objects *could be* sets. If we exhibit a *model* for each system we have introduced, and that model constructs 'concrete' versions of the axiomatised objects constructed out of sets, then we have shown precisely this. Thus exhibiting a system fleetingly expands the epistemic basis; but exhibiting a model of that system constructed of sets returns the epistemic basis to its original position (i.e., the ZF(C) axioms).

We will adopt this two-stage approach, namely the presentation of a system and then a concrete model, for all objects which are intuitively *sui generis*. Further examples of this kind, and subtleties associated with this approach, will be discussed in §7.5.1.

7.4.2 Identification

We will now describe a formal mechanism of *identification*. We will first describe the form and effect of identification, and then turn to the conditions under which a given identification may be made.

All of the identifications which we describe must have the essential form (cf. §5.4.1):

For X_1 a $\mathcal{D}_1$, X_2 a $\mathcal{D}_2$, ... and X_n a $\mathcal{D}_n$, we identify $\mathcal{N}_1(X_1, X_2, \ldots X_n)$ with $\mathcal{N}_2(X_1, X_2, \ldots X_n)$.

where $\mathcal{D}_i$ are N's and $\mathcal{N}_1(X), \mathcal{N}_2(X)$ are definite, singular noun phrases. In other words, the choice of words used to effect an identification may vary, but our theory only handles linguistic formulae which have the same semantic content as the statement just presented.

The formal effect of such an identification is equivalent to the assertion of the following axiom:

For X_1 a $\mathcal{D}_1$, X_2 a $\mathcal{D}_2$, ... and X_n a $\mathcal{D}_n$, $\mathcal{N}_1(X_1, X_2, \ldots X_n)$ is equal to $\mathcal{N}_2(X_1, X_2, \ldots X_n)$.

Additionally, the assertion of this axiom causes the types of the objects $\mathcal{N}_1(X_1, X_2, \ldots X_n)$ and $\mathcal{N}_2(X_1, X_2, \ldots X_n)$ to collapse into a single type.

Before we turn to the technical conditions under which identifications may be made, we will illustrate these remarks by giving an example of a statement with the above form. To do so, we will return to the very first instance of identification which we discussed, namely the identification of natural numbers and integers. The full details of this example will be given in §7.5.3; for now, we will only note that we introduce a 'system of natural numbers' and a 'system of integers', and then wish to identify each natural number with the corresponding integer. If we have set up terminology to label the natural numbers $0, 1, ...,$ and the integers $0_{\mathbb{Z}}, 1_{\mathbb{Z}}, ...,$ then an appropriate identification statement is:[26]

For n a natural number, we identify n with $n_{\mathbb{Z}}$.

The effect of this identification is equivalent to the assertion of the axiom:

For n a natural number, n is equal to $n_{\mathbb{Z}}$.

Assertion of this axiom also causes the type to which natural numbers belong and the type to which integers belong to collapse into a single type.

In §7.2.2, we noted that an approach taking identification to be equality did not work in a standard account of the foundations. The key advance which allows us to rehabilitate this approach is the existence of systems; because natural numbers and integers belong to different systems, they are *a priori* unrelated and we may assert that they are equal without causing a contradiction. The conditions which we give immediately below will ensure that this is the case in general.

Identifications may only be made when two specific conditions hold. The first of these is a local condition, which essentially requires that the two collections of objects being identified have the same structure in all relevant respects; the second is a global condition which ensures that if we make many identifications, these identifications 'fit together' in a technically correct way. We will describe these conditions in turn.

Local Condition

An identification of the form

For X_1 a $\mathcal{D}_1$, X_2 a $\mathcal{D}_2$, ... and X_n a $\mathcal{D}_n$, we identify $\mathcal{N}_1(X_1, X_2, \ldots X_n)$ with $\mathcal{N}_2(X_1, X_2, \ldots X_n)$.

may only be made if the following sub-conditions hold:

---

[26] In this case one can choose a more fluid choice of phrasing with the same semantic content, such as:

We will identify each natural number n with the integer $n_{\mathbb{Z}}$.

The syntactic variations among semantically equivalent phrasings can be completely captured by the theory given in Chapter 3, and so have no impact on the fundamentally semantic theory described here; we will not discuss them again.

Additionally, as we will shortly explain, each identification is licensed by a given pair of models. In practice, we might choose to emphasise this by writing, say:

Using Model 1.12 and Model 1.13, we will identify each natural number n with the integer $n_{\mathbb{Z}}$.

1. There exists systems $\mathcal{S}_1, \mathcal{S}_2$, independent of the X_i, such that all of the $\mathcal{N}_1(...)$ are objects created out of thin air in the system $\mathcal{S}_1$, and similarly all of the $\mathcal{N}_2(...)$ are objects created out of thin air in the system $\mathcal{S}_2$. (Note that according to the rules given in Chapter 5, this means that $\mathcal{N}_1(...)$ and $\mathcal{N}_2(...)$ necessarily belong to different types before any identifications take place.)
2. A model $\mathcal{M}_1$ of $\mathcal{S}_1$ has been explicitly presented, such that for every $\mathcal{D}_1\ X_1$, $\mathcal{D}_2\ X_2$, ... and $\mathcal{D}_n\ X_n$, the object in $\mathcal{M}_1$ corresponding to $\mathcal{N}_1(X_1, X_2, \ldots X_n)$ is just $\mathcal{N}_2(X_1, X_2, \ldots X_n)$.
3. As with 2., but with $\mathcal{S}_1 \leftrightarrow \mathcal{S}_2$, $\mathcal{M}_1 \leftrightarrow \mathcal{M}_2$, $\mathcal{N}_1 \leftrightarrow \mathcal{N}_2$.
4. Suppose that a term or piece of notation is defined in $\mathcal{S}_1$, and (treated as a sequence of tokens) that term or piece of notation would have an interpretation in $\mathcal{S}_2$ *if* the appropriate type collapse had occurred. Then the correlate of the term or piece of notation in $\mathcal{M}_1$ must be equal to its interpretation in $\mathcal{S}_2$.
5. As with 4., but with $\mathcal{S}_1 \leftrightarrow \mathcal{S}_2$, $\mathcal{M}_1 \leftrightarrow \mathcal{M}_2$.

We may illustrate this by returning to our example with natural numbers and integers. In this case, condition 1. specifies that $\mathcal{S}_1$ must be the system of natural numbers and $\mathcal{S}_2$ must be the system of integers. The next two conditions are:

2. A model $\mathcal{M}_1$ of the system of natural numbers has been explicitly presented, such that for every natural number n, the object in $\mathcal{M}_1$ corresponding to n is just $n_{\mathbb{Z}}$.
3. A model $\mathcal{M}_2$ of the system of integers has been explicitly presented, such that for every natural number n, the object in $\mathcal{M}_2$ corresponding to $n_{\mathbb{Z}}$ is just n.

In other words, for the identification to be made, there must be an explicitly presented model of the natural numbers in which natural numbers are just nonnegative integers, and an explicitly presented model of the integers in which nonnegative integers are just natural numbers. We will discuss the construction of models with these properties when we give full details of the construction of numbers, in §7.5.3.

Conditions 4. and 5. are like a 'structure preservation' requirement; they ensure that simple examples of notation which can be interpreted in both systems have the same meaning in both. To illustrate them in our concrete example, we need to first list the terms and pieces of notation defined in the two systems under consideration. (Cf. §7.5.3 for details.)

System of Natural Numbers   'natural number', '0', 'successor (of x)', 'Sx', 'sum of x and y', '$x + y$', 'product of x and y' and 'xy' (where x and y have type NATURAL NUMBER).

System of Integers   'integer', '0', 'sum of x and y', '$x + y$', 'difference of x and y', '$x - y$', 'minus x', '$-x$', 'product of x and y' and 'xy' (where x and y have type INTEGER). Also, for n having the type NATURAL NUMBER, one defines '$n_{\mathbb{Z}}$', the integer corresponding to n.

Identification causes the types NATURAL NUMBER and INTEGER to collapse into a single type. Consequently, out of the material introduced in the system of natural numbers, the following have an interpretation in the system of integers:

'0', 'sum of x and y', '$x + y$', 'product of x and y' and 'xy'.

Condition 4. therefore requires that in the model in which natural numbers are just nonnegative integers, each of these expressions refers to the same object whether interpreted using the language of the system of natural numbers, or the language of the system of integers. In other words, it requires that the natural number '0' is the same as the nonnegative integer '0_Z'; that $(x + y)_Z = x_Z + y_Z$; and so on.

In this case, we have a direct correspondence between notations in the two systems, so that conditions 4. and 5. are equivalent; in general this need not be the case. For example, if one system defines 'x^2' and a second defines 'x^n', then instances of 'a^2' may be interpreted in the second system, but instances of 'a^n' cannot be interpreted in the first system.

It is worth emphasising conditions 4. and 5. do not exclude ambiguity from arising during identification. In fact, ambiguity can arise in two independent respects. First, notation that is defined outside the system can become ambiguous. The canonical example is exponentiation (cf. §2.6 on reanalysis). Exponentiation of natural numbers and exponentiation of integers are distinct operations, and after the type of natural numbers and the type of integers are collapsed into a single type, the (typed) syntactic rules capturing the two operations are formally identical. Thus after identification, 'n^m' is indeed ambiguous. As discussed in §4.1.5, this constitutes an informational gap which can be filled in by making a statement such as

If n and m are integers, then n^m is unambiguous.

In some cases, such as during the reanalysis of an integer exponent into a real exponent, a reasonable amount of mathematics is needed to support statements of this kind (cf. §2.6).

The second source of ambiguity arises from 'transitive' identification. Suppose that we identify system A with system B, and system B with system C. If some notation is defined on systems A and C, but not on system B, that notation may become ambiguous. To take a concrete example, if we identify the natural numbers both with particular integers and with some other objects on which '$x - y$' is defined, '$-$' may end up having two meanings. Conditions 4. and 5. do not preclude this possibility. If it occurs — and we know of no case where it does — it would constitute an informational gap, which could be filled in using the mechanism discussed in §4.1.5. This 'lazy' approach is quite deliberate. As we saw in Chapter 4, mathematical language genuinely contains extensive ambiguity, especially global ambiguity which arises from independent local operations; any theory which attempts to completely exclude ambiguity both fails to reflect the actual data and (alarmingly) requires individual authors to be aware of the totality of mathematics.

The real function of conditions 4. and 5. is not to preclude ambiguity, but to restrict the formal notion of identification so that it more closely resembles our intuitive notion of what identification should be like. To take a specific example, these conditions prevent us from defining something that is like the integers but with notation for addition and multiplication switched, and then identifying a subset of this with the natural numbers.

The Local Condition and Isomorphism

In §7.2.9, we noted a number of problems with the idea that isomorphism of some kind licences identification. First, isomorphism licenses the identification of $\mathbb{C}$ with itself in a non-trivial way. Second, it is not clear in what respects structures must be isomorphic in order for an identification not to introduce properties that were not previously true. Third, it is possible to construct structures that are isomorphic in every conceivable respect, but which behave differently with respect to identification. In the course of presenting these problems, we considered a number of concrete examples which demonstrated the inadequacy of isomorphism as a licensing condition for identification.

Of the problems just listed, the first (related to the self-identification of $\mathbb{C}$) will be ruled out by the global condition, which is constructed to serve that specific end. The other two problems are handled correctly by the local condition. In this section, we will give some indication of why this is the case, and illustrate the way in which the local condition resolves the difficult examples from §7.2.9. We will continue to illustrate comments using the example with natural numbers and integers which was introduced earlier in this section; as noted there, full details of this example are given in §7.5.3 below.

The key to the functioning of the local condition lies in sub-conditions 2. and 3.. As we noted above, in the example we are considering, these reduce to:

2. A model $\mathcal{M}_1$ of the system of natural numbers has been explicitly presented, such that for every natural number n, the object in $\mathcal{M}_1$ corresponding to n is just $n_{\mathbb{Z}}$.
3. A model $\mathcal{M}_2$ of the system of integers has been explicitly presented, such that for every natural number n, the object in $\mathcal{M}_2$ corresponding to $n_{\mathbb{Z}}$ is just n.

That is, we have a model $\mathcal{M}_1$ of the natural numbers in which natural numbers are just nonnegative integers, and a model $\mathcal{M}_2$ of the integers in which nonnegative integers are just natural numbers.

Now, let us take any property of either system. For example, it is the case that in the system of natural numbers, $1 + 1 = 2$. Because $\mathcal{M}_1$ is a model of the natural numbers, $1 + 1 = 2$ inside $\mathcal{M}_1$; and because in $\mathcal{M}_1$ natural numbers are just nonnegative integers, we have that $1_{\mathbb{Z}} + 1_{\mathbb{Z}} = 2_{\mathbb{Z}}$ inside the integers. So the arbitrary fact that held of the natural numbers must also hold of the integers. Applying symmetry, we can see that the local condition tells us that the same facts must hold for both systems.

The key to the effectiveness of our formal version of identification is that this argument extends to facts like:

The set of natural numbers exists.

As before, because $\mathcal{M}_1$ is a model of the natural numbers, this fact is true inside $\mathcal{M}_1$; and because in $\mathcal{M}_1$ natural numbers are just nonnegative integers, it must be the case that

The set of nonnegative integers exists.

holds inside the integers. If we refer back to §7.2.9, we can see that this solves one of the major problems we discussed: it is guaranteed that when we identify (collections of) objects we are not introducing 'new facts', in a way that was not the case when we only checked the isomorphism of $(\mathbb{N}, +_{\mathbb{N}}, \times_{\mathbb{N}})$ and $(\mathbb{Z}'_{\geqslant 0}, +_{\mathbb{Z}'}, \times_{\mathbb{Z}'})$.

The other problem that we encountered was exemplified by the example about pseudo-integers, which were introduced in the same way as integers but for the following additional statement:

($*$) Pseudo-integers are not natural numbers.

Now that we have our formal machinery, it is easy to make this operation precise. The system of pseudo-integers looks exactly like the system of integers (which will be given in detail in §7.5.3), except that it refers to 'pseudo-integer' instead of 'integer' and contains ($*$) as a final line. And if we have constructed a model for the integers, as we will do in §7.5.3, we can construct another model for the integers by replacing each integer x with $(x, \mathbb{N})$. Since no object of the form $(x, \mathbb{N})$ can be an element of $\mathbb{N}$, we only need to shift terminology (from 'integer' to 'pseudo-integer'), to obtain a model for the pseudo-integers. Thus, from the perspective of systems and models, pseudo-integers are as valid as integers.

As we saw in §7.2.9, isomorphism failed to prevent the identification of natural numbers and nonnegative pseudo-integers. But the local condition requires us to give a model of the pseudo-integers in which non-negative pseudo-integers are just natural numbers. It is impossible to construct such a model, for the following reason. In order to give a model of the pseudo-integers, we need to check, one by one, that the assertions given in the system hold of the putative model. In particular, we need to check that in any putative model, ($*$) is true. And if we have constructed some candidate for modelhood in which pseudo-integers corresponds to natural numbers, it will clearly not be possible to prove that ($*$) is true. Thus one of the models required by the local condition cannot be constructed, and the local condition rules out the identification of natural numbers and nonnegative pseudo-integers in a way that isomorphism failed to do.

Global Condition

In order to state the global condition, we will introduce a category, called the *identification category*, which represents the (ontogenetic) state of mathematics after some of the formal mechanisms described in this section have been used. The category is defined as follows:

The objects of the category are collections, each with a label attached. (The use of 'collection' rather than 'set' is to distinguish from the mathematical uses of 'set' in this chapter; similarly while discussing the global condition we refer to things inside a system as 'entities', not 'objects', to avoid confusion. We will return to these points at the end of the discussion.) Thus more than one object may correspond to the same collection if different labels are used. The actual category contains one object for each system: each system is represented by the collection containing precisely those entities that are created out of thin air in that system. The object corresponding to a system is labelled with the name of the system.

The morphisms of the category are partial functions between the collections which function as objects, with composition of morphisms just being function composition. For each identification between two systems, the identification category contains a pair of inverse morphisms between the objects corresponding to those systems. Each morphism maps those entities that have undergone identification to the entity with which they have been identified. The only morphisms of the identification category are the identity morphisms on each object (which are total identity functions on the underlying collection), the morphisms 'corresponding to identifications' that we have just introduced, and compositions thereof.

We may illustrate this with respect to the examples given previously in this section. We have referred to three systems, namely the system of ordered pairs, the system of natural numbers and the system of integers; each of these will correspond to one object in the category. The identification between natural numbers and integers results in the creation of a pair of inverse morphisms between the corresponding objects. One morphism maps each natural number n to the corresponding nonnegative integer $n_{\mathbb{Z}}$, and the other morphism maps each nonnegative integer to the corresponding natural number. Thus the identification category is generated by:

Ordered Pairs   **Natural Numbers**   **Integers**
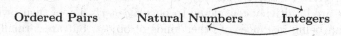

The global condition states that the identification category may not contain any maps from an object to itself which are not (total or partial) identity functions.

As we noted above, the global condition serves a narrow technical function. It ensures that two objects from the same system cannot be identified, and that each object from one system can be identified with at most one object from any other given system. By doing so, it excludes examples like the 'identification of $\mathbb{C}$ with itself along a non-trivial automorphism' (§7.2.4), whether such an illegal identification is performed in one step or indirectly via several other identifications.

In most of the cases we will consider, the global condition is trivially satisfied. We can introduce a more specific diagnostic. Consider the (multi)graph that contains one node for every system, and one edge for every identification, connecting the systems that have been identified. In the above example, this takes the following form:

Ordered Pairs   **Natural Numbers** ——— **Integers**

If this *identification graph* is acyclic, then it is easy to see that the global condition trivially holds. Note that this remark is a formalisation some of our informal comments in §7.2.7.

Finally, a technical caveat. The mathematical machinery (categories, collections, etc.) that we have used to describe the global condition should be taken as belonging to a meta-mathematical level of description. In particular, objects from this level may not be referred to by mathematical objects. Thus we may legitimately speak of 'the system of all sets' being represented in the identification category by 'the collection of all sets', or 'the system of all categories' being represented by 'the collection of all categories'.[27] In fact, very little machinery is actually needed to state the condition; the categories are all finite and the collections are all extensions of mathematical properties. Thus our use of mathematical terminology here is largely a matter of convenience rather than a matter of substance.

7.5   Application

This section illustrates the way in which systems, models and identification may be applied to develop foundational mathematics.

7.5.1   *Simple Objects*

As we noted in §7.2.1, many simple objects introduced in the foundations of mathematics are intuitively considered to be *sui generis*, i.e. of their own kind rather than being instances of other kinds of object, but are formally defined as sets. This causes both linguistic problems (due to collisions between the notations which are 'genuinely' defined on those objects and notations for sets) and philosophical problems (because Benacerraf's criticism applies). We can reverse these observations to construct two objective diagnostics for objects which are 'intuitively *sui generis*, but formally sets'. First, if an object A can participate in set notation — for example, by writing 'A^B' for the set of functions from B to A, or '$A - B$' for the set of objects that are in A but not B — then it is genuinely a set; if not, it is *sui generis*. Second, if an object could have been constructed in a different way without affecting its

---

[27] We do not necessarily need to regard sets and categories as part of systems, although there are certain advantages in doing so. See §7.5.5 for further discussion.

use in mathematics, i.e. with mathematicians using different versions able to communicate, then it is *sui generis*; otherwise it is a set. (Directly analogous diagnostics may be used to determine not just whether objects genuinely are sets, but whether they are of any given kind; for example, we will apply them in §7.5.4 below to determine whether cardinals really are ordinals.)

We know of no example on which these two diagnostics disagree. Applying them tells us that, for example, intersections, unions and products of sets are genuinely sets, as are equivalence classes; but ordered pairs, relations, functions and numbers of all kinds (including ordinals and cardinals), are *sui generis* and are not sets.

As we noted in §7.4.1, we can overcome these problems by adopting a two-stage approach to objects that are *sui generis*. When we need to introduce such objects, we will define them out of thin air in a system, as we did for ordered pairs in §7.4.1. By doing so, we are effectively axiomatising the objects directly, which avoids both the linguistic and philosophical problems at the cost of causing a separate epistemological problem. Second, we provide a concrete model for the system; by doing so, we neutralise this epistemological problem.

There are a number points worth noting here. First, there are very few cases in which simple objects are commonly axiomatised. (For example, the natural numbers are axiomatised via Peano's axioms, and real numbers via their characterisation as a complete ordered field.) Thus much of the content of systems will need to be created from scratch. Typically a system will consist of assertions that appropriate objects exist, followed by necessary and sufficient conditions for objects to be equal. Models, on the other hand, are rarely created from scratch; one adapts the standard set-theoretic definitions to construct a model, just as we did with Kuratowskian ordered pairs in §7.4.1.

Second, when we are constructing our 'concrete' model, we may safely use not only sets but objects introduced in other systems which have themselves been given concrete models. In effect, the necessary property that the objects in question could be sets will percolate up a pyramid of objects constructed in this way.

Third, we are always free to give more than one model of the system. This allows us to give competing constructions (e.g. Von Neumann's natural numbers and Zermelo's natural numbers) without needing to privilege one above the others. We are also free to give a new model for an old system at any point in (ontogenetic) time. For example, after encountering category theory, we can retroactively but monotonically give category-theoretic models for various of the systems we have encountered. Together with reanalysis (§2.6), which allows us to monotonically reinterpret pieces of existing notation as functors, this allows the theory to reflect the real ontogenetic development of mathematicians: one initially thinks of all objects in terms of sets, and then slowly shifts to thinking of the objects in many areas of mathematics in more category-theoretic terms.

Fourth, the fact that we have introduced certain objects axiomatically may force us to change the definition of other objects that genuinely are sets.

For example, defining ordered pairs in a system invalidates the definition of the product of sets A and B (which is a set of ordered pairs) as a subset of the power set $\mathcal{PP}(A \cup B)$.

Fifth, and last, both the above diagnostics and the use of a system and model may be applied to avoid concrete constructions in terms of objects other than sets. For example, sequences, vectors and matrices behave like functions but should not be defined as functions, both because this causes notational collision and because Benacerraf's criticism applies. Thus we should introduce each of these kind of objects in a distinct system and then construct a concrete model for each such system using functions. We will see another example of this kind when we discuss ordinal and cardinal numbers in §7.5.4 below.

We will illustrate these remarks with a two-stage example. The first stage builds on our 'ordered pair' example from §7.4.1 to introduce the product of sets A and B as a concrete set. The second stage will define the system of relations, and use products to construct a model of this system.

Defining the product of sets A and B is straightforward, as long as we are careful not to rely on the set-theoretic structure of the Kuratowskian ordered pair. We only need to state the following definition:[28]

Definition. If A and B are sets, then the product of A and B, $A \times B$, is the set

$$\bigcup \{\{(a,b) \mid a \in A\} \mid b \in B\}.$$

This definition gives $A \times B$ the homogenous type SET OF ORDERED PAIRS, and so supports the inference stating that members of a product are ordered pairs. (Cf. §5.3.5 and §5.4.4.)

The next step is to introduce relations. In order to do that, we first need to present the system of relations, i.e., to axiomatise what it means to be a relation. This particular axiomatisation is not commonly found in textbooks, and so must be constructed *ab initio*:

System 1.5 'Relations'

Let A and B be arbitrary sets. There are some objects called relations between A and B. If R is a relation between A and B, then for certain $a \in A, b \in B$, we say that R relates a to b and write aRb.

If X is a subset of $A \times B$, then there is a relation R between A and B such that for all $a \in A, b \in B$, aRb if and only if $(a,b) \in X$.

If R and R' are relations between sets A and B, and for every $a \in A, b \in B$, aRb if and only if $aR'b$, then $R = R'$.   □

---

[28] To see that this works, observe that if $A = \{a_1, a_2, \ldots a_n\}$ and $B = \{b_1, b_2, \ldots b_m\}$, then $\{\{(a,b) \mid a \in A\} \mid b \in B\}$ is just

$$\{\{(a_1, b_1), (a_2, b_1), \ldots (a_n, b_1)\}, \{(a_1, b_2), (a_2, b_2), \ldots (a_n, b_2)\},$$
$$\ldots, \{(a_1, b_m), (a_2, b_m), \ldots (a_n, b_m)\}\}.$$

Note that we have used the standard definition of a relation (as a subset of $A \times B$) in order to assert that sufficiently many relations exist. This development is characteristic of many systems introducing objects which are *sui generis*. (And note in particular that we did not say that a relation exists for every two-place formula with an appropriate shape; this would only have ensured that countably many relations existed.)

Introducing this system expands the epistemic basis, and we should immediately reverse this expansion by providing a concrete model of the system. We may do this as follows:

Model 1.6 of System 1.5 'Relations as Products'

Let A and B be arbitrary sets. A relation between A and B is a subset of $A \times B$. If R is a relation between A and B, and $(a, b) \in R$, then we say that R relates a to b and write aRb.

If X is a subset of $A \times B$, then X is a relation between A and B and for all $a \in A, b \in B$, aXb if and only if $(a, b) \in X$.

Suppose that R and R' are relations between sets A and B, and for every $a \in A$, $b \in B$, aRb if and only if $aR'b$. Then

$$R = \{(a, b) \in A \times B \mid aRb\} = \{(a, b) \in A \times B \mid aR'b\} = R'.$$

This model primarily consists of the usual concrete, set-theoretic definition of a relation; as we noted above, this reuse of concrete definitions inside models is typical.

Looking ahead, the next natural step would be the introduction of the system of functions, followed by the presentation of a concrete model of functions as sets. This system and model rely on relations in just the same way as the above system and model for relations relied on ordered pairs. First, one would state in the system that for every relation with a particular property, an appropriate function existed; and second, one would use relations as part of the construction of the concrete model of functions. However, in this case, the model would not simply be the standard construction, which is (as we noted in §7.1) technically incorrect in that it does not determine the co-domain of a function. Instead one could e.g. build a 'concrete' function as an ordered triple (A, B, X), where A is the domain of the function, B is its co-domain, and X is the relation determining the function. (A is unnecessary, but excluding it creates an ugly asymmetry between A and B.) If one chose to follow this approach, one would first need to introduce the system of ordered triples or the system of ordered n-tuples, and then provide a model for that system.[29]

---

[29] Note that the system of ordered pairs needs to be identified with (part of) the system of n-tuples; more specifically, one needs to identify ordered pairs and 2-tuples. Halmos (1960) gives pleasant definitions of ordered pairs and 2-tuples, but actually defines them to be distinct objects, without noticing the incongruity. Other authors ensure that ordered pairs are 2-tuples by giving very unwieldy definitions of n-tuples. By using systems, models and identification, we obtain the best of both worlds: we give the more attractive definitions, but can easily identify ordered pairs with 2-tuples.

Finally, a brief note about structures and systems. Under many accounts, structures are taken to be ordered tuples. Let us focus on a single example of structures, say groups, and evaluate this position. Applying the two diagnostics given at the beginning of this section, we see that groups do not support 'ordered tuple notation'. Additionally, groups could be defined in multiple ways, for example as the ordered pair of a set and a function, or the ordered pair of a function and a set; mathematicians using different definitions would remain able to communicate. Thus groups (and other structures) are not ordered pairs. We could certainly have applied the mechanism of systems and models to set up group notation: the behaviour of a group would be defined axiomatically in a system, and a model of this system involving an ordered pair of a set and a function would leave the epistemic basis unchanged. There are two problems with this approach. First, a separate system needs to be given for each kind of structure. Second, the general fact that a 'X together with a Y' can be treated as an 'X' (§5.4.8) would need to be manually encoded into each such system. In both of these respects, this approach fails to capture generalisations about the nature of structures. For this reason, we adopted a different approach to structures (§5.3.3): we allowed the elimination of structures via the expansion of each individual structure into several objects in the semantic representation. (So, for example, every group was expanded into a set and a function.) As we noted in §5.3.3, this was a theoretical move to avoid the need for new logical machinery; for practical purposes it is preferable not to make this expansion.

7.5.2   Natural Numbers

Natural numbers were our first examples of objects which were defined as sets, but which supported their own notation, colliding with set notation (§7.2.1). They were also the target of Benacerraf's original criticisms in Benacerraf (1965). Both of these problems arise because we intuitively think of natural numbers as being *sui generis*, but formally define them as sets for epistemological reasons. We may resolve both problems without violating epistemological considerations by applying the approach introduced in the previous section (§7.5.1): we create natural numbers out of thin air in a system, and exhibit a concrete model of that system using sets in order to satisfy the epistemological constraints.

The system of natural numbers gives one of the few cases where the necessary axiomatisation is already available, in the form of Peano's axioms augmented with axioms for addition and multiplication. We have a choice between stating the version that gives the axiom of induction in terms of properties (using higher-order language, as described in §8.2), and the version that gives the axiom of induction in terms of sets. The theory we have given above supports both versions equally fluidly; we will choose the latter variant in order to avoid the use of higher-order language, which we will not discuss until §8.2.[30] An appropriate axiomatisation is:

System 1.9 'Natural Numbers'

There are some objects called natural numbers. Further:

(i) One particular natural number is denoted 0.

(ii) Given any natural number n, there is a natural number called the successor of n and denoted Sn.

(iii) 0 is not the successor of any natural number.

(iv) If m and n are natural numbers and $Sm = Sn$, then $m = n$.

(v) Suppose that a set A contains 0, and that whenever A contains a natural number n, A also contains Sn. Then A contains all natural numbers.

If n and m are natural numbers, then there is a natural number called the sum of n and m and denoted $n + m$. $0 + n = n$ for any natural number n, and $n + Sm = S(n + m)$ for any natural numbers n and m.

If n and m are natural numbers, then there is a natural number called the product of n and m and denoted nm. $0n = 0$ for any natural number n, and $n(Sm) = nm + n$ for any natural numbers n and m. □

Having given this system, we need to construct a concrete model for it out of sets. Here we are on familiar ground: there is a standard construction which is given in many elementary textbooks, such as Halmos (1960) or Hamilton (1982). The material from such textbooks may be adopted unchanged into the model. As the construction itself is quite lengthy, we will only give an initial part of it, to convey the kind of statements that need to be made:

Model 1.10 of System 1.9 'Von Neumann's Natural Numbers'

We will say that a set X is a successor set if it contains the empty set and if, for each $y \in X$, we have $y \cup \{y\} \in X$ also. By the Axiom of Infinity, some successor set X exists.[31] Let

$$S = \{u \in \mathcal{P}X \mid u \text{ is a successor set}\}$$

and define ω to be $\bigcap S$.[32]

---

[30] In the version that states the induction axiom in terms of properties, axioms for addition and multiplication are required in order to correctly axiomatise natural numbers. We choose to also include them in the 'induction via sets' version as it is convenient to minimise the differences between the two versions.

[31] Note that this assertion about existence introduces a variable X into the discourse; cf. §3.5 for the discussion of this phenomenon.

[32] Note that 'ω' is the standard piece of notation like '0' or 'N'; accordingly we have defined it rather than introducing it as a variable.

Lemma. ω is a subset of every successor set.
Proof. Omitted.   □

A member of ω is called a natural number.

We define 0 to be the empty set; since 0 is a member of every successor set, it is also a member of ω. Thus 0 is a natural number.

Let n be a natural number. We call $n \cup \{n\}$ the successor of n and denote it Sn. Since n is an element of ω, it is also an element of every successor set. Hence $Sn = n \cup \{n\}$ is also an element of every successor set, and is therefore an element of ω. Thus Sn is a natural number.

Suppose that 0 is the successor of some natural number k. Then $\{\} = 0 = Sk = k \cup \{k\}$, so that $k \in \{\}$. But this is absurd; by contradiction, 0 cannot be the successor of any natural number.

[...]

                                                                      □

After this model has been presented, one may proceed to introduce the remaining terms and notation for the natural numbers. Note in particular that one can prove (using the set ω, induction, ϵ-recursion and the Axiom of Replacement) that the set of natural numbers exists, and then denote this set $\mathbb{N}$.

7.5.3 *Integers*

When constructing the integers, and only the integers, we face a situation-specific choice that is entirely orthogonal to our choice of approach for identification. We may either construct integers by taking the natural numbers and adding non-negative integers (essentially, relying on trichotomy), or by constructing *all* integers as entities that behave like differences of natural numbers.

Both of these approaches are technically possible, but the former is unsatisfying for two reasons. First, it misleadingly implies the existence of two dissimilar kinds of integer; it suggest that integers are *either* natural numbers *or* objects of some distinct kind. Second, it obscures the fact that the operation of constructing the integers is essentially closing the natural numbers under a certain operation, namely subtraction; and this in turn makes the construction of the integers look different from the subsequent construction of the rationals by closure under division and the reals by closure under convergence. (Another way to look at this is that there is no natural analogue of trichotomy for rational numbers or real numbers.) Thus we will not rely on trichotomy at all, but will only consider integers in their role as differences of natural numbers.

Our actual approach to integers will have three stages. First, we will describe the system of integers, by specifying appropriate axioms; this ensures that integers are not sets, avoiding notational collision and Benacerraf's criticism. Second, we will provide a concrete model of the integers to meet epistemological concerns. This model will be built out of both sets and other objects that have previously been given concrete models including, notably, natural numbers. Third, we will introduce an appropriate identification between part of the system of integers (specifically, nonnegative integers) and the system of natural numbers to ensure that natural numbers *are* integers.

This three-step approach is characteristic of our general approach to closure. First, the appropriate closure is described axiomatically using a system in order to avoid both notational collision and Benacerraf's criticism. Second, a concrete model of this system is given to satisfy epistemological concerns; in constructing this model we invariably make use of the collection of objects that are being closed (in the example above, natural numbers). Third, we identify the original objects with the elements of the closure to remove unwarranted distinctions (§7.2.2).

The System of Integers

Our first step is to axiomatise the integers as 'objects that behave like differences of natural numbers'. We will assume that the standard notation for the natural numbers has been set up after the system has been stated; so, for example, 1 has been defined, $<$ has been defined, $a + b \times c$ has been specified to mean $a + (b \times c)$, etc.. With this material in place, we may state the system of integers as follows:

System 1.11 'Integers'

There are some objects called integers. Given any natural numbers n and m, there is an integer called the difference of n and m and denoted $n -_z m$. Every integer is the difference of some natural numbers n and m, and if n, m, n', m' are natural numbers, then $n -_z m = n' -_z m'$ if and only if $n + m' = n' + m$. We will denote the difference of a natural number n and 0 by n_z.

If a and b are integers, then there is an integer called the sum of a and b and denoted $a + b$. Further:

(i) If a, b, c are integers then $(a + b) + c = a + (b + c)$.
(ii) If a and b are integers then $a + b = b + a$.
(iii) For every integer a there is an unique integer i such that $a + i = 0_z$; this integer is denoted $-a$.

Also, for any natural numbers n and m, $n_z + m_z = (n + m)_z$.

If a and b are integers, we will call $a + -b$ the difference of a and b and denote it $a - b$.

If a and b are integers, then there is an integer called the product of a and b and denoted $a \times b$. Further:

(i) If a, b, c are integers then $(a \times b) \times c = a \times (b \times c)$.
(ii) If a and b are integers then $a \times b = b \times a$.
(iii) If a, b, c are integers then $(a + b) \times c = a \times c + b \times c$.

Also, for any natural numbers n and m, $n_z \times m_z = (n \times m)_z$.

$\square$

There are two points to note here. First, the theory of typed parsing developed in Chapter 6 would have been able to handle this material even if we had not included the explicit disambiguating subscript on '$-_z$'; this subscript is present for clarity, not by necessity. Second, to make the presentation of models easier, the system is chosen to be minimal: we do not state important facts which can be derived from the included material, such as the fact that for $n \geqslant m$, $n_z - m_z = (n - m)_z$.

A Concrete Model of Integers

The next step is to give a concrete model for the system in terms of sets and objects of other systems which have been given concrete models, including specifically natural numbers. As with natural numbers, this requires us to follow an essentially mechanical process of adapting the concrete construction given in textbooks. For example, we begin by defining integers as equivalence classes of ordered pairs of natural numbers:

Model 1.12 of System 1.11

Let $\sim$ be the equivalence relation on $\mathbb{N} \times \mathbb{N}$ defined by $(n, m) \sim (n', m')$ if and only if $n + m' = n' + m$. The equivalence classes of $\sim$ are called integers. Given any natural numbers n and m, $[(n, m)]_\sim$ is called the difference of n and m and denoted $n -_z m$. Every integer is trivially the difference of some natural numbers n and m, and if n, m, n', m' are natural numbers, then

$$n -_z m = n' -_z m'$$
$$\Leftrightarrow [(n, m)]_\sim = [(n', m')]_\sim$$
$$\Leftrightarrow (n, m) \sim (n', m')$$
$$\Leftrightarrow n + m' = n' + m.$$

We will denote the difference of a natural number n and 0 by n_z.

[...]

The remaining material is essentially identical to that found in any textbook treatment of the construction of the integers; cf. for example (Hamilton, 1982, pp. 12–18).

Requirements for Identification

At this point, we will assume that standard terminology and notation for the integers have been introduced, and the basic properties of the integers have been proved. After this has been done, we only need to identify the natural numbers with nonnegative integers. We discussed this specific example in §7.4.2. In that section, we noted that the required identification may be effected by the statement

We will identify each natural number n with the integer n_z.

(Alternatively, one could use any syntactic variant that could be determined to have the same semantic content using the mechanisms described in the earlier parts of the book.)

We also noted that in order to licence the identification, we needed to explicitly exhibit

1. A model of the natural numbers in which natural numbers are just non-negative integers, and
2. A model of the integers in which nonnegative integers are just natural numbers.

We also needed to satisfy the global condition for identification, but this is trivial as the identification graph becomes

Natural Numbers ——— Integers

As this graph is acyclic, the global condition is trivially satisfied.

Model of Natural Numbers as Nonnegative Integers

Constructing the model of natural numbers as nonnegative integers is technically straightforward, but runs into real problems involving our use of language. Specifically, inside the model, we ignore all the material introduced in the system of natural numbers and construct natural numbers afresh. But our system of integers *referred* to natural numbers, and so our integers themselves depend upon natural numbers. When we attempt to refer to integers inside the model, it is not clear what ought to happen.

This problem is difficult to tackle directly. Fortunately, we can illuminate the situation by considering a closely related problem. We will return to the example given in §7.2.4, wherein we identified the complex numbers with themselves 'along the nontrivial automorphism'. This corresponds to a presentation of a model $\mathcal{M}_{conj}$ for the system S of complex numbers, such that each $a + ib$ in S corresponds to $a - ib$ in $\mathcal{M}_{conj}$. (We will discuss the details of the system of complex numbers in §7.5.4; for the moment we will quote the sections that we need.)

Identification of $\mathcal{M}_{conj}$ and S is prohibited by the global condition on identification, as noted in §7.4.2; but $\mathcal{M}_{conj}$ itself is a perfectly valid model.

Presentation of this model expresses something mathematical; it tells us that whenever we have something that satisfies the axioms comprising the system of complex numbers, i.e., whenever we have a model of the system of complex numbers, we can construct another model (by 'pointwise conjugation'). But although $\mathcal{M}_{\text{conj}}$ is valid, it is very difficult to state. For example, the system of complex numbers states:

> There exist some objects called complex numbers. If a and b are real numbers, then there exists a complex number denoted $a + ib$.

When we construct a model of this system out of real numbers, we may state:

> A complex number is an element of $\mathbb{R}^2$. An element (a, b) of $\mathbb{R}^2$ is denoted $a + ib$.

But although we know what the corresponding definition that we need to make in $\mathcal{M}_{\text{conj}}$ is, we cannot state it. All we can do is to write:

> A complex number is a complex number. A complex number $a - ib$ is denoted $a + ib$.

This is not as nonsensical as it appears; it is in essence an attempt to state that

> A [complex number]$_{\mathcal{M}_{\text{conj}}}$ is a [complex number]$_{\mathcal{S}}$. A complex number $[a - ib]_{\mathcal{S}}$ is denoted $[a + ib]_{\mathcal{M}_{\text{conj}}}$.

In other words, the real problem is ambiguity between references to the system and references to the model. As in the above except, this ambiguity may be removed by the use of explicit subscripts. But requiring explicit disambiguation of this kind makes models very hard to read. Because $\mathcal{M}_{\text{conj}}$ and similar models 'of a system using itself' are in practice entirely useless, we have stipulated that a model may not refer to material introduced in its own system (§7.4.1).

Returning to our main example, in which we want to construct a model of natural numbers as nonnegative integers, we encounter an analogous problem. We want to make assertions like:

> A natural number is a non-negative integer. [...] The sum of natural numbers a and b is the sum of the integer a and the integer b.

Phrases like 'the integer a' are *a priori* ambiguous; 'integer' could either be interpreted to refer to integers relative to the original system of natural numbers, or integers relative to the model currently being constructed. Purely on grounds of convenience, we stipulate that the former is the case. That is, although we are giving an alternative account of what natural numbers 'might be', any references to integers will be taken to refer to our original conceptions of integers, not an induced alternative account of what integers 'might be'.

More technically: suppose that we have $\mathcal{S}_1$ and $\mathcal{S}_2$, $\mathcal{S}_2$ is stated in terms of material introduced in $\mathcal{S}_1$, and we are trying to provide a model $\mathcal{M}_1$ for

$\mathcal{S}_1$ which uses material from $\mathcal{S}_2$. $\mathcal{M}_1$ may not refer to material introduced in $\mathcal{S}_1$ (it is trying to give an alternative account for that same material), but it may refer to material from $\mathcal{S}_2$, and that material is interpreted in its original sense.

This convention removes most of our problems concerning the use of language in the case of the model we are trying to construct. (After we have constructed the actual model, we will give a more detailed account explaining the exact function of the model and, in particular, explicitly exhibiting the fact that this convention does not cause circularity.) Unfortunately, there is one residual problem. In our model, in which natural numbers are to be just the nonnegative integers, we want to define the natural number 0 to be the integer $0_\mathbb{Z}$. The convention given above ensures that this is noncircular, but we still face a technical difficulty. When we refer to the integer $0_\mathbb{Z}$, we are using a compositional combination of reference to the natural number 0 and the notation '$\bullet_\mathbb{Z}$' that we defined in the system of integers. And the reference to 0 remains invalid. We could introduce some further convention, like the subscripts above, to try and disambiguate this; but that would involve extra technical machinery and we would have to take particular care to distinguish between, say, our technical subscripts and mathematical subscripts. (More generally, it is hard to find notation that has not been used by mathematicians!)

Because we only face a problem in a very local area of theory, we will adopt an economical approach and work around the problem by introducing extra definitions. In this concrete case, we will define, say, $0^\mathbb{Z}$ to be $0_\mathbb{Z}$ *before* specifying the model; then the principles given in §7.4.1 make it clear that $0^\mathbb{Z}$ is referring to an integer.[33]

After we have settled these issues, constructing the actual model is straightforward. The definitions are all forced (i.e., we have no choices to make), and all the relevant properties of natural numbers follow directly from properties of integers. Thus we obtain:

We define $0^\mathbb{Z}$ to be $0_\mathbb{Z}$ and $1^\mathbb{Z}$ to be $1_\mathbb{Z}$. If a and b are integers, then we define $a +^\mathbb{Z} b$ to be $a + b$ and $a \times^\mathbb{Z} b$ to be ab.

Theorem 1.13 'Induction for Integers'
Suppose that a set A contains $0_\mathbb{Z}$, and that whenever A contains a nonnegative integer n, A also contains $n + 1_\mathbb{Z}$. Then A contains all nonnegative integers.

Proof. Define $B = \{n \in \mathbb{N} \mid n_\mathbb{Z} \in A\}$. Then B contains 0, and B contains Sn for every $n \in B$. By the Principle of Induction, $B = \mathbb{N}$, and the result follows. $\square$

---

[33] There is some risk of notational collision here, in that we are introducing a definition that does not exist in mathematics. A safer option would be to define an integer which was also called '0', etc., and rely on the mechanisms introduced in previous chapters to remove all of the subsequent ambiguity. We will not follow this approach here as it makes the actual presentation of the model considerably harder to follow.

Model 1.14 of System 1.9 'Natural Numbers as Nonnegative Integers'

A natural number is a nonnegative integer. Further:

(i) The natural number 0^Z is denoted 0.

(ii) If n is a natural number, then $n +^Z 1^Z$ is called the successor of n and denoted Sn.

(iii) Suppose that 0 was the successor of a natural number k. Then $0 = k +^Z 1^Z$ and so $k = -(1^Z)$. But natural numbers are nonnegative. By contradiction, 0 is not the successor of any natural number.

(iv) If m and n are natural numbers and $Sm = Sn$, then $m +^Z 1^Z = n +^Z 1^Z$, so that $m = n$.

(v) Suppose that a set A contains 0, and that whenever A contains a natural number n, A also contains Sn. By Theorem 1.13, A contains all natural numbers.

If n and m are natural numbers, then $n +^Z m$ is called the sum of n and m and denoted $n + m$. $0 + n = n$ for any natural number n, and $n + Sm = n +^Z (1^Z +^Z m) = 1^Z +^Z (m +^Z n) = S(n+m)$ for any natural numbers n and m.

If n and m are natural numbers, then $n \times^Z m$ is called the product of n and m and denoted nm. $0n = n$ for any natural number n, and $n(Sm) = n \times^Z (m +^Z 1^Z) = (n \times^Z m) +^Z n = nm + n$ for any natural numbers n and m. □

We should also explain in detail what systems and models are achieving in this case, not least to emphasise the fact that there is no circularity. Suppose that we have any model A of the system of natural numbers, whose objects are 0_A, 1_A, and so on. (For example, we might have constructed this model out of sets.) The material which we presented before discussing identification allows us to construct from this a model B of the system of integers, whose objects are elements like $0_B = [(0_A, 0_A)]$, $1_B = [(1_A, 0_A)]$ and $-1_B = [(0_A, 1_A)]$.

Now, the material just given allows us to take any system of integers and construct from it a model of the natural numbers. In particular, we can take B and construct a model C of the natural numbers which has $0_C = 0_B = [(0_A, 0_A)]$, $1_C = 1_B = [(1_A, 0_A)]$, and so on. By showing that we can construct this model, in conjunction with earlier material, we have also shown that given any model A of the natural numbers it is possible to construct a pair of models (B, C) of integers and natural numbers respectively, such that the natural numbers of C are integers in the sense of B. This in turn tells us part of what we need to identify natural numbers with certain integers; when we make that step, we are excluding A from being a legitimate model of the natural numbers, but our universe remains consistent partly *because* we have shown that the model of the natural numbers C exists. Note in particular that even though A is no longer a legitimate model of the natural numbers, it still exists a concrete construction; thus our construction of C remains valid.

Model of Integers with Nonnegative Integers as Natural Numbers

Finally, we need to exhibit a model of the integers in which the nonnegative
integers are just natural numbers. Our approach here is to take the concrete
model of the integers we constructed above, in which integers are equivalence
classes of ordered pairs of natural numbers, and apply manual replacement
(§7.2.7) to produce a model with the appropriate structure. More specifically,
we will construct the set

$$(\mathbb{N}^2/\sim) \underbrace{-\{[(n,0)]_\sim \mid n \in \mathbb{N}\}}_{\text{Remove equivalence classes}} \cup \mathbb{N}.$$

and then 'lift' all of the terms, notation and results from our concrete model to
this new model by using an explicit bijection between $\mathbb{N}^2/\sim$ and the above set.
Essentially, we are mechanically relabelling elements of the concrete model
presented above to construct a new model. A technical presentation of this
process is entirely unilluminating, and so we will omit it.[34]

As we noted in §7.2.7, manual replacement is an extremely ugly operation
involving an inhomogenous set (cf. §5.3.5). However, because we have very
explicitly defined models in such a way that nothing stated inside the model
has any impact on subsequent mathematics (§7.4.1), both the inhomogenous
set and the linguistic problems they would cause are completely contained by
the model. In effect, the set constructed by manual replacement is constructed
in a very local way and then thrown away. Note also that because this set is
only used locally, we do not encounter any of the technical problems noted
in §7.2.7, which all derive from defining the integers to *be* elements of this
inhomogenous set.

7.5.4   Other Numbers

Reaching the Reals

The construction of the rational numbers from the integers can be performed
exactly as the construction of the integers from the natural numbers. First,
we introduce the rational numbers as a system; second, we exhibit a concrete
model, using material drawn almost verbatim from textbooks; and third, we
perform the identification associated with the statement

We will identify each integer a with the rational number $a_\mathbb{Q}$.

The two models required to support the identification correspond exactly to
the two models used to identify natural numbers and nonnegative integers.
The first model takes the rational numbers of the form $q/1$ and shows that
these form a model of the integers; the second takes the concrete model from

---

[34] Ideally we would refer to the details in a textbook, but all textbooks utilising
'manual replacement' that we know of similarly omit the details.

the second step and applies manual replacement (§7.2.7) to construct a model
of the rational numbers in which integers really are integers, but all other
numbers are equivalence classes of ordered pairs of integers. Additionally,
the identification graph is just the path

Natural Numbers ——— **Integers** ——— **Rational Numbers**

which is trivially acyclic; thus the global condition of identification is trivially
true.

The construction of the real numbers from the rationals can be made in
exactly the same way. As noted in §7.5.1, one is free to give either the Cauchy
construction of the real numbers, or the Dedekind construction, *or both*, as
models. This reflects the way in which mathematicians really think about
real numbers, and is a consequence of the fact that we have addressed the
heart of Benacerraf's criticism.

One point that we should emphasise is that our development of numbers
is made in full accordance with isochrony; every class of numbers is treated
in the same way as every other. In particular, as we completely introduce
one class of numbers (say, the rationals) before we begin to introduce the
next (say, the reals), it is clear that we are not making any use of the benefit
of hindsight. Thus we have given an ontogenetically satisfactory account of
the numbers. One consequence of this is that our approach can be extended
indefinitely; it can cope with an arbitrary number of closures to wider kinds
of number.

Complex Numbers

Complex numbers need to be treated in a slightly different way to integers,
rational numbers and real numbers. It is the case that they are the algebraic
closure of the real numbers. However they are not usually introduced in this
way; as we noted in §7.2.7, the complex numbers are usually introduced
long before the Fundamental Theorem of Algebra, which states that they are
algebraically closed (and are therefore the algebraic closure of the reals), is
proved. Thus, in most treatments, complex numbers are initially introduced
in a relatively unmotivated way, as ordered pairs of real numbers.

Ontochronic considerations require us to follow the usual order of development. Thus we will introduce complex numbers essentially as ordered pairs of
real numbers, and after some (ontogenetic) time has passed, come to identify
them with the algebraic closure of the reals. We will still not introduce
complex numbers *as* ordered pairs; as usual, this would cause notational
collision, open us to Benacerraf's criticism and close off the possibility of
identifying real numbers with complex numbers. Thus we will introduce
complex numbers in a system, which begins as follows:

System 1.25 'Complex Numbers'

There are some objects called complex numbers. Given any real numbers x and y, there is a complex number denoted $x + iy$. Every complex number can be written in the form $x + iy$ for some real numbers x and y.

[...]

After this, we proceed in the same way as with previous number classes; that is, we give a concrete model (in terms of ordered pairs of real numbers) to show that the complex numbers can be constructed, and then identify the real numbers with complex numbers of the form $x + i0$ via the construction of an appropriate pair of models. Much later, after we have proved the fundamental theorem of algebra, we use the mechanism of identification in order to identify the complex numbers with the algebraic closure of the real numbers (which is also introduced in a system).

Ordinals and Cardinals

The theory developed above also extends to treat ordinal numbers and cardinal numbers without any difficulties. For the usual reasons, we introduce ordinal numbers in a system and leave the concrete construction for a model. The same is true of cardinal numbers, but here the point is worth emphasising because the concrete construction of cardinal numbers is given in terms of ordinal numbers rather than in terms of sets. That is, we do not make a definition such as:

Definition Given any set X, the cardinal number of X, written card X, is the smallest ordinal number which is equinumerous with X.

(Hamilton, 1982, p. 223)

To see that this definition causes notational collision, observe that under this definition $\aleph_0 = \omega$ but $\aleph_0 + 1 \neq \omega + 1$. Thus '+' means something different when applied to cardinals and ordinals, and we require them to be of different types. As usual, Benacerraf's criticism accompanies notational collision, as there are other ways of defining cardinal numbers. (For example, if one uses Von Neumann-Bernays-Gödel-style class theory, one can define a cardinal as a class containing all sets that can be put in bijection with a given set.)

As usual, systems and models dissolve all of these problems. We define the system of cardinal numbers in terms of the essential properties that cardinal numbers need to have, by writing:

System 1.25 'Cardinal Numbers'

There are some objects called cardinal numbers. Given any set X, there is a cardinal number called the size of X and denoted $\#X$ or $|X|$. Every cardinal number is the size of some set, and two sets X and Y have the same size if and only if there is a bijection from X to Y.

[Definitions of addition and multiplication follow]   □

We then give a concrete model of this system, in which cardinal numbers are initial ordinals.

One point of interest here is that finite cardinals are usually identified with natural numbers. This is another example of late identification, and proceeds in the usual way: we construct a model of the natural numbers in which natural numbers are finite cardinals, and a model of the cardinals in which finite cardinals are natural numbers, and check that the overlapping terminology (for addition and multiplication) is consistent.

One particular consequence of this identification that is worth noting is that the type CARDINAL NUMBER is collapsed together with the type NATURAL NUMBER. Since NATURAL NUMBER is itself collapsed with INTEGER, RATIONAL NUMBER, etc. by the identifications listed above, we end up with a single type containing all numbers; this is the type we have denoted NUMBER earlier in the book. Or, more accurately, we should say that the type we called NUMBER is an arbitrary label we use to denote the type that contains natural numbers (among other objects) *at whatever stage in ontogenetic development we are considering*: depending on which identifications have taken place, the label may denote different types.[35] This reflects an observation made in §5.3.5, that types need to be able to 'expand' as ontogenetic time passes and closures occur.

It is also worth noting that if by some unusual path of development one obtains a system of cardinal numbers and a system of real numbers, without having a system of the natural numbers, the finite cardinals and the 'whole' (i.e. nonnegative, integral) real numbers can be identified using the mechanisms described in §7.4.2: one gives a model of the cardinals in which finite cardinals are whole real numbers, a model of the real numbers in which whole real numbers are finite cardinals, and check that the overlapping notation agrees. This case is worth noting for two reasons: first, it indicates that the theory can handle quite extreme ontogenetic variations as long as they are internally coherent, and second, it indicates that the mechanism of identification copes with the case where neither of the systems being identified becomes a proper subset of the other.

7.5.5　Sets and Categories

Digressing briefly, we may note that the theory developed here may be applied to a standard foundational problem in category theory. Typically, one has two conflicting motivations when setting up category theory. On the one hand, one does not wish to expand the epistemic basis; that is, one does not wish to posit axioms beyond the ZF(C) axioms. This is possible, but under standard accounts involves non-monotonically redefining 'set' to mean

---

[35] In our experience, attempting to directly encode the 'ontogenetic time' as part of the name of a type causes confusion rather than clarity; it is simpler to regard a type with a fixed name as changing over ontogenetic time.

'small set'. This conflicts with the second motivation, which is simply that of developing mathematics monotonically.

If one is willing to introduce sets themselves as part of a system, then the exact same mechanisms used above to construct integers and other numbers (§§7.5.3, 7.5.4) can be used to circumvent this dilemma. To do this, we begin by introducing the system of sets, which contains a declaration that there are some objects called sets and lists the standard ZF(C) axioms. We then introduce the system of categories, which asserts that there are some objects called categories, and lists appropriate axioms that categories satisfy. Next, we formally exhibit a model for the system of categories using sets; the existence of this model shows that the ZF(C) axioms are epistemologically sufficient for category theory. Finally, we show that the appropriate conditions hold and monotonically identify sets with elements of the category **Set**; this produces the correct ontological picture, in which some categories are not sets.

Notwithstanding these remarks, we anticipate that having a 'system of sets' may be philosophically contentious. In particular, this approach would mean that the respect in which mathematics can be derived from the ZF(C) axioms is not absolute, as it would be if those axioms were stated outside a system. Rather, it follows from the fact that one can (directly or indirectly) construct models for all other systems out of sets.[36] Accordingly, except for the notes in this section, we have developed the theory in this chapter without committing ourselves either way concerning the existence of a system of sets; we leave the discussion of this issue to further work.

7.5.6 Numbers and Late Identification

To close this section, we will use the examples we have developed to illustrate the notion of late identification (§7.2.7).

In many senses the clearest and most mathematically significant example of late identification is that of the identification of $\mathbb{C}$ with the algebraic closure of $\mathbb{R}$; the Fundamental Theorem of Calculus (needed to motivate and underpin this identification) is a sufficiently substantive result to make it completely

---

[36] It is also worth noting that this approach would also allow us to give alternative foundational accounts within a single mathematical text. For example, we could provide an alternative system of sets using axioms other than those of ZF(C), and show that a model for the standard system of sets could be constructed using these alternative sets; we would then have formally shown that the alternative axioms were sufficient for doing mathematics. Thus we could formalise some notion of relative foundations; i.e. we could formally express the fact that mathematics could be built up from any one of a number of axiom systems. Again, we anticipate arguments as to whether this an attractive property, or whether one should enshrine the status of the ZFC axioms in an absolute way, without the use of a system of sets.

clear that considerable ontogenetic time needs to pass between the introductions of complex numbers and algebraic closures and the identification of $\mathbb{C}$ with $\mathbb{R}$. Unfortunately, this example is technically complex for two reasons. First, the notion of an algebraic closure of a field depends on the field k being considered; while the theory can handle this, it makes the example substantially harder to follow. Second, as noted in the previous section, we have deliberately avoided the question of whether *sets* are part of a system. Because fields are themselves sets, this choice has technical ramifications for the example. For these reasons, we will present a different example of late identification, chosen for its simplicity rather than because it is a naturally occurring example in mathematics. .

For our actual example, we will build on the material we have already discussed. In §7.5.4, we noted that the rational numbers could be introduced by closing the integers under division, using exactly the same line of development that we used to introduce the integers in §7.5.3. But this is not the only way of reaching the rational numbers. In fact, this way of reaching the rational numbers does not match psychological ontogeny: most people do not learn about negative numbers before they learn about fractions. Thus an alternative way of reaching the rational numbers is to proceed from the natural numbers to construct (a system of) nonnegative fractions and to reach the rational numbers from these.

To a considerable degree, the theory we have described already handles this. One may give two different constructions of the rational numbers as separate models; the first will be the construction via the integers, and the second will be the construction via the nonnegative fractions. This approach is entirely adequate *if* one realises that they yield the same result immediately after both constructions have been presented. But if we look beyond this example, in general, in mathematics, this is not the case; just as we continue to discover new mathematical objects, we continue to discover connections between objects. Sometimes we discover that two objects have the same structure and fulfil the same role, and conclude that it would be convenient to identify them. As we noted in §7.2.7, our ontogenetic constraint of isochrony, which requires us to work without the benefit of hindsight, means that our theory has to cope with this kind of late identification.

In our theoretical framework, late identification corresponds to the need to identify two systems after they have been constructed. Because some time passed between the introduction of the systems and our realisation that we needed to identify them (or, alternatively, because the systems correspond to material given by different authors in different textbooks), we are genuinely dealing with two systems; we cannot simply rewrite history to consider one as the 'true system', and the other as a model.

In the case at hand, the two systems are:

- A system of rational numbers$_A$, constructed from the (system of) nonnegative fractions via closure under subtraction, in the manner outlined in

§7.5.3. The system of nonnegative fractions is itself constructed from the system of natural numbers of §7.5.2 via closure under division.

- A system of rational numbers$_B$, constructed from the (system of) integers of §7.5.3 via closure under division, again in the manner outlined in §7.5.3.

Before we can identify the systems, we need to construct a isomorphism pairing up the two versions of the rational numbers; that is, we need to define a bijective function $i : \mathbb{Q}_A \to \mathbb{Q}_B$. This is not difficult, but we will spell out the details to remove any doubt. The easiest approach is to start by showing that each rational number$_A$ can be written in the form $(a/b) - (c/d)$ for some natural numbers a, b, c, d with $b, d \neq 0$ and that each rational number$_B$ can be written in the form $(a' - b')/(c' - d')$ for some natural numbers a', b', c', d' with $c' \neq d'$. (By choosing these natural numbers, we are effectively picking representatives for certain equivalence classes.) We then define the map i by

$$i\left(\frac{a}{b} - \frac{c}{d}\right) = \frac{ad - bc}{bd - 0}$$

We then need to show that i is well defined; this is a laborious but routine exercise in high school algebra.

Once we have our map i, we can formulate the statement that identifies the two systems as follows:

We will identify each rational number$_A$ q with [the rational number$_B$] $i(q)$.

(The part in square brackets may be omitted, but we prefer to leave it in for stylistic reasons.)

In order for this statement to be legitimate, we need to satisfy the local condition and the global condition (§7.4.2). Considering the local condition first, we find that the requirements for models are as follows:

2. A model $\mathcal{M}_1$ of the system of rational numbers$_A$ in terms of rational numbers$_B$ has been explicitly presented, such that for every rational number$_A$ q, the object in $\mathcal{M}_1$ corresponding to q is just $i(q)$.
3. A model $\mathcal{M}_2$ of the system of rational numbers$_B$ in terms of rational numbers$_A$ has been explicitly presented, such that for every rational number$_B$ q', the object in $\mathcal{M}_2$ corresponding to q' is just $i^{-1}(q')$.

In this instance, because there is a one-to-one correspondence between *all* objects in the two systems being considered, or equivalently because we are identifying all objects in both systems, we have no freedom of choice in constructing the models; the local condition specifies exactly what both models need to be. Speaking loosely, to licence the identification, we essentially have to show that the rational numbers$_A$ are a model of the rational numbers$_B$ and vice versa. To satisfy the remainder of the local condition, we also have to show that notation matches in the two systems, i.e., that

$$i(q +_A r) = i(q) +_B i(r)$$

and so on. It is in fact convenient to perform these steps in the other order. First one shows, essentially, that i is an homomorphism with respect to all of the declared notation, and then one uses this fact to demonstrate that the two putative models are indeed models. Again, this is essentially a protracted exercise in high school algebra; for example, in order to check that $i(q +_A r) = i(q) +_B i(r)$, one actually has to show that

$$i\left(\left(\frac{a}{b} - \frac{c}{d}\right) + \left(\frac{a'}{b'} - \frac{c'}{d'}\right)\right) = i\left(\frac{a}{b} - \frac{c}{d}\right) + i\left(\frac{a'}{b'} - \frac{c'}{d'}\right)$$

by expanding out the definition of i given above.

Thus checking the local condition is routine, if tedious. It is the global condition that is of more interest. This is the first case where we are considering an identification graph which contains a cycle (cf. §7.2.7 and §7.4.2); thus this is the first case where the global condition does not follow trivially. In this case, we will actually have to work via the identification category. The category is generated by:

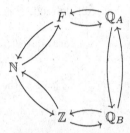

The pairs of morphisms are by definition mutually inverse. Thus in order to check that the global condition, which states that there are no morphisms from an object to itself which are not (total or partial) identity morphisms, we have to check that going 'around the large cycle' brings us back to the point at which we started. To do this, all we need to do is to check that the following diagram commutes:

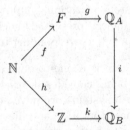

Here F is the set of nonnegative fractions, and the remaining functions are the obvious inclusions, i.e. the functions defined by $f(n) = n/1$, $g(x) = x - (0/1)$, $h(n) = n - 0$, $k(a) = a/(1 - 0)$. Thus for n a natural number, we have

$$i(g(f(n))) = i\left(g\left(\frac{n}{1}\right)\right)$$
$$= i\left(\frac{n}{1} - \frac{0}{1}\right)$$
$$= \frac{n.1 - 1.0}{1.1 - 0}$$
$$= \frac{n - 0}{1 - 0}$$
$$= k(n - 0)$$
$$= h(k(n))$$

as required.

As in this case, verifying the global condition usually amounts to checking that a particular diagram is commutative. Indeed, the only reason why we did not formulate the global condition in terms of a commutative diagram is because that approach makes it harder to represent the identification of a category with itself (as occurs in our example from §7.2.4, involving a nontrivial automorphism of $\mathbb{C}$).

Thus our theory copes with late identification without difficulty. By doing so, it conforms to the highest ontogenetic standard; it copes not only with the ongoing introductions of new mathematical objects, but with the ongoing discoveries that certain of the objects we construct should be regarded as being one and the same.

7.6 Further Work

Our ontogenetic approach opens up three distinct topics in the philosophy of mathematics. The first uses late identification to argue against *realism*, the position asserting that timeless mathematical objects really exist and have objective properties. The second uses the fact that identification happens at a specific (ontogenetic) time and the conventional status of identification to argue against certain features shared by contemporary varieties of *structuralism*, the position arguing that the identities of mathematical objects are less significant than the structures formed by their relationships to each other. The third topic is the development and defence of a novel *formal structuralist position* in the philosophy of maths, based on the material treated in this chapter. We intend to treat each of these topics in subsequent work.

8

Extensions

There are a large number of minor topics in the language of mathematics which do have not have space to describe in depth. §8.1 and §8.2 give brief outlines of our approach to these miscellaneous topics in textual and symbolic mathematics respectively. §8.3 discusses a final major topic.

8.1 Textual Extensions

Anaphora

The typed parsing algorithm of Chapter 6 is fully capable of using type information to determine anaphoric antecedents. Notwithstanding this, examples where this is needed (as, for example, are given in (Ranta, 1994, p. 8)) seem to be rare in real texts.

Definite Descriptions

We follow the DRT-specific approach of van der Sandt (1992) closely. In particular, we treat the presuppositions associated with definite descriptions by introducing generalised anaphors which can have presuppositional material attached to them. It is worth noting that the distinction between binding and accommodation is misleading when applied to mathematics; in all cases, the appropriate way in which to treat presuppositions attached to definite descriptions is to verify that an object with the appropriate properties exist. If there is an explicit antecedent to which one may bind, this is trivially the appropriate object; if not, the object is not explicitly available and a non-trivial proof may be required to verify that it exists.

Prepositional Phrases

An extension of our combined syntactic-semantic rules to allows slots which are tagged with prepositions as well as slots that are tagged with numbers, which allows treatment of prepositional phrases. The typed parsing algorithm can resolve PP attachment ambiguity using type information; because our analysis of prepositional phrases does not overgenerate, this resolves all cases of PP attachment ambiguity that we have encountered in texts.

A

The meaning of the ubiquitous determiner 'a' can vary in meaning depending on its position in the sentence,[1] as in

A [every] domain is simply connected.

0 is **a** [some/one] natural number.

A simple extension to our framework handles this.

8.2 Symbolic Extensions

Higher-Order Constructs

Mathematicians very rarely make explicitly higher-order remarks, preferring to rephrase said remarks in terms of Zermelo-Fraenkel set theory. The most significant instances in which such rephrasing is not possible are the ZF Axioms of Separation and Replacement themselves; examining the presentation of those axioms in a range of textbooks shows that these are *all* informal or incorrect to some degree. We describe one possible way to correctly describe higher-order constructs, designed to fit seamlessly into real mathematical texts.

Further, certain notation is invariably defined for specific mathematical objects but subsequently applied to arbitrary terms; for example, $\lim_{x\to\infty} \bullet$ is formally defined on functions, but subsequently may be applied to arbitrary terms. This 'superficially higher-order' notation may be related to the mechanisms previously introduced.

Ellipsis

Ellipses occur in expressions like '$1^2 + 2^2 + \cdots + n^2$'. There are examples showing that this notation cannot be extensional. Both the dependence of the '$\cdots$' notation on the natural numbers and the existence of finite and infinite variants of '$\cdots$' mean that the notation must be analysed as being introduced by a definition, rather than being built in to our analysis of mathematical language itself. It turns out that the same mechanism used to handle higher-order constructs can be used to introduce ellipsis via definitions.

---

[1] An analogous phenomenon in Dutch mathematics is discussed in (De Bruijn, 1982, p. 86).

Chained Infixed Formal Relations

'Overlapping' mathematical formulae may be compressed into a single long formula, as in the use of:

$$a_0 < a_1 < a_2 < a_3$$

for

$$a_0 < a_1 \text{ and } a_1 < a_2 \text{ and } a_2 < a_3.^2$$

The illegal example '$*a < b > c$' shows that this usage is restricted; there are technical conditions that license it. Again, a straightforward extension to the theoretical framework handles this construction.

Term Lists

Comma-separated lists of terms may be used to abbreviate similar formulae or sentences, as when '$a, b \in \mathbb{N}$' is a shorthand for '$a \in \mathbb{N}$ and $b \in \mathbb{N}$'. Illegal examples such as '$x \in a, b$' suggest that this may only be done at the start of a formula. There is a simple way of handling term lists within the framework of Chapter 3, without extending it, by introducing a single grammatical category.

Exposed Formulae

Exposed formulae are formulae that are used as if they were terms, as in:

For every real number $\epsilon > 0$, there exists a real number $\delta > 0$ such that ...

These always occur at the textual/symbolic boundary: the exposed formula must be used as a noun phrase, not a term. (Cf. '*Then $\epsilon \in \mathbb{R} > 0$'.) Further, exposed formulae must start with a variable, like ϵ, δ above. (Cf. '*For every $0 < \epsilon$, ... '.) The same grammatical category used to handle term lists also enables us to handle exposed formulae without altering the theoretical framework.

Concrete Numbers

We treat concrete numbers such as '114' and '3.1415' by introducing an invisible marker '$\oplus_d$' between adjacent digits. Syntactic and semantic interpretation of $\oplus_d$ may then introduced for specific domains via definitions. This allows material after the decimal point to be interpreted right-to-left, as in '$.1(415) = .1 + (.415)/10$' and material before the decimal point be parsed

---

[2] Cf. (De Bruijn, 1987, p. 926).

left-to-right, as in '$(114)2 = 114 \times 10 + 2$'. It also allows tensors, such as g in, say, general relativity, to support the notation g_{11}, where '11' does not indicate the number eleven but two distinct subscripts, '1' and '1'.

Symbols and Symbol Conventions

In individual mathematical texts, authors sometimes explicitly state that particular *symbols* are conventionally used to indicate specific kinds of object, as when e.g. 'p' is used to denote primes. Such conventions carry across to *derived symbols* such as 'p'' and 'p_0'. We have developed an analysis of the internal structure of symbols and of symbol conventions that can handle the phenomena found in textbooks.

8.3   Covert Arguments

Motivation

As we noted in §5.3.3, it is not necessary to have dependent types in order to understand the linguistic structure of a piece of mathematics. That is, we never need types like ELEMENT OF THE GROUP G or $n \times n$ MATRIX OF NUMBERS in order to determine the syntax of a piece of mathematics, or to resolve the overloading of notation. Nevertheless, there are cases where it is desirable to encode in the semantic representation the kind of information that might be carried by dependent types (such as the group in which an element g lies, or the size of a matrix). The classic example is when one encounters an expression

$$gg'$$

where both g and g' are elements of some group G. Here one would like to obtain as semantic representation not simply

$group\_product(\mathbf{g}, \mathbf{g'})$

but rather

$group\_product(\mathbf{g}, \mathbf{g'}, \mathbf{G})$.

That is, one would like to encode as part of the semantic representation the group in which the product is evaluated.

We know of a clear (and, to our knowledge, novel) diagnostic characterising precisely those cases in which one wishes to infer information of this kind. The diagnostic is as follows:

Suppose that one encounters a definition with the essential form (§5.4.1):

LHS is defined to be RHS.

or

> We say that LHS if RHS.

If the RHS refers to a variable available from the context (§2.5, §3.5) and that variable does not appear on the LHS, then the variable corresponds to an invisible *covert argument* in the semantic function or predicate being defined.

For example, consider one possible definition of the product of elements of a group:

> If g and g' are elements of a group G, then we will write gg' for $m(g,g')$, where m is the multiplication function of G.

Here the right hand side refers to a variable G from the context, but left-hand side ('gg'') does not. Thus G corresponds to a covert argument in *group_product*.

Given the above diagnostic, it is easy to find further examples of covert arguments. For example, the trace of a matrix may be defined as follows:

> Let A be a $n \times n$ square matrix A. The trace of A is defined to be

$$\mathrm{Tr}(A) = \sum_{i=1}^{n} A_{ii}$$

Here both the new N' 'trace [of $\bullet$]' and the new piece of notation '$\mathrm{Tr}(A)$' rely on n for their meaning but do not have it as part of their syntactic realisation. Thus both term and notation refer to a covert argument. Similarly, when defining the product of a $n \times k$ matrix and a $k \times m$ matrix one finds that all of n, k, m appear as covert arguments.

Framework

In the typed parsing process, we simultaneously derived and used a large amount of semantic information because it was necessary to do so; as we showed in detail in Chapter 4 and elsewhere, this information was necessary to derive the syntactic structure of a piece of mathematics. As we have noted, information about covert arguments is *not* needed to deduce syntactic structure; it is never the case that a piece of mathematics will have a different structure depending on, say, which group a product is evaluated in, or the size of matrices being multiplied. Even when one forms illegal expressions — for example by trying to multiply object from different groups or by trying to multiply matrices of incompatible sizes — this can simply be analysed as presupposition failure; we know of no case where illegal operations of this kind should be analysed as having a fundamentally different reading. Note in this respect that it is crucial that *only* objects which have no fundamental type may have a relational type (§5.4.3). This means that, for example, the product of a vector x and a matrix A cannot be analysed as a product of ELEMENTS OF SOME GROUP, because x and A have fundamental types.

As information about covert arguments is never needed to determine syntactic structure, we do not deduce it as part of the typed parsing process. This is partly for parsimony, but it also ensures that expressions which have the same meaning are always treated in the same way by our approach to covert arguments, regardless of their syntactic form; this is an attractive property.

Our first step in handling covert arguments is to introduce extra slots in the semantic functions and predicates. The typed parsing process will simply fill such slots with placeholders which we will denote '$-$'. So, for example, 'gg'' will be translated into

$\quad$ *group_product*$(\mathbf{g}, \mathbf{g'}, -)$.

We then deduce the identity of the covert arguments purely by examining the semantic representations, using means sketched out below.

Note that the use of placeholders is a form of underspecification; the semantic representations produced by the main theory are underspecified with respect to covert arguments. The key point here is that this use of underspecification *separates* the problem of determining covert arguments from the material discussed in the body of this book: each can be considered entirely independently of the other.

Subtleties

Now that we have shown that the problem of determining covert arguments is separable from the other material discussed in this book, we will sketch the remaining points more rapidly. We will concentrate on the example involving products in a group. First, some quick points:

Presentation. For exactly the same reasons given in §5.3.4, i.e. because one can erect a group structure on any set, we are interested not in whether an object is an element of a group, but in whether it has been *explicitly presented as* an element of a group.

Reasoning. Consider the case where we have subgroups H and K of a group G. If we see the expression 'hk', where $h \in H$ and $k \in K$, we need to interpret this as a product in the group G, not a product in either H or K. In particular, we cannot only rely on the way in which h and k have been directly presented as elements of H and K respectively; we also need to utilise the fact that H and K have been explicitly presented as subgroups of G. In other words, some degree of *reasoning* is required.

Ambiguity. If H is a subgroup of a group G, and we see a reference to 'hh'', where $h, h' \in H$, then the product may be interpreted either in H or in G. i.e. we have ambiguity with regard to what the covert argument should be. In this case the ambiguity is spurious: 'hh'' has the same meaning regardless of which candidate is adopted as the covert argument.

The next point is crucial. Consider the following example:

> Assume that we have a sequence of groups G_1, G_2, ..., such that G_n is a subgroup of G_m if and only if n divides m. (An example of this kind genuinely occurs when one is giving a concrete construction of the algebraic closure of the p-adic numbers.) Now, suppose that $g_k \in G_k$ for each k, and we see a reference to the product '$g_n g_m$'. In what group(s) does the multiplication take place? The answer is that the multiplication may be interpreted in G_k where k is any multiple of the highest common factor of n and m.

The key point of this example is that although in *most* cases determining covert arguments requires very little reasoning, it is difficult to put a hard upper bound on the strength of reasoning that is required. We expect there to be very few cases which require us to compute something more complicated than a highest common factor, but we are not confident in asserting this as a uniform upper bound.

Mechanism

Stepping back, we can see that we have exactly the same situation we encountered in §6.5. In particular:

1. There is no theoretical bound on how difficult examples may become. One can contrive an example where G_n is a subgroup of G_m if and only if $P(n, m)$ holds, where P is an arbitrary property. (Examples like this will never occur in practice but are completely legitimate from a mathematical point of view.) Interpreting '$g_n g_m$' then involves deducing arbitrary facts about P. I.e. the general problem is halting equivalent.
2. There is no hard, uniform upper bound on the strength of reasoning that is required to resolve examples that occur *in practice*.
3. On the other hand, the required strength of reasoning tails off rapidly relative to the complexity of examples; one finds fewer and fewer instances of harder and harder examples.
4. From a *computational* perspective, we would like a mechanism that a) resolves the vast majority of practical cases and b) detects extremely hard or contrived cases rather than beginning an extremely expensive computation (i.e. the mechanism should be 'resilient to sabotage').

The mechanism we adopt will tackle this problem in a very similar way to the mechanism of §6.5; the major difference will be that when it detects an excessively hard problem it will not produce an error, but fall back to an implicit specification of the covert argument using modal logic. The key features of the mechanism are as follows:

1. In examples like the one above, involving G_1, G_2, ..., there are too many
   mathematical objects are us to keep track of facts about each one individually. Instead of doing so we will keep track of facts about *intensions*, like
   '$G_\bullet$'; each intension will refer to a family of objects.
2. For each intension, and each explicitly presented relationship that might
   be relevant in determining covert arguments (such as '— is a member of
   the group —' or '— is a subgroup of —'), we keep track of upper and lower
   bounds for the collection of relationships. (The reference to 'relevance' of
   relationships is a rough expression of a technical property.) Note that if one
   is not dealing with sequences of groups, etc., but simply a small number
   of individual objects like G, H and K, then we are keeping track of all
   relevant relationships between individual objects.
3. We ensure that these relationships remain closed under inference; for example, if we know that 'h is a member of the group H' and 'H is a subgroup
   of G', we deduce that h is a member of the group G.
4. Suppose that we have conditional inferences, i.e. we have (explicitly presented) facts that look like:

   > If g is a member of the group G and H is a subgroup of G and *[arbitrary
   > fact holds]*, then g is a member of H.

   where the arbitrary fact is *not* a relevant relationship. When we encounter
   concrete examples where this rule might apply, we will not attempt to
   determine whether the arbitrary fact holds. Instead we will allow the lower
   and upper bounds to diverge from each other: we will add 'g is a member
   of H' to the upper bound for the collection of relationships, but *not* to the
   lower bound. By doing so we encode the fact that 'g *might* be a member
   of H'.
5. The separation of upper and lower bounds also arises when one has definite
   information about a single object that cannot be encoded at the level of
   the intension; for example, a definite fact about G_2 needs to be encoded
   as a fact that might be true about $G_\bullet$.

When we come to try to fill in a covert argument, we take the relevant
relationships, list all the relevant candidates, and extract the lower and upper
bounds for them. For example, when we encounter gg' and know that both g
and g' have the type ELEMENT OF SOME GROUP, we extract the lower and
upper bounds for the relationships

> g is a member of the group —

and

> g' is a member of the group —.

Effectively, we find which groups g is *certainly* an element of, and which
groups g *might* be an element of, and similarly for g'.

We then determine from these relationships a collection of objects that *can* or *might* be used as the covert argument. In this case, this involves determining which groups multiplication certainly could take place in and which groups multiplication might take place in. Suppose that the lower and upper bounds match, i.e. that we are sure of exactly what the candidate groups are. In this case, we construct a *presupposition* to the effect that it does not matter which candidate we choose, and take one as the covert argument. (So, for example, in the example given under the heading of 'Ambiguity' above, where $h, h' \in H$ and $H \leqslant G$, we would construct a presupposition to the effect that '$h *_H h' = h *_G h'$'.) Where we are dealing with intensions like '$G_\bullet$', we universally quantify over the intension, for example presupposing that we can interpret the product in any G_n and the choice of n does not matter.

In the case where the lower and upper bounds do not match, we fall back to a different method involving modal logic. Suppose we have an atomic predicate $P(x_1, x_2, \ldots, x_k, -)$ involving a covert argument, and that we have definite candidates $d_1, d_2, \ldots d_n$, and possible candidates $p_1, p_2, \ldots p_m$ for that covert argument. It turns out that we can construct predicates R_i such that p_i is an candidate if and only if $R(x_1, x_2, \ldots, x_k, p_i)$ *necessarily* holds.

For example, suppose that we have a subgroup H of G and elements $g, g' \in G$. G is a definite candidate for the group in which the product gg' is evaluated; suppose also that we know that H is a possible candidate (due to some conditional inference). Then H is an actual candidate if and only if we could have proved that both g, g' lie in H (using sufficiently strong reasoning). But being able to prove that g and g' lie in H is equivalent to g and g' lying in H in all models;[3] and that in turn can be encoded as '$\Box(g, g' \in H)$', where $\Box$ is the 'necessary' operator from modal logic.

Once we have the R_i, we may simply replace $P(x_1, x_2, \ldots, x_k, -)$ with $\exists h. P(x_1, x_2, \ldots, x_k, h)$, where h carries the presupposition that:

$$P(x_1, x_2, \ldots, x_k, h) \Leftrightarrow P(x_1, x_2, \ldots, x_k, d_1) \wedge$$
$$P(x_1, x_2, \ldots, x_k, h) \Leftrightarrow P(x_1, x_2, \ldots, x_k, d_2) \wedge$$

$$\vdots$$

$$P(x_1, x_2, \ldots, x_k, h) \Leftrightarrow P(x_1, x_2, \ldots, x_k, d_n) \wedge$$
$$(\Box R_1(x_1, x_2, \ldots, x_k, p_i) \Rightarrow (P(x_1, x_2, \ldots, x_k, h) \Leftrightarrow P(x_1, x_2, \ldots, x_k, p_1))) \wedge$$
$$(\Box R_2(x_1, x_2, \ldots, x_k, p_i) \Rightarrow (P(x_1, x_2, \ldots, x_k, h) \Leftrightarrow P(x_1, x_2, \ldots, x_k, p_2))) \wedge$$

$$\vdots$$

$$(\Box R_m(x_1, x_2, \ldots, x_k, p_i) \Rightarrow (P(x_1, x_2, \ldots, x_k, h) \Leftrightarrow P(x_1, x_2, \ldots, x_k, p_m)))$$

---

[3] Or at least, this is true up to considerations of undecidability, which turn out to be irrelevant here.

I.e. we assert that it makes no difference which of the definite candidates is chosen, as all are provably equivalent; and we assert that it makes no difference which of the *actual* potential candidates is chosen, as all are provably equivalent. The key operation we have used is to displace the (potentially arbitrary hard) problem we need to decide into the logical representation, rather than actually attempting to solve that problem inside our linguistic theory.

The case where the covert argument appears in a term is essentially identical. First one removes functions from the semantic representation by introducing extra variables (essentially reversing the process of §3.3.3), so that e.g. $f(g(x)) = y$ is replaced with

$$\exists a.(a = g(x) \wedge \exists b.(b = f(a) \wedge b = y)).$$

Then one handles each expression of the form '$a = f(x_1, x_2, \ldots, x_{k-1}, -)$' (involving a k-ary function f) that includes a covert argument exactly as if it were a $(k + 1)$-ary predicate '$P_f(a, x_1, x_2, \ldots, x_{k-1}, -)$'.

Notes

This approach is extremely resistant to artificially hard problems (i.e. 'sabotage') in exactly the same way as our method in §6.5. Suppose, for example, that we set up groups H and K such that K is a subgroup of H if and only if the Riemann hypothesis is true. This will cause lower and upper bounds to diverge from each other but will not result in any expensive computations or other problematic behaviour. If the divergence of the bounds becomes relevant, i.e. if we have a case in which a multiplication *might* be interpreted in K depending on whether or not the Riemann hypothesis is true, this will simply be encoded into a piece of modal logic that essentially asserts:

> If the Riemann hypothesis is provable (i.e. necessarily true), then multiplication in K must give the same answer as multiplication in H.

It is worth emphasising that we do need the operator $\square$. To see this, suppose that we are considering not the Riemann hypothesis but some property $P(H, K)$ involving H and K. It may be that H are K entirely unrelated, and so $P(H, K)$ is not provable, but that $P(H, K)$ holds *in some models*; for example, the groups C_2 and SO_3 are unrelated, but happen to have elements in common *in some models*. Nevertheless, if $P(H, K)$ is false, we do not want to check that

> If $P(H, K)$ holds *in some model*, then *in that model* multiplication in K must give the same answer as multiplication in H.

Rather, because H are K unrelated, K is irrelevant; we want to say nothing about it at all. (To continue with our example, just because the base sets of C_2 and SO_3 may overlap in some models, we do not want to force them to have compatible group structures in those models.) Thus we *must* check that the property $P(H, K)$ is provable, i.e. holds in all models, before licensing K as a candidate in any model; and to do this, we need the operator $\Box$.

Is also worth noting that we have simplified the above description slightly regarding the treatment of spurious ambiguity. If we have been explicitly shown facts like

If H is a subgroup of G, then $h *_H h' = h *_G h'$.

then we can use these facts to avoid constructing presuppositions. The key to doing this is grouping the candidates for the covert argument into equivalence classes with respect to the relevant notion. For example, in our 'hh'' case, when we need to list the candidates for the group in which the multiplication takes place, we should not state that

H is a definite candidate; G is a definite candidate,

but rather that

H or G is a definite candidate (and it makes no difference which we choose).

This approach can also reduce the number of cases in which we need to fall back to modal logic. For example, if we have a state

G is a definite candidate; H *might* be a candidate,

and we know that H and G give the same result, then we can reduce to the state where

G or H is a definite candidate (and it makes no difference which we choose).

Here fusion of the possible candidate H with the definite candidate G has squeezed out the modality: we know *for certain* that 'G or H' is a definite candidate, and so modal logic need not be utilised. This last point is important because in many real cases elements of a group G could turn out to be elements of some subgroup H by some indirect chain of reasoning, and we prefer not to be forced to invoke modal logic in all such cases.

9

Conclusion

In §1.1, we outlined the main challenges faced in this book. The summary from that section is reproduced here:

> **Breadth.** The theory must be able to describe all of pure mathematics.
>
> **Full Adaptivity.** All mathematical content must be extracted from mathematical text.
>
> **Words and Symbols.** We will need to analyse all phenomena in mathematics by giving a unified description of their relationships to both the words and symbols in mathematics, despite the fact that these are highly dissimilar.
>
> **Ambiguity.** We will find that ambiguity is utterly pervasive in mathematics, and that it crosses the line between words and symbols in an unprecedented way. Resolving this will require novel techniques.
>
> **Belief and Behaviour.** We will need to resolve disparities between the claims mathematicians make about certain mathematical objects and the linguistic behaviour of those objects.
>
> **Time.** We will discover a novel notion of time underlying mathematics, and all accounts of the language of mathematics and the foundations of mathematics will need to be compatible with this.

We will close the book by discussing the way in which we overcame these challenges.

First of all, we required that the theory be able to describe all of pure mathematics. This requirement pervaded the work described in this book, although its impact was rarely explicit. Had we been giving a theory suited to one or two domains, large portions of the book would have been unnecessary. For example, if we had only been concerned with real analysis, then all of our discussions of structures and relational types would have been unnecessary. If we had only been concerned with combinatorics, our extensive discussion of the number system could have been dispensed with. (And so on.) More importantly, if we had only been discussing individual domains, we would

not have found many of the generalisations which we did; for example, it
is unlikely that we would have discovered a general mechanism that could
track both the dimensions of a matrix and the group in which a particular
instance of group multiplication occurred (§8.3). Thus our requirement of
generality exerted a quiet but continual pressure throughout the book, forcing
us to discover deeper patterns rather than giving superficial analysis of the
phenomena at hand.

Our second requirement was that of full adaptivity. Its direct purpose
was to support the first aim by maximising our chances of handling mathematics yet to come (cf. our discussion of time, below). But it raised its
own specific difficulties. Large parts of our analysis were motivated by the
need to handle particular elementary phenomena in an adaptive way. For
example, without our insistence on handling set theory adaptively we would
not have had to tackle inferential types, type inference, parametric types
or any higher-order material (§5.4 and §8.2), and we could have formulated
our typed parsing algorithm (Chapter 6) with reference to a fixed set of
type assignment mechanisms. Equally, if, in a moment of weakness, we had
described the familiar kinds of numbers directly in the theory then we would
have avoided the central problem motivating our entire discussion of the
foundations (Chapter 7). But, ultimately, we would have paid the price for
these concessions. If we had not handled set theory adaptively, then we would
have faced severe difficulties when we reached category theory, which is like set
theory but substantially more complicated; we would have had to rewrite our
entire theoretical framework to explicitly include category theory. Similarly,
if we had not concentrated on handling numbers adaptively we would never
have found the ontogenetic perspective of Chapter 7, which is one of the
major advances of this work; and as a result, our theory would be far more
likely to break down when it encountered future mathematics.

The next two points are naturally discussed together. The need to give a
unified analysis of textual and symbolic phenomena was an ongoing theme in
Chapter 3. It led us to heavily modify Discourse Representation Theory so
that it could account for symbolic phenomena as well as textual. As we saw, a
wide range of symbolic phenomena could be naturally handled by modifying
Discourse Representation Theory, including the (non)interaction of symbolic
terms with anaphor, variables, mathematical donkey-like sentences, symbolic
presuppositions, the asymmetric substitutability of terms for noun phrases,
and the persistence of variables between sentences (§3.3 and §3.5). Yet the
real force of the requirement for a unified analysis only became apparent
when considered in conjunction with ambiguity, which we shall turn to next.

As we showed in §3.2, the extent to which ambiguity was a major challenge
in the work described here arose from the fact that we were considering
many domains, that is, from our first requirement that we model all of
pure mathematics simultaneously. In §4.2, we showed that textual ambiguity
was a substantial problem in its own right: many of the kinds of ambiguity
that occur in natural language also occur in mathematical language, and, in

particular, the specific phenomena that can cause the degree of ambiguity to grow exponentially with sentence length exist in textual mathematics. Symbolic mathematics introduced an even more challenging kind of ambiguity; it allowed the number of types, corresponding to syntactic categories, to increase as time passed (§3.2; cf. our discussion of time, below), and types themselves crossed the boundary between properties and syntactic categories in a way that had no precedent in the literature (§3.6). We needed to disentangle two deeply confused notions of type (§5.1 and §5.2) and delve deeply into mathematical usage (§5.4) before understanding how types could be used to remove symbolic ambiguity.

Yet the hardest problems faced in this volume arose not from textual ambiguity or symbolic ambiguity alone, but when the two were considered in conjunction. As we showed in §3.6, a variable introduced inside a textual sentence could carry syntactic information from one part of the sentence to another. Effectively, we are allowed to introduce a word in one part of a sentence, and declare its part of speech in another; and this operation has no analogue in natural language. Worse, as we showed in §4.3, symbolic ambiguity and textual ambiguity are inextricably intertwined: we cannot determine the textual structure of a sentence and then separately analyse the symbolic material. Thus we needed a joint disambiguation mechanism for both textual and symbolic material. This forced to generalise our notions of type so that they applied to natural language; we had to consider issues like the application of type to textual categories, and the flow of type information around textual sentences, issues which do not have even remote analogues in the literature. In Chapter 6 we resolved such issues and thereby constructed technical machinery, unlike anything in linguistics or computer science, which removed all textual and symbolic ambiguity. Out of all the material discussed in this book, this machinery comes closest to the heart of the language of mathematics; it treats it not as a hybrid or union of textual and symbolic sub-languages, but as a single seamless language of which text and symbol are superficial facets.

After these last points, which led us deep into the heart of the language of mathematics, our fifth point related to the relationship between the language of mathematics and the underlying mathematics itself. More specifically, it arose from the discovery of a gap between the way in which mathematicians manipulate mathematical objects and the properties which they claim those objects have (§5.3.2). We showed that where such disparities arise, it is the use of language rather than the formal ascription of properties that matches mathematicians' actual intuitions (§7.1). As a result, we began our search for a new account of the foundations of mathematics that gave the right linguistic predictions by virtue of reflecting mathematicians' actual intuitions. This search revealed that our linguistic issues interconnected with issues in the philosophy of mathematics, including those raised in Benacerraf's seminal *What Numbers Could not Be* (Benacerraf, 1965, cf. §7.2.1) and concerns about the ontology and epistemology of mathematical objects (§7.3).

Ultimately we introduced a novel notion of time (discussed below) and used this to find the precise points of weakness in all existing foundational accounts; we then built on the intuitions gained by applying this notion of time to construct a new account of the foundations. As well as aligning mathematicians' intuitive beliefs about mathematical objects with their formal properties, and so dispensing with the linguistic problems, this account overcame all of the philosophical difficulties.

Finally, we turn to our novel notion of time itself. Of all the novel concepts discovered in this work, this was the most unexpected and exciting. The more one analyses the language of mathematics, the more central is the role which it takes. Initially, it surfaces only in an awareness of the temporal nature of definitions and of the ordering of texts (§1.2.2); later, one encounters phenomena like reanalysis, which involve an intrinsic notion of irreducible notion of change over time (§2.6); and finally, when one examines the foundations of mathematics, the ontogenetic character of this notion of time becomes clear and it governs all of our analyses of both linguistic and philosophical issues (Chapter 7). In particular, it requires that all of our analyses be able to 'keep pace' with real mathematicians as they continue to learn mathematics: it treats mathematics not as a fixed, unchanging tapestry, but as a living and growing subject. By doing so, it gives our theory of the language of mathematics the best possible chance of expanding to encompass both the mathematics we ourselves have not encountered and the mathematics that is yet to come. In other words, it gives us a strategy for realising our first goal, of describing all of pure mathematics, to a much greater degree than would otherwise be possible. And, out of all the advances presented in this book, this new notion of time is that opens up the largest number of new areas of research (§7.6). We look forward to applying it in future work.

References

Aho, A.V., Ullman, J.D.: The theory of parsing, translation, and compiling. Parsing, vol. I. Prentice-Hall (1972)

Asher, N., Lascarides, A.: Logics of conversation. Cambridge University Press (2003)

Atiyah, M.F., Macdonald, I.G.: Introduction to commutative algebra. Addison-Wesley (1969)

Barendregt, H.P.: The lambda calculus. North-Holland (1984)

Barendregt, H.P., Wiedijk, F.: The challenge of computer mathematics. Philosophical Transactions: Mathematical, Physical and Engineering Sciences 363, 2351–2375 (2005)

Benacerraf, P.: What numbers could not be. The Philosophical Review 74(1), 47–73 (1965)

Birkhoff, G., Mac Lane, S.: A survey of modern algebra. Macmillan (1941)

Blackburn, P., Bos, J.: Working with Discourse Representation Theory: an advanced course in computational semantics (2009), Draft downloadable from www.blackburnbos.org

Bollobás, B.: Graph theory: an introductory course. Springer (1979)

Briscoe, E.J.: Modelling human speech comprehension: a computational approach. John Wiley & Sons (1988)

Burgess, J.P.: Book review: Stewart Shapiro. Philosophy of mathematics: structure and ontology. Notre Dame Journal of Formal Logic 40(2), 283–291 (1999)

Cardelli, L.: Type systems. In: Tucker, A.B. (ed.) The Computer Science and Engineering Handbook, pp. 2208–2236. CRC Press (1997)

Carl, M., Cramer, M., Kühlwein, D.: Landau in Naproche, ch. 1 (2009), http://naproche.net/downloads/2009/landauChapter1.pdf

Chernoff, P.R.: Nonassociative addition of unbounded operators and a problem of Brezis and Pazy. Bulletin of the American Mathematical Society 78(4), 562–563 (1972)

Chomsky, N.: Syntactic structures. Mouton (1957)

Church, A.: A formulation of the simple theory of types. Journal of Symbolic Logic 5(2), 56–68 (1940)

Church, K., Patil, R.: Coping with syntactic ambiguity or how to put the block in the box on the table. American Journal of Computational Linguistics 8(3-4), 139–149 (1982)

Conway, J.H.: On numbers and games. A. K. Peters (2001)

Cooper, R.: Quantification and syntactic theory. Studies in Linguistics and Philosophy. Springer (1983)

De Bruijn, N.G.: Taal en structuur van de wiskunde (1982), http://alexandria.tue.nl/repository/books/238171.pdf

De Bruijn, N.G.: The mathematical vernacular, a language for mathematics with typed sets. In: Dybjer, P., et al. (eds.) Proceedings of the Workshop on Programming Logic, Report 37, Programming Methodology Group. University of Göteborg and Chalmers University of Technology (1987) ISSN 0282-2083

Dummit, D.S., Foote, R.M.: Abstract algebra, 3rd edn. John Wiley & Sons (2003)

Eisenbud, D., Harris, J.: The geometry of schemes. Springer (2000)

Enderton, H.B.: Elements of set theory. Academic Press (1977)

Erdös, P., Rado, R.: A partition calculus in set theory. Bulletin of the American Mathematical Society 62, 427–489 (1956)

Ferdinands, J.: $G_{n,3}(C)$ is prime if n is odd. Topology and its Applications 86(3), 233–251 (1998)

Floyd, R.W.: Syntactic analysis and operator precedence. Journal of the ACM 10(3), 316–333 (1963)

Geach, P.T.: Reference and generality. Cornell University Press (1980)

Geis, M.L., Zwicky, A.M.: On invited inferences. Linguistic Inquiry 2(4), 561–566 (1971)

Gödel, K.: Die vollständigkeit der Axiome des logischen Funktionenkalküls. Monatshefte fur Mathematik und Physik 37, 349–360 (1930)

Gordon, M.J.C., Melham, T.F. (eds.): Introduction to HOL: a theorem proving environment for higher order logic. Cambridge University Press (1993)

Grattan-Guinness, I.: Companion encyclopedia of the history and philosophy of the mathematical sciences. Johns Hopkins University Press (2003)

Grigoriev, D., Singer, M., Yao, A.: On computing algebraic functions using logarithms and exponentials. SIAM Journal on Computing 24(2), 242–246 (1995)

Halmos, P.R.: Naive set theory. Springer (1960)

Hamilton, A.G.: Numbers, sets, and axioms: the apparatus of mathematics. Cambridge University Press (1982)

Hamilton, A.G.: Logic for mathematicians. Cambridge University Press (1988)

Hardy, G.H., Wright, E.M.: An introduction to the theory of numbers. Oxford University Press (1960)

Harris, M., Shepherd-Barron, N., Taylor, R.: A family of Calabi-Yau varieties and potential automorphy (2006), preprint at www.math.harvard.edu/~rtaylor

Hartshorne, R.: Algebraic geometry. Springer (1977)

Hatcher, A.: Algebraic topology. Cambridge University Press (2002)

Henle, J.M.: An outline of set theory. Springer (1986)

Jech, T.: Set theory. Springer (2002)

Jurafsky, D., Martin, J.H.: Speech and language processing. Prentice-Hall (2009)

Kamp, H., Reyle, U.: From discourse to logic: introduction to model-theoretic semantics of natural language, formal logic and Discourse Representation Theory. Studies in Linguistics and Philosophy, vol. 42. Springer (1993)

Karttunen, L.: Discourse referents. In: Proceedings of the 1969 Conference on Computational Linguistics, pp. 1–38. Association for Computational Linguistics (1969)

Koepke, P.: Naturalness in formal mathematics (2009),
    http://www.math.uni-bonn.de/people/koepke/Preprints/
    Naturalness_in_formal_mathematics.pdf

Kolev, N.: Generating proof representation structures (2008),
    http://naproche.net/downloads/2008/2008%20kolev%2001.pdf

Korta, K., Perry, J.: Pragmatics. In: Zalta, E.N. (ed.) The Stanford Encyclopedia
    of Philosophy. The Metaphysics Research Lab. (2008)

Kuhlwein, D., Cramer, M., Koepke, P., Schröder, B.: The Naproche system (2009),
    http://www.naproche.net/downloads/2009/emergingsystems.pdf

Kurtzman, H.S., MacDonald, M.C.: Resolution of quantifier scope ambiguities.
    Cognition 48(3), 243–279 (1993)

Lakatos, I.: Proofs and refutations: the logic of mathematical discovery. Cambridge
    University Press (1976)

Lang, S.: Algebra. Addison-Wesley (1993)

Maehara, R.: The Jordan curve theorem via the Brouwer fixed point theorem.
    American Mathematical Monthly 91(10), 641–643 (1984)

Martin-Löf, P.: Intuitionistic type theory. Bibliopolis (1984)

Milner, R.: A theory of type polymorphism in programming. Journal of Computer
    and System Sciences 17(3), 348–375 (1978)

Montague, R.: Universal grammar. Theoria 36(3), 373–398 (1970a); Reprinted in
    Montague, pp. 222–246 (1974)

Montague, R.: English as a formal language. In: Visentini, B., et al. (eds.) Lin-
    guaggi nella Società e nella Tecnica, pp. 189–224. Edizioni di Comunità (1970b);
    Reprinted in Montague, pp. 188–221 (1974)

Montague, R.: The proper treatment of quantification in ordinary English. In:
    Hintikka, K.J.J., Moravcsik, J.M., Suppes, P. (eds.) Approaches to Natural
    Language, Dordrecht, pp. 221–242 (1973); Reprinted in Montague, pp. 247–270
    (1974)

Montague, R.: Formal philosophy: selected papers of Richard Montague. Yale
    University Press (1974)

Pierce, B.C.: Types and programming languages. MIT Press (2002)

Quine, W.V.O.: Mathematical logic. Harvard University Press (1940)

Ranta, A.: Type Theory and the Informal Language of Mathematics. In: Barendregt,
    H., Nipkow, T. (eds.) TYPES 1993. LNCS, vol. 806, pp. 352–365. Springer,
    Heidelberg (1994)

Ranta, A.: Syntactic Categories in the Language of Mathematics. In: Dybjer, P.,
    Nordström, B., Smith, J. (eds.) TYPES 1994. LNCS, vol. 996, pp. 162–182.
    Springer, Heidelberg (1995)

Ranta, A.: Context-Relative Syntactic Categories and the Formalization of Mathe-
    matical Text. In: Berardi, S., Coppo, M. (eds.) TYPES 1995. LNCS, vol. 1158,
    pp. 231–248. Springer, Heidelberg (1996)

Ranta, A.: Structures grammaticales dans le français mathématique: I.
    Mathématiques, Informatique et Sciences Humaines 138, 5–56 (1997a)

Ranta, A.: Structures grammaticales dans le français mathématique: II-(suite et
    fin). Mathématiques, Informatique et Sciences Humaines 139, 5–36 (1997b)

Reinhart, T.: Definite NP anaphora and c-command domains. Linguistic In-
    quiry 12(4), 605–635 (1981)

Robinson, D.J.S.: A course in the theory of groups. Springer (1996)

Rotman, J.J.: An introduction to the theory of groups. Springer (1995)

Rudin, W.: Principles of mathematical analysis. McGraw-Hill (1964)

Schumacher, C.: Chapter zero: fundamental notions of abstract mathematics. Addison-Wesley (1996)

Serre, J.-P.: Local fields. Springer (1979)

Shapiro, S.: Philosophy of mathematics: structure and ontology. Oxford University Press (1997)

Silverman, J.H.: The arithmetic of elliptic curves. Springer (2009)

Stewart, I., Tall, D.: The foundations of mathematics. Oxford University Press (1977)

Stoll, R.R.: Set theory and logic. Dover Publications (1979)

Sutherland, W.A.: Introduction to metric and topological spaces. Oxford University Press (1975)

Trybulec, A.: The Mizar-QC/6000 logic information language. Bulletin of the Association for Literary and Linguistic Computing 6(2), 136–140 (1978)

Tuganbaev, A.A.: Projective modules over Dedekind prime rings. Russian Mathematical Surveys 55(1), 188–189 (2000)

van Dalen, D., Doets, H.C., de Swart, H.: Sets: naive, axiomatic and applied. Pergamon Press (1978)

van der Sandt, R.A.: Presupposition projection as anaphora resolution. Journal of Semantics 9(4), 333–377 (1992)

Wasow, T., Perfors, A., Beaver, D.: The puzzle of ambiguity. In: Orgun, C.O., Sells, P. (eds.) Morphology and the Web of Grammar: Essays in Memory of Steven G. Lapointe. CSLI Publications (2005)

Weisstein, E.W., et al.: MathWorld. Wolfram Research (2009), mathworld.wolfram.com

Whitehead, A.N., Russell, B.: Principia mathematica. Cambridge University Press (1910)

Wiedijk, F.: Formalizing 100 theorems (2009), http://www.cs.ru.nl/~freek/100/mizar.html

Wittgenstein, L.: Philosophical investigations. Blackwell (1953)

Wolska, M., Kruijff-Korbayová, I.: Analysis of mixed natural and symbolic language input in mathematical dialogs. In: Proceedings of the 42nd Annual Meeting of the Association for Computational Linguistics, pp. 25–32. Association for Computational Linguistics (2004)

Index